George Grant in Process

Edited by Larry Schmidt

George Grant in Process:

Essays and Conversations

ANANSI   **TORONTO**

Published with the assistance of the Ontario Arts Council and the
Canada Council.

House of Anansi Press Limited
35 Britain Street
Toronto, Canada M5A 1R7

Cover Photo: Dorothy Richardson
Cover Design: John Grant

        78 79 80 81 82 83   6 5 4 3 2 1

Canadian Cataloguing in Publication Data
    Main entry under title:
    George Grant in process
    Bibliography: p.
    ISBN 0-88784-065-5 bd. ISBN 0-88784-064-7 pa.

    1. Grant, George P., 1918-   2. Philosophy,
    Canadian — 20th century. I. Grant, George P.,
    1918-   II. Schmidt, Lawrence, 1942-

    B995.G74G46   191   C77-001723-1

Acknowledgements

Grateful acknowledgement is here expressed to the *Queen's Quarterly* for permission to reprint Lawrence Lampert's "The Uses of Philosophy in George Grant". The editor also wishes to thank the Canada Council for a Conference grant which enabled participants to come to the symposium at which the conversations in this volume were taped. The symposium was sponsored by Erindale College, The Religious Studies Department of the University of Toronto, and the Toronto School of Theology.

It is impossible to express one's gratitude to everyone who helped with this volume. But the following individuals must be thanked: Professor Herbert Richardson who helped in the organization of the symposium, contributed extensively to the discussions, and made helpful suggestions regarding publication; Miss Virginia Jaklic for her excellent typing of the taped conversations; the participants in the symposium: the contributors to this volume, Miss Joan Lockwood and Professor Danny Drache; James Polk of Anansi Press for his perceptive editorial assistance; and Dr George Grant who could not have been more gracious from beginning to end.

Annotation

Footnotes for the essays are collected at the end of the book. References to Grant's work are given the following abbreviations: *PMA, Philosophy in the Mass Age,* 2nd edition, (Vancouver, 1966); *LN, Lament for a Nation: The Defeat of Canadian Nationalism,* (Toronto, 1970); *TE, Technology & Empire: Perspectives on North America*, (Toronto, 1969); *TH, Time as History*, (Toronto, 1971).

Contents

Contents

Introduction

George Parkin Grant, who will celebrate his sixtieth birthday this year, is now established as Canada's foremost political philosopher. His importance has continued to grow from the time when *Philosophy in the Mass Age* was published in 1959, through the Diefenbaker years when he was particularly concerned with Canadian nationalism, and into the last decade when he has been preoccupied with the relationship between technology and justice.

However, one cannot but think that George Grant has become important without becoming influential, and that this gives some indication of how unphilosophical a nation he inhabits. It was, after all, a sign of the health of their *polis* that the Athenians could be disturbed enough by what a philosopher said to kill him. Though Canadians have acknowledged Grant's importance, they have largely ignored what he has to say.

Instead of reading his works and participating in his relentless ethical quest, men of Grant's own generation have been content to make him a fellow of the Royal Society. The men between forty-five and sixty who now run this country saw Grant more and more as an anachronism when he attempted to shake them from their liberal and continentalist assumptions by analyzing the demise of the Canadian nation. *Lament for a Nation* became a classic without being accepted. These same men have been tolerant of Grant's eccentric critique of modernity because it could be safely deemed irrelevant, or so they thought.

Ironically, however, George Grant has never seemed irrelevant to the younger generation which is now between thirty and forty-five. In the 1960s they may have misinterpreted his criticism of the Vietnamese war as a call to revolution, but they did take him seriously. The result is that, ten years later, having experienced and reflected on the "intimations of deprival" of which Grant writes, younger political scientists, philosophers, historians and theologians still look to him for an illumination of the darkness of the technological society. They acknowledge the gravity of the questions he has raised, and are forced into dialogue with him. This book is but one manifestation of that dialogue.

The essays in this volume were, with one exception, written for a symposium held at Erindale College in April of 1977 to discuss issues raised in the social, political and religious writings of George Grant. The meetings were intellectually stimulating and fruitful, especially since Dr Grant himself was present. It was felt that the prepared papers were of such good quality that they were worthy of publication. When House of Anansi Press read the papers, they were enthusiastic about publishing them but felt they would be incomplete without a contribution by George Grant himself. Professor Herbert Richardson, who had been instrumental in planning and organizing the April meeting, suggested that we tape and transcribe a lengthy group discussion with George Grant. A second symposium was quickly planned for October, and Dr Grant graciously agreed to participate. The conversations are based on edited transcripts of the delightfully relaxed dialogue which transpired.

The essays and conversations are divided loosely into four sections: Canadian Politics, Intellectual Background, Theology and History, and Philosophy. The essays examine aspects of Grant's thought on themes determined by the writers according to their scholarly interests. Though many aspects remain to be treated, the important task of elaborating the process by which Grant has come to his unique understanding of the modern world is begun. The essays demonstrate that from the outset of his career as a philosopher, he has always been in process. His mind has changed often as he has attempted to think deeply about the implications of the modern enterprise. But his commitment to the good has remained a constant in his philosophical quest.

Because all Grant's ideas are interrelated, it is almost impossible to divide his thought into four neat categories, and the very nature of conversation precludes such simple categorization. Nevertheless, the conversations illustrate the agility and the lucidity of Grant's mind when engaged by a group of friendly but probing colleagues. And since these are George Grant's own words, they are both thoughtful and thought-provoking, for he has given a lifetime to consideration of the issues that confront us in Canadian society. They are neither the last nor the definitive words from him. He is still among us, and, I am sure, he is still talking.

— Larry Schmidt
Erindale College,
University of Toronto

I
CANADIAN POLITICS

PART I. CANADIAN POLITICS

Conversation

Question: Let's look back at *Lament for a Nation* eleven years later. First, do you still think that Canada's disappearance as a nation is a matter of necessity? Do you think that nationalism has a future as far as Canada is concerned?

Grant: Obviously no sane person predicts the details of the future. It is quite clear that the central ruling class of the great corporations, national or multi-national, do not think in terms of Canadian independence. Beyond that I find it very hard to believe that the general English-speaking bourgeois want anything particularly distinctive to be built on the northern half of this continent. They seem to want the same things as other North Americans – although sometimes they want these things with a Canadian sign. As for young people and the American dream, I just don't know.

Question: I have a question that relates to that point. Many of the critics of the Parti Québécois today (and I mean those critics who are favourably disposed to the Parti Québécois, who try to assess what's going on from within it, and who identify with it), are saying that the whole dream, the alternative that was envisaged by the dreamers of this party, is slowly evaporating, is giving way to something that looks much more like the technological society, and that one can see this in figures like Parizeau, in particular, but also in Camille Laurin. Now this is being said by very sympathetic people, so the question is not only about the anglophones in Canada, but is it not a question also about the whole culture? Doesn't it have something to do with the inevitability of technocracy?

Grant: I think people such as Premier Lévesque and Dr Laurin were brought up, like everyone of my generation, to assume that an advancing technological society went with an advancing humanness. That has been taken for granted so long in the western world that it is almost impossible to doubt it. In Dr Laurin's case he found in his psychiatric work something beyond this. He found that much of the mental illness he encountered came forth from the fact that his patients lived in a culture which was imposed on them from outside. I am sure that much of the Parti Québécois leadership takes for granted that the expansion of technology is almost automatically good. But at the same time they want it to take place as Frenchness, and in that they have to break with established power structures.

Question: You were making the point that the survival of Canada would depend upon attitudes of the anglophone community particularly, and I'm suggesting it's a question of the technocratic mind set and momentum.

Grant: What you say is quite true. Obviously the universalizing and homogenizing power in a technological society is very great. That is the central fact of our destiny. It is for that reason that I have turned in my own work from thinking about the details of Canadian life to the nature of technological society. That is the big question. Also, of course, at a shallow level there has been a lot of phony Canadian nationalism which is simply imitation Americanism. If they have *Portnoy's Complaint*, we have *Duddy Kravitz*. We'll have movies and universities just like their movies and universities, etc., etc.

Question: In your analysis of Diefenbaker in *Lament for a Nation* one of the striking things is the ambiguity in his nationalism. He didn't recognize the rights of community. Isn't one of our problems that we haven't had anyone in Canada who has recently been able to articulate a nationalism that's at all appealing, significant, or attractive to the English-speaking community?

Grant: I think it's very hard to do. The modern experiment went against this – at the centre of the modern experiment was the universal and homogeneous society. Those who spoke against it (Coleridge, Swift) were speaking against something that made them seem "out of it." How can a belief in anything else but the universal and homogeneous state seem real to people, particularly in a place like North America? How can such thought have much meaning in terms of the 20th century?

Question: In relation to French Canada then, how do you understand their nationalism at the moment?

Grant: They had roots in something much greater than anything the English-speaking world had. They had roots in a very great Catholicism. Their high level of education also put them outside modernity. They had a great tradition that was outside modernity. They were a minority, a people being brought into technology late, far behind, terribly exploited by an alien people.

I don't see English-speaking Canada paying much attention to its nationalism or caring much for its nationalism. Therefore it seems to me good that the French should try some other way of defending themselves for their survival.

Take Trudeau, for example; he always speaks and acts (at least to English-speaking audiences) as if all was really great with Canada, except for a bunch of crazy separatists in Quebec, and he is the man to deal with that. Yet since he came in in 1968, our indebtedness to the U.S. has grown by leaps and bounds. We have gone on with the policy of selling our national resources and the ownership of our country to the U.S. Why should the French believe that their enormous problems of survival as a French-speaking nation of six million, in a continent of 250 million English-speakers, is being helped by being one with English-speaking Canada, which has shown so little interest in its own independence? It's beyond me to conceive why one isn't glad that the French-Canadians have put up a fight against integration.

Question: But who is the fight against?

Grant: Not against anybody. They are being attacked. They want to continue to be something. This is what makes genocide so hideous: once you destroy a people it's destroyed, as a species often becomes extinct. There are no more carrier pigeons in Ontario and one is sad — why? Because it adds to the diversity of being. Why is genocide more terrible to me than individual murder? Because it wipes out a people who can never be again. I'm not talking of race and racial purity, but there is something about a group of people.... The French stuck down in North America have produced something that is nowhere else. Do you want to see them disappear?

Question: You misunderstand me. I'm not saying I'm in favour of the French Canadians disappearing, not at all.

Grant: They were threatened.

Question: I understand that. They've been threatened for three or four hundred years.

Grant: Yes, but this is one of the worst threats.

Question: But what is the threat? Is the threat English Canada, as a number of people in Quebec suggest, or is the threat the universal homogeneous state?

Grant: Obviously the big question in the modern world is what alternative there is to the universal and homogeneous state. But in the meantime, what are people to do if they are going to do anything practical? I think the Québécois are in a very difficult position. I rejoice because they haven't chosen to go down easily. They are rejoicing because they felt themselves as a conquered people for a long time. After all, English-speaking people have not for many centuries lived in a position where they felt they were conquered.

Comment: After the November 15th election a French man said to me, "I think we may now have another child."

Grant: Clearly the French are interested in getting control of their technology. They are behind. The universal language of the most powerful technology is English. The only choice they have for control over the technological life of their country is to hold onto French as the language of their society. Their language is the only advantage they have in trying to redess the balance of what has been English-speaking control of their technology. That advantage might give them ten years to catch up in technological education.

Now technology is a given destiny of the whole modern world, and one may well say that, whatever happens, they are going to be caught up in the massive imperial system of the western multi-national corporations.

Question: But to talk that way is to assume that technology is neutral and can be used for good or ill. And this ignores your central point: that in a sense you can't use technology except in one direction.

Grant: I am sure that people in Quebec are going to find that out. We in the West are in the midst of a destiny which we have given ourselves, which carries us only in one direction. But in the meantime, what are practical people to do? Are they to put up no resistance to the destruction of their culture? Doesn't a person such as Parizeau say, "If I'm not in charge of the Quebec economy, then Lalonde will be, and isn't it clear that I, Parizeau, care more about the continuance of French society than Lalonde?"

Isn't it just a question of function? For somebody such as myself, the job is to think through what technology is, and to try to show what it portends for the future. But that makes me quite impotent in the practical realm. People whose job is to live and try to do things in the practical realm, have to have feasible immediate alternatives – in this case, alternatives for saving their culture – but this immersion in the practical means they can't be concerned with the long-range questions of destiny.

Question: Don't you think that the present nationalist establishment of Quebec has deliberately uprooted itself from those traditions which you say are the sort of thing that make Quebec nationalism workable? I mean, René Lévesque really is a renegade liberal.

Grant: Yes, I think that is in a certain sense quite true. What the PQ want is that their technology be in their own hands. But you have to see something more in Lévesque. Why did he turn away from success in the English world? He was a star, and something in him said *no* to this. Also Lévesque has been too busy doing important and vital things to think through the nature of the technological society. This is surely one of the complexities of life – that those who are taken up with doing necessary and practical things just don't have the time to think through the central issues of their society. This is the cause of the division between the practical and philosophic lives.

Question: I don't understand why you're so happy about the Parti Québécois and this resurgence of French nationalism, when that appears to be having the effect of weakening Canada and making the process of integration of the whole of Canada into the American empire just that much more simple.

Grant: My answer would be something like the following. Canadian politics has had two main questions: first, how to maintain some independence while sharing this continent with the most powerful modern empire; second, how to maintain workable relations between the French- and English-speaking communities. Those two very complex questions can only be thought about clearly if they are thought about together.

This country was made up of two founding groups who weren't very friendly to each other, but who made a contract because they thought such a contract would help each of them achieve their own particular ends – but these ends were different.

The present constitutional crisis has arisen because some of the Quebec élite have received the backing of many voters, particularly young voters, under the affirmation that that contract does not serve their purposes, and therefore must be terminated or perhaps clarified.

Question: Do you have any fear that what is going on in Quebec may cause disorder and violence, which are things not to be sought after, almost under any circumstances? I'm thinking of the argument against French-Canadian nationalism, which says that what is happening is an attack against a deliberately balanced system of order, and that an attack on this system opens the door to violence.

Grant: I would say two things. First, that system of order has not been serving the French in recent years. Take the breakup of traditional Catholicism, and the use of the birth-control pill in Quebec. This meant that if they were going to survive, they had to have control over immigration policies in their society. But second, and more important, people often delude themselves when they say the violence has come from the French Canadians. This is six million people in a sea of 250 million English-speakers. After all, the last big case of violence was the federal government bringing in its troops in 1970 to meet two kidnappings. The English-speaking people pushed technology into Quebec and rushed for fast technological development. There is something analogous in the relations of the Russians to western Europe.

People are always saying that the Russians are the chief aggressors in the world. But it was western Europe that time and again invaded Russia. I see Marxist communism as the Russians taking a very brutal and terrible technological system, so that they would have the power to stand up to the expansionist western Europeans. It has been horrible medicine for the Russians – but this was always Stalin's argument: "If you don't have an authoritarian technological system, you can't stand up to the rest of the world." In the same way the French Canadians have had modernity pushed in upon them under English-speaking auspices, and they have decided they want to control it for themselves. The James Bay project is, after all, their big ace in the game they are playing.

Now of course when you move a people quickly into technological society, as Quebec has been moved, there is a lot of political craziness around. But is there any more craziness there than in our society? The great question is whether in such a situation there is going to be enough political moderation on either side to work something out. Of course, the first priority for English-speaking Canadians is to think what we want, and first in that is to think whether we want to be a country in the northern half of this continent, and what we need to do if we want to continue such a country. There is something specious and dishonest about English-speaking Canadians saying to French people – "the only difficulty is you. We really want to be a country" – when in fact we have done so little to protect our own society. We have in fact let it go in the interests of making a quick buck, quickly.

Question: In an article you and your wife wrote on abortion, you seem to base your whole argument on the inalienable rights of individuals. Aren't you then drawing heavily on the very same liberal tradition you attack elsewhere?

Grant: What one says depends on where one writes. We were writing that piece for the Anglican Church, of which we are members. It was written to persuade the particular members of our church that they ought to be horrified by the mass foeticide that's going on, and in which our church seems to acquiesce. But nearly all Anglican church members are modern bourgeois Canadians and such people take the language of liberalism as the only moral language they've got. Therefore one has to use it in speaking about such matters. One has to be ironic, in the classical sense.

This takes me back to something which is central to any discussion of politics at all. Certainly I don't believe that one should be easily cut off from the practical life around one. Also practical or political life is concerned with doing the best that seems possible, however bad the circumstances. Thomas More's statement about politics is my favorite: "When you can't make the good happen, prevent the very worst from happening." There are some good things left in modern technological Canada; among them, certain legal traditions from liberalism. One doesn't want to attack them – even though they're going down the drain because of other influences.

Question: Are you saying that the origin of the legal tradition in the classical 18th and 19th century liberalism is laudable?

Grant: No. But remember that the common-law tradition has its roots in something long before Locke and Bentham – in the Natural Rights traditions of the West. Also there are worse accounts of politics than Locke's. There are worse views of the world than that the end of life is comfortable self-preservation. There's even Montesquieu's argument that the English constitution is higher than the Athenian because it substituted commerce for honour, and commerce is a more feasible basis for society than honour. I think we have all suffered enough from capitalism to know that is not true. Nevertheless, we also know that there are worse regimes than plutocratic democracy. There was a lot of good in the English constitution.

Question: You've introduced the category of irony as the sense that one has when one lives within a double vision: eternal justice and those caricatures of justice which parade before us in the conventional world for our approbation. It's a very consistent Platonism – the sense of having been outside the cave, but having to live, because one has children, most of one's life inside the cave. One carries around with oneself a kind of doubleness, and I take it that you do in that way.

Grant: I will say yes to that, without saying that I have been outside the cave, because that I don't know. Life teaches one all kinds of ironies. I think irony is necessary if you're going to have your car fixed, and you can hardly live without a car in twentieth-century North America. How can one live as a Christian in a modern university without irony? If a Christian spoke frankly in a modern multiversity, he would have to leave. Yet is one just to give up these institutions? Therefore I don't think irony is dishonest or wrong at such points. All of you know that.

Question: The difference between calling it irony and calling it realism is that the realists believe that this realm of convention is what is ultimately valuable; and the ironists know that it's ultimately trivial, and that the eternal realm is ultimately valuable.

Grant: That I think is quite right. In dealing with the gas station, the realists might carry the irony so far that it would be unjust, and that must be avoided.

Question: To get back to nationalism, I would like to question the general assumption that Canadian nationalism would be a desirable thing. I can understand your being concerned to prevent the universal and homogeneous culture of the Great Republic from flooding Canada, and wanting to preserve alternative values and calling for a Canadian response in defence. But it's one thing to seize upon nationalism as a defence against nationalism, and another thing to laud nationalism as a good thing. If there's any insidious part of modernity it is the idea of nationalism, which goes hand in hand with technology. Nationalism is precisely the idea that produces the universal and homogeneous state. It becomes in France, for example, the way of generalizing the Parisian culture and destroying Britanny. It became in the United Kingdom the principle for the generalization of Anglophone culture and destroying the Scots. If nationalism is our salvation in Canada, we will buy into the worst of modernity. How could anyone like yourself, rooted in the truly cosmopolitan Greek and Christian tradition be seeking salvation from nationalism?

Grant: I think, in terms of the modern world, the practical political choice has often been between nationalism and cosmopolitanism. But cosmopolitanism has generally been a mask for a particular imperialism. In the Canadian case the opposite to nationalism has always been said, by people like Pearson and Trudeau, to be cosmopolitanism. But what that, in a word, comes down to is immersion in the culture of the United States, and subservience to the purposes of the American empire in the world. Also, cosmopolitanism is an appeal to a universal culture which is shallow beyond measure, and denies all the particularities of our roots. It means, as well, the loss of politics as a real activity for human beings. In the great cosmopolitanising of our English-speaking society we are all retreating into private life, and there is no place for people to take part in politics in a meaningful way. Is that not a real loss? Is it not right to lament it?

Question: I certainly think it's a loss, but I think the ideology of nationalism is the major factor contributing to the demise of politics in the modern world, and my argument would run something like this. By nationalism I mean that general conviction that the life, purpose, and organization of a people is rooted in, and a function of their being part of, a nation, which is usually defined as a linguistic cultural group. This allows the government to assume that it knows what the general good of the whole people might be, rather than consulting either the individual or particular institutions which have structures utterly transcending the nation. The differentiated character of society, as composed of many different institutions having different functions, is overlooked. Individuality is overlooked. So is the aloneness and separateness of the soul before God, if one wants to think about Simone Weil. I think that politics arises precisely when persons become aware of a life in God which calls them to stand to some extent within, and to some extent over against, the present situation, and in that primal way the world is differentiated. That's why I see nationalism as the enemy of politics. Bernard Crick, in his little book, *In Defense of Politics*, makes this very point far better than I.

Grant: That is a very powerful case. Also what I have said about it being good to take part in politics is a strong case. How do you put together the truth of both these sides? Very difficult. I am not sure that I know.

Question: How do you understand the relation between politics and nationalism? It seems to me that at some points you see nationalism as necessary to the retaining of politics.

Grant: I don't know about that, because the nation is a different thing from the *polis*. Whether you can have politics in a nation is another matter. I found myself brought up in a society which was made up of two traditions that were in some sense deeply distinct from the traditions of the United States, and it may have been those traditions that made me very hostile to the sort of capitalist individualism of the United States. I thought of nationalism as a governmental means of preserving and allowing to expand certain traditions that were different from those of the United States.

Question: Would you accept the distinction between nationalism and patriotism, and accept the idea that, generally speaking, nationalism now functions as a progressive force at the leading edge of modernity, introducing more and more homogeneity? Patriotism could and in some cases does have the opposite effect. It could be a force for the maintenance of tradition.

Grant: I agree with that. What it seems to me to come down to is the tension between love of your own and love of the good. That is a very deep tension. On the one hand, love of one's own must ultimately be a means to love of the good. On the other hand, people who are deracinated, so that they have nothing which is really their own, rarely can move to the good. How to express a proper love of one's own within a Christian life? That is very hard — a very difficult question. And yet I know that most people who are cosmopolitan lack something essential. That is one reason I distrust Trudeau so greatly. He is such a cosmopolitan. You feel in him a real dislike of ordinary French-Canadian life, and even a dislike of the deeper roots which made French Canada distinct. Whatever Lévesque's mistakes, one does not feel that superior cosmopolitanism in him. One feels a love of his own in all its rough particularity.

A Imperio usque ad Imperium:
The Political Thought of George Grant
by Barry Cooper

Die Krähen schrein
und Ziehen schwirren Flugs der Stadt:
bald wird es schnein, –
weh dem, der deine Heimat hat!
Nietzsche, Vereinsamt.

Now this predicament is too enormous in the history of the race to
permit one to say: I'm against it, or I'm for it. The main thing,
you know, in my life, is just to see what it is.
George Grant.

A Man of Common Sense

We are so little used to commonsensical discussion in philosophy and
political thought that when it intrudes upon our consciousness we consider
it illegitimate. Immediately we deflect the force of a genuine argument
looking for ulterior motives, or dismissing all thought as opinion. In the
more desiccated language of political science we speak of value-preference
and ideology, but the effect is the same: we avoid the question of whether
what is being said is true. To raise such a question, at least in polite
scholarly company, is considered tasteless, evidence of inadequate sociali-
zation. Such, or something like it, seems to be the general verdict rendered
by academics about George Grant's work. Particularly fine examples of the
technique of the studied refusal to discuss have been written by foreign
sociologists, employed at the time in instructing young Canadians. For
their part, Canadian historians, when not pillaging his rhetoric and
arguments, defuse them by placing Grant in a "tradition", so he need not
be taken seriously in the present.

A sympathetic reader has called him a prophet.[1] Provided we
emphasize the immediacy of the prophetic word, the existential urgency
of the message, such a description is not misleading, for all Grant's writings
have proceeded from a reflective encounter with particular and concrete
historical contingencies. Another has observed that Grant's work is not
"professional." He does not engage in merely intellectual exercises, and
consequently his "is philosophy in a sense that would exclude it from
most philosophy journals."[2] In his own writing Grant has gone out of his
way to avoid identifying his work as philosophy. Lament for a Nation, for
example, was "not based on philosophy but on tradition" (p. 96);
Technology and Empire did "not presume to be philosophy" but was
"written out of the study of the history of political philosophy" (p. 11).

One reason for this reluctance to identify his enterprise with philosophy results from what philosophy has come to mean. Reason is understood today not as an instrument of spiritual diagnosis but as a means to control nature and nature's fortune; at best philosophy is considered to be a *Glasperlenspiel* for the impotent clever. Yet those who know of the archaic origin of philosophy may find something familiar in Grant's writing.

Philosophy originally was a public and therefore a political act. It was, moreover, an act of resistance to that spiritual disorder whose most obvious political manifestation was injustice. Only in its decadence did it retreat behind the walls of Epicurus's garden or turn away from a truculent public to mock it and be mocked in turn. Grant has refused the garden-asylum that is professional philosophy in the modern university as he has refused irresponsible cynicism. He has addressed a general public, often over the CBC or in popular rather than scholarly periodicals, and he has addressed them as equals, as fellow citizens concerned about right and wrong in the world. He has asked us to be serious for a moment, to wonder about our doing, and to think how it is to be judged. In short, Grant makes real demands upon us, which is to say that his work is essentially a practical affair. Precisely because his writing deals with practical, common, lived experience, an imaginative act is required of his later readers if they are to recapture the significance of writings such as *The Empire, Yes or No?* or *Lament for a Nation*, which were addressed to specific questions of policy. Not that Grant's writings are dated but that we must attend to the historical contexts of their composition if we hope to understand how his argument transcends the occasions that inspired them.

By characterizing his work as commonsensical, one means, in the first place, that Grant has tried to take stock of our common reality as it presents itself to him. But in addition, as Eric Voegelin has pointed out, "commonsense is a compact type of rationality" and is to be distinguished from the aspirations of philosophy.[3] It is, however, a particularly appropriate mode for public discourse about political things because it "never aspires to universally valid knowledge and it never attempts exhaustive communication. Its concern is the concrete and particular. Its function is to master each situation as it arises."[4] Or, in the words of Thomas Reid, the eighteenth-century "commonsense philosopher," we are called upon "to judge of things self-evident." Now it is, of course, true that commonsense is incomplete of itself, even while it strives towards philosophical generality or serves as its necessary beginning. Accordingly, if Grant is right to refuse the title "philosopher" it is not simply because of that word's public meaning. Having devoted much effort to understanding the thought of other men, Grant must know that anyone, especially anyone today, who claimed the dignity of philosophy for his political thoughts showed by the immodesty of that claim that he was not one. In the end we may judge Grant a philosopher, but we must begin a consideration of his thought on its own terms. It is, then, as a practical citizen and man of commonsense that we approach Grant's political reflections.

Conservatism and Empire

Grant's first political writings appeared in the period immediately following World War II. Germany and Japan had been defeated but the configuration of post-war politics was still uncertain. In theory, it would be a world of united nations, but ruled by the four "great powers," the United States, Great Britain, the Soviet Union and, with American help, China. Later, France, which had been crushed during the war, gained similar status in the form of a permanent seat on the United Nations Security Council. Canada's contribution to the San Francisco conference, which established the U.N. organization, was minimal. There was some pious talk about the international rule of law; a new self-definition emerged: Canada was something called a "middle power." When the Canadian delegation attempted to modify the veto-power of the "Big Five" they learned that "middle-power" status was honorific.

Equal to the United Nations in importance for Canadians was the Commonwealth and Empire. Specifically, our place in what Bartlet Brebner had called the North Atlantic Triangle was not yet fully clear. In 1944, for example, Lord Halifax, the British Ambassador to the United States, speaking in Toronto, appealed for greater cooperation and "closer unity of thought and action" with respect to defence, economic and foreign policy. Great Britain, he said, did not have the real power that went with its status of "greatness." Not Britain alone, "but the British Commonwealth and Empire must be the fourth power in that group upon which, under Providence, the peace of the world will henceforth depend." To the Prime Minister, who was "not so much a Canadian citizen as a citizen of North America,"[5] and his Department of External Affairs, Commonwealth cooperation meant imperial centralization, an evil to be mightily resisted. With the Canada-United States defence agreements of 1947 and the establishment of NATO two years later, both of which were formal military pacts, Canada ended up much more subservient to American direction than ever it had been to British. However that may be, when Grant wrote first of Canada's political opportunities, the implications of wartime cooperation with the United States were still ambiguous.

In two pieces published during 1945 Grant pondered two questions: "Have we a Canadian Nation?"[6] and *The Empire, Yes or No*?[7] Nationalism, he said, was a phenomenon "embodied in an individual culture ... capable of unique contributions to the world." It was the *de facto* principle of political particularity: "the colour and glory of life are not found in uniformity but in diversity." It was, moreover, the foundation of interstate politics. In Europe nationalism developed from a linguistic or territorial or cultural sense of belonging, a sense that took centuries to mature. In Canada, however, the time had been too short, and Canadians, especially in the first generation, still retained ties to what, without prejudice, they called their homelands. Canadian nationalism, therefore, must be "created around some principles. It must be consciously based on certain conscious ideas." The chief principle has been our refusal to break with the past by revolution. "This meant first of all that we were a conservative nation" not in the sense of defence of property alone, but in "that we were a nation who believed that the past could tell us something of the future. A nation that realized that true progress can only be made step by step – layer on layer – if it is going to stick." There was nothing glorious in breaking with the past but much to be lost. Certainly there was no danger of being a British colony: "it might have been true in 1870 or 1900. But this is 1945. And in 1945 the danger to our nationhood does not come from any colonial feelings to the British, but rather the danger of becoming a satellite of the U.S.A." Indeed, those who spoke so vehemently about ending a non-existent "colonial relationship" with Britain were mendacious, a danger to Canadian nationhood because their rhetoric of independence covered an actual policy of increasing subordination to the United States.[8]

Here Grant saw a special role for the British Commonwealth and Empire. The world, he said, was divided into three parts, "the two immense continental empires of the U.S.A. and the U.S.S.R., and the maritime empire of Great Britain." Continental regionalism would not mean world unity: "It inevitably means a division of the world." In light of the dangers of continental bi-polarity, the Commonwealth, spanning several continents, might act as a counterforce to regional isolation. As its interests were world-wide it could never itself become isolationist; it was decentralized and acted by consent and the practical cooperation of free nations. The Commonwealth was, in short, "the ideal the world must strive for. The Commonwealth shows it can be achieved." Grant was clearly at one with Lord Halifax. Two years later, however, President Truman announced in his famous "Doctrine" that the world had been divided into two, and only two, camps. An opportunity had been lost through lack of initiative and the rare ability, which is not yet exhausted, of Canadian politicians to deceive themselves and fight the battles of 1870 and 1900 over again.

The British Empire was an imperial political order as well as the maritime organization of former settlement colonies. Imperialism "after all ... is nothing but the expansion of one vital people from its own native heath into other areas." Some of this vital expansion is brutal and some is peaceful, but it is in any case necessary for reasons of military security and for "the development of retarded people." In this respect, the tutelage of the British Empire "stands for the ordered helping of people in backward areas to move towards fuller political consciousness and the modern use of their resources," and is the sole alternative to "the mercy of private investors and private companies who are responsible to no one." The only practical question, therefore, was whether British responsibility and experience were to be put to use or whether some other power would step in. "Our aim must be the upward climb of mankind to a perfect and effective world government, and on the ladder upwards the British Commonwealth is an important step." Beyond the desirability of maritime diversity and the great effectiveness of British experience in the "development of backward peoples towards political democracy and economic maturity," the Commonwealth was "the mainstay of Western Christian Civilization. ... Western Christian Civilization has little chance of survival if the British Commonwealth and Empire goes down."

In these two early works Grant alluded to the political maturation he had personally achieved during the war. Through the 1930s it seemed he had indulged himself with "the pious talk of idealists" but the war instructed him more deeply about the *cose del mondo*. He knew that politics involved hard choices, and that next to wisdom, the most important political virtue in an imperial age was courage. His untimely insistence on the point assured that his contemporaries would find offensive his remarks that the United States was "something a lot worse" than the British connection, whereas to present readers, grown secular and soft on a rich diet of propaganda concerning good feelings, peace, and cooperation among all the peoples of the world, Grant's words about the backward and retarded people appear most shocking.

He was, one might say, a progressive conservative. He found a genuine purpose and meaning to political and economic "development," world government seemed to offer the possibility of international cooperation among gentlemanly democratic regimes, and so forth. At the same time, Grant's progressivist faith was tempered by a distrust for revolutionary breaks with the past in the American and Soviet fashion. One may assume that the main reason why the British Empire appeared as the mainstay of Christian civilization was because of its embodied tradition and not because of any active commitments by the British people or their leaders. Grant's faith in progress was sufficient innoculation against the chief vice of conservatism, a retiring and sentimental nostalgia, but it was no substitute for thought and eventually would conflict with the commonsense that informed his analysis of Canada's prospects. He was silent about explicitly political matters until 1965. During the interval he worked through the implications of his progressive conservatism and by the time *Lament for a Nation* was published he had passed beyond the ideological inadequacies of his earlier formulae. The slow purgative was found in his reflections upon technology.

Liberalism and Technology

As early as 1951 Grant had argued that the effective purpose of Canadian universities was to serve "as technical schools for the training of specialists."[9] The significance of this fact was unclear to him, owing to the Hegelian idiom Grant favoured at this time.[10] Knowledge was described, for example, as "any means that brings the human spirit to self-consciousness." Likewise, "the highest moment known to finite mind" was declared to be the activity "wherein the knowledge of [one's] own mind leads [one] to the presence of the absolute mind."[11] Now Hegel's thought is much more seductive and subtle than that of his more famous pupil, Marx. The great charm of the Hegelian dialectic is that it orders a host of disparate contingencies upon what Hegel called "the chain of absolute necessity."

It was in this Hegelian mood that Grant wrote of the emancipation of social scientists from protestantism to humanism. Of itself it was an act of foolishness upon which "it is hard to look with anything but sadness" for "so much wisdom has been forgotten. Nevertheless a lot of error has been discarded too." The negative side of the revolt against Christianity was spent: "all partial grounds for hope have been wiped away." The exemplar here was Sartre. The non-existence of God was clearly an embarrassment to Sartre; but there it is. Sartre called upon us, Grant said, to recognize that "human condition is anguish. As despair becomes an open possibility to the sensitive and intelligent in our society, the opportunity for a profound adult education will become unlimited. When men encounter nothingness they are at last driven to seek reality. As in the pointless universe the days are spent in the beauty parlors, at the cineramic feelies or in the search to prolong a dying virility, in the days when there is always economic plenty and even cruelty has become tedious, then will be the moment to speak to men of education, of the journey of their minds to liberation."[12] Such counsel was ambiguous: how does one judge when jaded tastes have been sated? Only after the fact, when the former habitué of movie theatres, beauty parlours and the like turns to adult education?

But then what assurance do we have that what joined his inner experience with his external act was in fact that dialectic whereby an encounter with nothingness transformed itself into a search for reality? And what if our man without qualities, to use Musil's phrase, learns to live with possible realities? Not progressivist faith this time, but the sophistication of Hegel, pushed contingency in the sought-for direction.

A year later, in a second article on adult education, Grant turned from the certain untruth of an Hegelian resolution to the uncertain truth of commonsense. Now he saw an inherent dilemma, not a contradiction straining towards its own dissolution, in the contemporary position of higher education. Grant has always insisted that universities and schools reflect the commitments and opinions of the important members of society. If universities were technical schools, this was because society was one that "holds that the control of nature by technology is the chief purpose of human existence and so from that belief a community is built where all else is subordinated to that purpose."[13] Such an historical situation Grant called "the expanding economy." The problem was this: "an expanding economy has given us a society in which more people than ever have a chance for education," but "in the building of that economy we have created a world in which the idea of real education is darkened in the human soul as perhaps it has not been since the end of the Roman Empire."[14] Relying now for guidance on Simone Weil rather than Hegel, Grant noted that one could consider the true purpose of education to be the cultivation of a capacity for attention. In the past most people learned to attend to small and eventually great things by means of physical labour, whereas a few learned by disciplined study. As technological change liberates increasing numbers of people from the discipline of toil they either must submit themselves voluntarily to the discipline of thought or they will lose the capacity for attention. "And the faculty of attention is just our freedom,"[15] which is to say the capacity to do what is right.

Increasingly, however, freedom has come to mean the capacity to do as we like. The origin of this interpretation of freedom lay in Puritanism,[16] in the emphasis on the utter transcendence of God, the hiddenness of His purposes, and the inscrutability of His will, all of which served in the first instance to discount all authority, tradition, and established order as guides to conduct and salvation. One may argue, of course, that Calvin's *Institutes* were more authoritative and precise than any prior teachings about natural law; for Grant, however, the crucial point was that there was released an impulse to act for the best in the world, where the best was understood as securing visible evidence of having attained the highest ends.

Apart from the ambiguous Cromwellian interlude, Puritanism was never a dominant religious or political movement in Europe. In contrast, in

North America Puritanism was intensely held, being the product of a persecution now left behind. In the language of *Technology and Empire*, it is a major component of our "first presence" or "primal." In time, the way men have conceived of their highest ends has changed. The early Puritans acted in order to serve God's will; later "inner-worldly ascetics" identified God's will with their own economic advancement. Today the highest ends, the way our society understands its salvation, is found, Grant said, in technique.[17] From early Puritan to modern technician, one thing remained constant: "always the control of the world is seen as the essentially moral" (*PMA*, p. 87). The great problem with salvation by technique is not simply that it is as uncertain as salvation by faith, that "man's domination of nature can lead to the end of human life on the planet, if not in a cataclysm of bombs, perhaps by the slow perversion of the process of life" (*PMA*, pp. 78-79), but that having conceived action as essentially moral, and having no purposes beyond the sphere of action, one is deprived of standards by which the goodness of an act might be judged. The early Puritans could abide in this ambiguity because they trusted in God. God in the end would call His own to Himself and His judgement would be right. But when faith in God has left us, we are alone before the self-understanding of technologically inclined secular Puritans who excuse their own deeds as necessary, which is to say, beyond good and evil. The political expression of that self-understanding, Grant said, is liberalism, the ideology of the technological society striving to fulfill its own immanent entelechy.

Liberalism in Canada is both the professed ideology of the major political party and a principle of historical interpretation. Before considering Grant's account of the structure of Canadian history, to which some brief allusion has already been made, a short account of the liberal version (or Liberal, for the two are indistinct) may be in order. It is not too much of an exaggeration to say, with Professor Creighton, that the regnant notion of the Canadian nationality in its liberal form has been shaped by "a preoccupation, amounting almost to an obsession" with the twin achievements of Responsible Government and Dominion Status, that is, with the process of emancipation from Great Britain.[18] Britain, they say, opposed the forces of Canadian nationality gallantly represented by a series of Liberal politicians: Baldwin won Responsible Government, Blake diminished the powers of the Governor General, Laurier was constantly battling the Colonial Office, King had his famed quarrel with Byng and eventually gained us the Statute of Westminster, St Laurent stopped appeals to the Judicial Committee of the Privy Council, Pearson gave us our own flag, and Trudeau, if the English language permits it, intends to "patriate" the British North America Act. This is the potted history that most Canadian school-children learn.

The liberal interpretation of Canadian history, as the whig interpretation of British history, consists in the study of the past from the standpoint of present preoccupations; it is distinct, therefore, from narrative or analysis of the self-understanding of the historical actors. Liberal historians, as Liberal politicians, have thought and acted as though the creation of Canada took place wholly within the British Empire and not also within North America. Whether the persistent reluctance to deal with the struggle for a separate political existence in North America was deliberate and studied, a conscious act of continentalist propaganda, or merely a *suppressio veri, suggestio falsi*, we need not decide.[19] It is enough to point out that slogans known to every Canadian child, such as "good neighbour," or "the longest undefended border in the world" badly describe the long, and often armed struggle to maintain Canadian separateness. The liberal history of Canada is essentially a progressivist history, in our instance, the progressive integration of the continent so that there can be no point in defending the border. But, as Grant pointed out, "progressivist historians do not write much about the losers of history, because belief in progress often implies the base assumption that to lose is to have failed to grasp the evolving truth. Nevertheless, the losers existed and they are worth reading now that we see what kind of society the winners have made" (*TE*, p. 67).

As we saw in Grant's writing just after the war, he thought that Canadian independence had chiefly to be maintained against the might of the United States, and that Britain would serve as a helpful counterweight to the preponderant presence of the United States. Two things vitiated Grant's argument. First, he had underestimated the damage done by King in dissolving the links to Britain and forging them to the United States. Second, he had not yet witnessed the total collapse of Britain as a major power. One can see, if one had eyes for it, that the Ogdensburg Agreement of 1940, which gave the United States bases in Newfoundland, Bermuda and the West Indies in return for a motley collection of over-age destroyers, was both the first step in the creation of an American military empire in North America and a signal to Canada that we could no longer look to Britain for help.

If, as has been argued, Canadian conservatism is what Macdonald and his successors *did*, not what Burke and his successors *said*, then Grant was surely right in declaring that after 1940 "nationalism had to go hand in hand with some measure of socialism. Only nationalism could provide the political incentive for planning; only planning could restrain the victory of continentalism" (*LN*, p. 15). If, that is, preservation of political independence is the defining characteristic of Canadian conservatives, when the main challenge to that independence was economic (rather than, say, military, as in earlier days), then there is nothing paradoxical in advocating so-called socialist programmes to meet the threat. What is socialism, Grant asked, "if it is not the use of the government to restrain greed in the name of social good?" (*LN,* p. 59). After 1940 Canadian conservatives were "red tories" or they were nothing.[20]

In the event, they were nothing. The conservative dilemma was this: conservatism meant socialism, but a socialism without either the hard doctrine of class struggle or the soft one of altruistic cooperation among equals, both of which have contended for prominence within the CCF and its successor. There is, of course, the Conservative Party, yet to support that party as the incarnation of conservatism "means *de facto* to justify the continuing rule of the business man and the right of the greedy to turn all activities into sources of personal gain ... which is the very symbol of the unlimited and the disordered. ... Thus it is almost impossible to express the truth of conservatism in our society without seeming to justify our present capitalism" (*PMA,* p. 109). Diefenbaker, whose failure was analyzed with such power in *Lament for a Nation*, was skewered on the horns of just this dilemma. His failure was double: he failed as a politician because he approached the corporate economy with the perspectives of a prairie lawyer, and he failed as a conservative because this same "free enterprise" prejudice ensured that he would be unwilling to use government power to direct the economy. What rescued his failure from banality was his determination not to jump when orders came from Washington.[21] His behaviour during the defence crises of 1962 and 1963 were no worse than naive inasmuch as he thought that NATO was an alliance, not an instrument of the Pentagon, and that Canadian defence policy was formed in Ottawa. It was a naiveté not untouched with nobility.

More generally, Diefenbaker's failure was that he could do no more than evoke memories. What was his vision of the north but a romantic prolongation of the Laurentian dream, which had been obsolete for 30 years? "Memory is never enough to guarantee that a nation can articulate itself in the present. There must be a thrust of intention into the future" (*LN,* p. 12). For Canada, as ever, that meant a definition of purpose distinct from the American dream, freedom for endless consumption. None was available, since no Canadians in positions of power seemed able to think or act outside the terms that made the American dream so seductive. Canadians increasingly gave a higher loyalty to prosperity than independence. Thus, when Grant declared "the impossibility of Canada" (*LN,* p. 68), he meant no more than that the nation had finally abandoned a common intention to preserve itself politically. Our common intentions were, and are presently, expressed in the non-political desire for consumer goods.[22] To the extent that we have become if not satisfied, then at least content, in being plugged with such goods, we are the creatures of technique, good liberals, and last men.

Towards the Universal and Homogeneous State

In the introduction to the Carleton Library edition of *Lament for a Nation* Grant reflected on his statement of five years earlier. The problem was the same: "in what ways and for what reasons do we have the power and the desire to maintain some independence of the American empire." It was easier in 1970, during the war in Vietnam, to see undesirable aspects of the United States than it had been during the salad days of Camelot. Yet even in the original book there lay, behind immediate questions of policy, determined by Canada's position within the empire, "the deeper question of the fate of any particularity in the technological age. ... How much difference can there be between societies whose faith in 'the one best means' transcends even communist and capitalist differences?"

It was not simply that a succession of Liberal leaders had betrayed their country to foreigners. Rather, for increasing numbers of people, the distinction between native and foreign was fading. In *Lament for a Nation* Grant had pointed to the self-contradiction of a manifesto, published in May, 1964 in *Cité Libre* and *The Canadian Forum* and signed by seven French-speaking intellectuals including Marc Lalonde, Maurice Pinard, and Pierre-Elliott Trudeau, that appealed for a new and vital federalism in terms of certain apparently universal values. "The faith in universalism," Grant commented, "made it accurate to call the authors liberal. But how can a faith in universalism go with a desire for the continuance of Canada? The belief in Canada's continued existence has always appealed against the wider loyalty of the continent." It was true that Canadian nationalism was less parochial than French-Canadian nationalism, but "if one is a universalist, why should one stop at that point of particularity?" (*LN*, p. 85). That is, as Canadians, including French-speaking Canadians, the least modern citizens in the country, increasingly saw themselves as modern progressives and, as it were, abandoned St Thomas or Hooker for Locke (*LN*, pp. 62-65), simultaneously their highest public aspirations included no need for political separateness.

A second contradiction appeared in the document. The authors deplored the "victimization" of Indians, Métis, Orientals, Doukhobors, Hutterites and dissidents of all kinds, and called for the protection of those cultures. But universal values, whatever they may be, can be truly universal only if they are apprehended as such. And they can be so apprehended only if the individuals who undertake to judge them are led to see things the same way. Now, we see things differently in part at least because of the tacit instruction of differing cultures. Truly universal values, which are understood to be universal, imply a homogeneous culture through which the values may be apprehended as universal. Did these men not know, Grant asked, "that liberalism in its most equivocal form (that is, untinged by memories of past traditions) includes not only the idea of universality but also that of homogeneity? The high rhetoric of democracy was used when the Doukhobors were 'victimized' under a French-Canadian Prime Minister" (*LN*, p. 85). Far from protecting cultural diversity, liberalism turns as by an instinct to violence and war when cultural separateness shows signs of becoming serious, which is to say, political.[23]

Let us briefly summarize the argument so far: Grant has said that Canada became increasingly liberal under the guidance of King and the Liberal Party. The defining feature of liberalism was the opinion that the essence (if that scholastic term makes any sense in this context) of man was freedom. A secularized pioneering Puritanism, we saw, held that what chiefly concerns man in this life is to shape the world as we want it (*TE*, p. 114), the major agency for which is technique. The identification of technique with the goals of liberalism "makes our drive to technology still more dynamic than the nihilistic will to will which is emptied of all conceptions of purpose" (*TE*, p. 27).[24] In North America we are agreed upon our purpose, which is freedom, the freedom of everyone to realize one's capacities, the freedom to do as one will by willing the freedom of all. One consequence is that politics has become administration and political debates are essentially tactical disputations. In St Laurent's apposite phrase, Socialists were just Liberals in a hurry. There are no *real* differences: it's all a matter of timing.

The regime that incarnates the claims of Liberalism and is predicated upon the triumph of technique over chance in natural and human affairs has been called the universal and homogeneous state. The phrase was invented during the 1930s by Alexandre Kojève, a Russian emigré lecturing on Hegel in what we might call the graduate department of religion at the University of Paris. As we cannot presently consider the argument of Kojève in detail,[25] let us simply accept Grant's summary statement: "The universal and homogeneous state is the pinnacle of political striving. Universal implies a world-wide state, which would eliminate the curse of war among nations; homogeneous means that all men would be equal, and war among classes would be eliminated. The masses and the philosophers have both agreed that this universal and egalitarian society is the goal of historical striving" (*LN*, p. 53). Such a goal was fatal for any local and particular culture, especially one in close proximity to the heartland of modernity: "our culture floundered on the aspirations of the age of progress" (*LN*, p. 54).

Considered abstractly, one might think that because we have realized most fully the potentiality of the technological society, we should be most competent to account for it. Yet in actuality the same dilemma Grant noted earlier with respect to an expanding economy and adult education reappeared. "The very substance of our existing, which has made us the leaders in technique, stands as a barrier to any thinking which might be able to comprehend technique from beyond its own dynamism" (*TE*, p. 40). The barrier is not insurmountable, as Grant's work and the authorities upon which he relied so clearly shows. Nevertheless, it is true that thinking outside the assumptions of expansionist practicality makes one a stranger to public discourse (*TE*, p. 28), a statement that may serve as the equivalent with respect to theory that the previously noted remark on the impossibility of conservatism stands with respect to political action. But Grant is not a total stranger to the public realm. His books are read and studied for their arguments. Likewise, while conservatism may indeed be futile in the sense that it does not inform the deeds of human beings, it is not absolutely futile. It can still provide, if not an interpretation of those deeds, then perhaps the motivation for one. Indeed, Grant characterized his own relationship to conservatism in approximately those terms (*TE*, pp. 68-69). In moving from a lament for the dissolution of the tradition that once expressed the Canadian nationality to an account of the agent of that dissolution, modern technique, and the emerging social order, the universal and homogeneous state, one moves from conservatism to theory or, if you like, to philosophy. In passing from conservatism and tradition to philosophy we may be able to judge the goodness of the universal and homogeneous state.

Grant's purpose, we said earlier, was practical; here we have just maintained that the basis for judgement is philosophy or theory. There is no contradiction involved, for philosophy transcends the distinction between theory and practice. As all readers of Plato know, it is a way of living whose most obvious manifestation to those who live in other ways is irony.[26] Grant's theoretical account is practical in another way as well. Most people order their lives on the basis of commonsense judgements about phenomena and not on the basis of a considered reflection on the truthfulness, for example, of Xenophon's account of tyranny. Grant has undertaken such reflections and has grasped thereby something of the essential characteristics of tyranny and technology. Thus is he able to evoke those contingent everyday appearances that serve as evidence to describe the present regime and its approximation to the "ideal" of universal and homogeneous state. Most of Grant's readers, if they are persuaded to think, will have been so moved by the rhetorical irony and wit that gives pungency to his descriptions. And rhetoric is a practical art.

All readers of Grant's work doubtless have discovered his evocative power: "the space programme, necessary imperial wars and the struggle for recognition in the interlocking corporations can provide purpose only for a small minority. Purpose for the majority will be found in the subsidiary ethos of the fun culture. It will meet the needs of those who live in affluence but are removed from any directing of the society. One is tempted to state that the North American motto is: 'the orgasm at home and napalm abroad,' but in the nervous mobile society, people have only so much capacity for orgasm, and the flickering messages of the performing arts will fill the interstices" (*TE*, p. 126). Or again: "differences in the technological state are able to exist only in private activities: how we eat; how we mate; how we practise ceremonies. Some like pizza, some like steaks; some like girls, some like boys; some like synagogue, some like the mass. But we all do it in churches, motels, restaurants indistinguishable from the Atlantic to the Pacific" (*TE*, p. 26). Or again: "How can we escape the fact that the necessary end product of the religion of progress is not hope, but a society of existentialists who know themselves in their own self-consciousness, but know the world entirely as despair?" (*TE*, p. 58). In sum, Grant's rhetoric informs us that, as our society approaches the universal and homogeneous state, it is peopled with spiritless voluptuaries who ask for nothing but comfort and entertainment. "This is the price the race has to pay for overcoming two millennia of Christianity" (*TH*, p. 33).

Beyond the Last Men

Grant's first writings on politics showed him to be a progressive conservative. The contradictions of this position were slowly resolved; *Lament for a Nation* was an angry and simply conservative pamphlet. The distance and indirection of his later thought, which has grown detached from the heat of daily policy, suggest not a fading eros but the power of a soul that has experienced the cold lostness suggested by Nietzsche in one of the epigraphs to this paper. The loss of traditions deeply held and deeply loved must needs be painful. This is so, independently of the more speculative question of whether or not the universal and homogeneous state is (or would be) a planetary tyranny against which the continued existence of the nation would be a barrier, however modest. Simple patriotism, then, tells us we are right to lament the defeat of Canadian nationalism. But conservative lamentation can avoid degenerating into sentimentality only by courageously thinking through the meaning of our fate. And one does not begin the task of thinking unless one recognizes what is lamentable. The most obvious aspect of our fate as citizens of the universal and homogeneous state is that we are surrounded by nihilists and last men. The terms, of course, are Nietzsche's, and in his last book Grant spent some time discussing their significance.

Grant turned to Nietzsche because he "thought the conception of time as history more comprehensively than any other modern thinker before or since" (*TH*, p. 22). The phrase, "time as history" refers simply to "the idea that the events of human society have a meaning in their totality as directed towards an end" (*PMA*, p. 46). Nietzsche accepted not only the concept but the concrete experiential meaning that the concept carried. "He articulates what it is to have inherited existence as a present member of western society" (*TH* p. 24).[27] Specifically, he saw through the intellectual swindle that sustains the religion of progress. During Nietzsche's lifetime this religion found expression in terms of the increasing rationality of history. The learned pointed to science, the rest to railroads and the vicarious excitement of imperial conquest. Nietzsche understood that the same science that had no need, as Laplace said to Napoleon, for the hypothesis of God, also was unable to account for its own goodness. It was, therefore, an unjustifiable act of courtesy or cowardice to call a purposeless historical process rational, progressive, or good. Likewise, the fundamental teachings about man, God, society, and nature, by means of which the lives of most people are guided, the horizons, as Nietzsche called them, within which we live, were understood to be historical contingencies and not at all fundamental. When we know our horizons to be horizons, to be arbitrary and contingent, not rational, true, natural, necessary, etc., that is, when we live out the glib vocabulary of value-preferences, then follows, according to Nietzsche, the crisis of the modern will.

Much of Nietzsche's story is already familiar from Hegel's teaching: mastery of the earth through technological conquest of nature and imperial conquest of the "underdeveloped" world had as its objective the building of the universal and homogeneous state. In Europe and North America the objective was more or less realized and Nietzsche, unlike Hegel, had to live with success. The cry of the French Revolution, *"liberté, égalité, fraternité,"* could make sense only because those who gave it still retained a fiduciary commitment to God (or to a secular horizon with an equivalent psychological meaning). But when God has died and the horizon of horizons is gone, we are forced to live in an indifferent cosmos—or rather in a limbo between cosmos and chaos. We can subject other human beings, but we know there is no point to it. Unlike the pointless imperialism of the ancient world, so perfectly expressed by Scipio weeping as he beheld the destruction of enemy Carthage, there can be no good news. We have seen through pious as well as impious frauds.

The citizens of the universal and homogeneous state, we said, are of two varieties, last men and nihilists. The last men believe in the slogans of the French Revolution but even more they believe in the pursuit of happiness. Since they believe in equality, the happiness they pursue must be the same for all, which is to say, an animal happiness exhausted in the gratification of our several orifices (*TE*, p. 130). Or, in Kojève's terms, the re-animalization of mankind is the true meaning of the American way of life. The nihilists, on the other hand, despise the last men and seek fulfillment in resolute acts of will. They choose to be self-assertive but cannot know why. Nor does it matter to them: they will to will and that is enough. "The question is whether there can be men who transcend the alternatives of being nihilists or last men" (*TH*, p. 35). As to whether such men would appear, Nietzsche could not say. He was clear, however, as to what sort of men they would be: they would be ones who had overcome (or had been delivered from; the language is ambiguous) a will to revenge. Most profoundly, the will to revenge operates not upon one's contemporaries, the last men and the nihilists, but upon the past. Accordingly, the true "superman" is one who can say of the past that he would have sought it. The height of the human achievement is the act of *amor fati* "willed in a world where there is no possibility of either an infinite or finite transcendence of becoming or willing" (*TH*, p. 41). Having attained the *amor fati* beyond the horizons of good and evil, the Nietzschean "superman" can joyfully will to will.

Grant studied Nietzsche, we saw, because he most explicitly and comprehensively expressed the purposes of modern human beings as found in the concept of time as history. Yet, Grant added, "the conception of time as history is not one in which I think life can be lived properly. It is not a conception we are fitted for. Therefore I turn away from Nietzsche and in so turning express my suspicion of the assumptions of the modern project" (*TH*, p. 45). Grant's rejection of Nietzsche was similar to Scheler's: how is it possible for the *amor fati* to be freed of resentment if it grows from the experience of the death of God whose murder was (and is) undertaken from a spirit of revenge and jealousy? How, Grant asked, can anyone love fate unless "there could appear, however rarely, intimations ... of perfection (call it if you will God) in which our desires for good find their rest and their fulfillment" (*TH*, p. 46). If, nevertheless, one affirms the *amor fati* as absolute, how can one avoid Nietzsche's fate?

One need not read Nietzsche in order to be suspicious of the modern project. Indeed, Grant's several apologies for treating Nietzsche, and his warnings about trivializing his thought as shocking entertainment for the dull and bored, suggests that he did not expect many readers to open Nietzsche's works or, having done so, to study them. Other evidence to justify our suspicions is implied in Grant's statement that we are not fit for time as history. In an older language, to live time as history is unnatural.

That human beings have a natural and an unnatural way of living and conducting their common affairs is not a proposition that commands much acceptance today. It is far too late in an essay grown over-long to enquire into the meaning of nature for Grant. Nor is such a difficult task needful for our purposes. To put the matter plainly and in the crude language of commonsense, whether we accept what is natural and true makes no difference to nature and truth. If we live in a way for which we are not fit, then we shall suffer for it, not least of all in our inability to understand and put into words what we have done and what is being done to us. "The Platitude" that closes *Technology and Empire* is an attempt to instruct us on this matter. Liberalism, we know, is the great solvent of traditions, myths, philosophy and revelation. It excludes meaning. Politically, liberalism is institutionalized in the universal and homogeneous state, the regime of nihilists and last men; philosophically it amounts to the spiritual disorders of Nietzschean "supermen." What we do not know, however, is what we have lost through the triumph of liberalism, even if we know we have lost something and why: "all languages of good except the language of the drive to freedom have disintegrated, so it is just to pass some antique wind to speak of goods that belong to man as man. Yet ... if we cannot so speak, then we can either only celebrate or stand in silence before that drive. Only in listening for [and not speaking of], the intimations of deprival can we live critically in the dynamo" (*TE*, p. 14).

Whether what we hear, if we hear anything at all, is essential, just as what we yet may do in, and to, the world, is yet unknown. "For example, how far will the race be able to carry the divided state which characterises individuals in modernity: the plush patina of hectic subjectivity lived out in the iron maiden of an objectified world inhabited by increasingly objectifiable beings" (*TE*, p. 142). Is there a kind of critical mass where such division turns into rage, anxiety, or the fitful violence of the desperate? But not just our doings to each other are ambiguous: technology is first of all the manipulation of non-human nature. "Is the non-human simply stuff at our disposal, or will it begin to make its appearance to us as an order the purposes of which somehow resist our malleablizings?" To act against such an order ensures only our doom. It will appear to us, modern creatures of will, as sheer rebelliousness. "Are there already signs of revolts in nature?" (*TE*, p. 142).

It would be the height of pessimism,[28] Grant said, "to believe that our society could go on in its present directions without bringing down upon itself catastrophes. To believe the foregoing would be pessimism, for it would imply that the nature of things does not bring forth human excellence."[29] There is no account of the whole, of all that is, that shows the superiority of *posse* to *esse*. The attempt seriously to live that inversion may serve as a fittingly modern definition of madness. If we do not choose madness, we must cope with deep uncertainties; "it would be lacking in courage to turn one's face to the wall, even if one can find no fulfillment in working for or celebrating the dynamo. Equally it would be immoderate and uncourageous and perhaps unwise to live in the midst of our present drive, merely working in it and celebrating it, and not also listening or watching or simply waiting for intimations of deprival which might lead us to see the beautiful as the image, in the world, of the good" (*TE*, p. 143). Listening, the act of those who might hear the word; watching, the act of the theorist who would see what is; and for the rest, waiting, for we know our own uncertainties, though not, perhaps, what they mean. In the epoch of the universal and homogeneous state, Grant's intentions can still be called patriotic. He reminds us that while we may have forever lost the *patria* of our fathers, we need not go homeless in the world.

George Grant's Anguished Conservatism
by John Muggeridge

These days a conservative's lot is not a happy one. He is torn between his dislike of the reigning progressivism and his sense of duty to the society which preaches it. His rejection of officially accepted wisdom turns him into what George Grant calls "a stranger to the public realm," and yet his esteem for community and tradition makes him long for a public realm to feel at home in. He is a heretic with orthodoxy in his soul, a scorner of grape boycotts and a petitioner for the return of the Latin Mass. The world calls him divisive, moralistic and irrelevant. He sees himself as a defender of order, morality and belief in eternity. The trouble is that the world and he use different dictionaries. For him philosophy truly means the pursuit of wisdom; for him ideas are indeed real and possessed of consequences. For the world, the only consequences that count are those which can be measured by scientists; for the world, a philosophy incapable of being tested in the laboratory is useful only, as Frank Underhill, Canada's most distinguished modernist, once remarked, "to make us feel more comfortable, not to make us see more clearly."[1]

The Canadian writer who most profoundly expresses this conservative predicament is George Grant. Again and again he stresses how deeply rooted in western Christian tradition is modernity. It is a gnosticism, the oldest of all heresies, and the one which most closely reflects genuine Christian fervour. The modern spirit, Grant argues in *Philosophy in the Mass Age*, may *look* like the antithesis of the religious.[2] In fact it is a secular form of the religious. The age of progress far from being a departure from the age of faith, is a logical outcome of it. "The Christian idea of history as the divinely ordained process of salvation, culminating in the kingdom of God" he sees naturally developing into "the futuristic spirit of progress in which events are shaped by the will of man," and the only mediating term between these two contrasting views of history is freedom.[3] It is all very well, therefore, to throw in one's lot, as Grant does, with the ancients and to stand aside from the mass society plumping for traditional morality, but this "act of philosophy," to use Grant's words, "is not only a continual negation of the self, a continual self-transcendence; it is often also a negation of what is most dear in one's own society."[4]

In Grant's opinion, then, progressivism is not something imposed on us from outside by power-hungry pragmatists; rather, it reflects a lawlessness written in our collective heart. The technological society remains inevitable while our deepest concern is for the sort of freedom which only untrammelled technology can provide. And who dares stand against freedom? "Those who criticize our age," Grant warns, "must contemplate pain, infant mortality, crop failures in isolated places and the sixteen-hour day."[5] If such physical and cultural deprivations are indeed considered the only absolute moral evils, then the claims of progressivism are irrefutable, necessity and goodness do indeed march together, and those symptoms of global homogeneity so chillingly described by Grant — emerging technocracy he calls "Fellini's *Satyricon* plus techne" — simply indicate that the liberal universe is unfolding as it should. 'Tis madness to resist or blame the force of angry heaven's flame' — especially when the heavenly flame in question promises a vaccine against venereal disease and birth control in the municipal water supply.

But what proves most clearly to conservative thinkers such as Grant the invincibility of progressivism in western society is the fact that the state has become its established church. We live in a liberal theocracy whose dogmas are inculcated through our system of public schooling. Thus "values education," the closest equivalent to religious instruction permitted in Ontario secondary schools, turns out to be a celebration of moral relativism, while even privately financed Roman Catholic high schools have found it necessary to put "Man in Society" in place of "Religion" on their curriculum. This is entirely understandable. Theocracies cannot allow citizens to be held by rival religious loyalties. In British Columbia in the fifties, pluralism stopped short at allowing Doukhobors' children to stay out of state schools, while in Alberta in the seventies Mennonites are barred from teaching their children traditional morality during school hours, even at their own expense. As Grant points out in the introduction to "Religion and the State," the only interpretation that technological liberalism allows to survive is "that part of it (e.g. the thought of Teilhard) which ... plays the role of flatterer to modernity."[6]

Grant argues, moreover, that most North Americans are believing members of the established church of progressivism. There was much talk in the sixties about the alternative society, but how alternative was it? In the seventies its leaders have for the most part become pillars of the Establishment, and its once inflammatory rhetoric is today the stuff of Sunday sermons. Grant's essay, "In Defence of North America," written in 1969 at the height of the anti-Viet Nam War movement, shows how dissent, even then, was being institutionalized, the demands of the fashion and record industries overshadowing those of protest and revolution.[7] "The directors of General Motors," he writes, "and the followers of Professor Marcuse sail down the same river in different boats," while our political arguments he refers to as "squalls on the surface of the ocean" taking place "within the common framework that the highest good is North America moving forward in expansionist practicality."[8]

Despite everything, however, Grant refuses to embrace today's fashionable revolutionism. He is neither an integrist working to restore some unrecoverable golden age, nor a futurist hoping with bombs or broadsheets to usher in a new age. For all his anguished conservatism, he is scrupulously loyal to the system under which he lives. Thus he rejects Edgar Friedenberg's definition of the state as a self-legitimating conspiracy, and in particular he rejects the contractualist view of political relationships which such a definition implies. For Grant, good Platonist that he is, the state must always be something more than a mere contract which generations of unscrupulous politicians have turned into an instrument for their own self-aggrandizement. In Grant's eyes the state has religious connotations; men naturally set up governments to create an atmosphere of order in which they may pursue virtue; order and morality go together, as do disorder and immorality. No wonder, then, that in his debate with Friedenberg he defends the practice of shooting looters. It is not that he has an inordinate love for the institution of private property, but rather that he believes in the sanctity of order. On the same grounds he praises the way in which, in the Canadian West, authority preceded settlement.

He is able to do so all the more whole-heartedly admiring as he does the principles for which that authority stood. These were Christian principles. Grant is a Christian. In British societies, he claims, there was a natural tendency for Peace and Order to be accompanied by Good Government because British jurists have traditionally stressed the connection between positive and God-given law, and British social reformers appealed directly to Christian values. In the nineteenth century the religious impulse sent missionaries to the heathens, but it also prompted the setting up in British territories of a system of legal and political rights which Sheila and George Grant in their contribution to *The Right to Birth* call "the crown of our heritage." "The very idea of rights," they contend, "is founded on the Biblical assumption that human beings are children of

God."[9] They go on to argue that once law-makers discard this assumption, all rights are threatened. Hence the strenuousness with which the Grants oppose legalized abortion. It reduces men at a certain stage in their development from the status of living souls to that of unwanted tissue. It augurs the end of humane society. Already unborn children have been officially stripped of all rights to existence in the United States. "Are we," the Grants ask, "going to let it happen in Canada and open the gates to all the consequences of tyranny that will follow?"[10]

Twenty years ago George Grant noted that Canadians did not yet consider abortion as a simple matter of convenience because in this country "the old tradition about this matter lives on."[11] It died officially with the passing of the Omnibus Bill in 1969. Under the moral and legal tutelage of Mr Trudeau we have reaped where the Wolfenden report sowed. The once widely held notion that society in Canada has a more conservative tone than that in the United States is no longer valid. Canadians today are in the modernist vanguard.

For a conservative such as George Grant, however, the death of a particular tradition does not remove the obligation to defend the values that it once enshrined. Values are not subject to change. Nor can true philosophy ever be made totally to depend on the prevailing intellectual climate. Grant shuns both historicism and determinism. We may indeed be moving inexorably towards what C.S. Lewis called the abolition of man, but there is always the possibility of setting up road blocks, and who knows what the future holds? Grant answers Friedenberg's campus anarchism in the words of his favourite conservative hero, Saint Thomas More, spoken, significantly enough, from the scaffold: "When you can't get the good to happen, prevent the very worst from happening."[12]

Grant's Platonist political outlook is perhaps most clearly reflected in his devotion to the idea of Canada. He has all of Socrates' passionate commitment to the laws of his society. Indeed he is the only modern Canadian writer one can even remotely imagine talking to a personification of them. "As some form of political loyalty is part of the good life," he writes concerning the disappearance of his fatherland, "we must be allowed to lament the passing of what has claimed our allegiance."[13] Critics have called *Lament for a Nation* an expression of nostalgia for the Victorian past.[14] There is, however, nothing very nostalgic about its tone of white-hot indignation. It was written in the rough and tumble of a federal election to expose a campaign of vilification, directed, as Grant saw it, against one of the party leaders. It is about the way in which the idea of Canada espoused by that leader has been betrayed, which for Grant means how Canada has been betrayed. National betrayal is hardly a fit theme for nostalgia.

But Grant is more than just an inflexible Canadian. He is a Canadian-minded conservative. Canadianism is the medium through which he expresses his conservatism. To be a Canadian for him is to be *per se* a conservative. When he thinks about Canada he thinks about reality, and when he thinks about the destruction of Canadian independence he thinks about the ways in which modernists distort reality. Hence that unexpected mixture in all his writings of philosophical analysis and references to the current North American scene. No inquiry by him into the origins and growth of progressivism is complete without a comment on the Americanization of the Halifax skyline, or a remark about the deepening control of multi-national corporations based in the United States over the social life of southern Ontario. His point is that these things go together. Capitalism is an economic manifestation of the idea of progress. The United States is the heartland of world capitalism. Thus the idea of progress speaks with an American accent. More than that, it is the mark of American government. To embrace it involves taking out citizenship in the continental empire of the United States. To resist it presupposes a desire to live under a different flag. This, according to Grant, was the central insight of the Loyalists. They were the first and most authentic Canadian nationalists.

The man Grant sees as the modern embodiment of this conservative-separatist impulse in North America is, of course, John Diefenbaker. In Diefenbaker, Grant hears the last strangled voice of his pre-modernist Loyalist ancestors. Diefenbaker stood for something beyond efficiency. His very absurdity is an unprogressivist mark in his favour. He wooed all the wrong friends and alienated all the wrong enemies. It was obvious at the time that Diefenbaker and educated Canadians belonged to different worlds. Many thought their government in the hands of a maniac; others more charitably viewed the prime minister as a Canadian Don Quixote who had ridden out of Prince Albert having had his head turned by reading too many books about Sir John A. Macdonald. This in Grant's opinion was the inevitable fate of a Loyalist in the age of progress. In such times standing up to continentalist giants was bound to look like tilting at windmills.

Grant's picture of Diefenbaker as the last of the Loyalists has some validity. Loyalists hold fast to that which seems good; modernists, to that which seems expedient. Diefenbaker holds fast to the idea of a single British Canada. This is what makes him look so out of step with his contemporaries. In modernist Ottawa he came to resemble a fundamentalist preacher at a convention of new-wave theologians. He actually believed in the Confederation Agreement and voted against the Official Languages Act in order to uphold it. The sincerity of Diefenbaker's

Loyalism is apparent from the degree of hostility and ridicule which it provoked. In 1963, as Grant shows, he managed to unite Washington, Colorado Springs and most of Ottawa against him, while in 1969, when the truly Loyalist strand of moral conservatism in his thinking prompted him to lead his party in voting against the Omnibus Bill, supporters of that enlightened legislation called across the House to invite him into the twentieth century.

But of course Diefenbaker was very far from being a parfit gentle Loyalist knight. As a political leader he had glaring faults, and George Grant is well aware of them. *Lament for a Nation*'s original title was *A Defence of Mr. Diefenbaker*, but it does little to raise Diefenbaker's reputation in the eyes of the reader. Grant's defence consists in refuting the libels of Diefenbaker's enemies; nowhere does he make a concerted attempt to justify his subject's conduct, nor does he ever hide the fact that as a statemen he prefers Howard Green. The truth is that *Lament for a Nation* is not chiefly concerned with polishing Diefenbaker's image as a hero of Canadian conservatism. It is concerned with using Diefenbaker's fate to illustrate the author's favourite thesis: that preserving a truly conservative tradition in North America depended on preserving Canada as a truly separate national community. *Lament for a Nation* is sub-titled *The Defeat of Canadian Nationalism. The Defeat of North American Conservatism* would have served just as well.

Grant's equating of nationalist and philosophical purposes has its dangers. A philosophy expressed in nationalist terms above all runs the risk of losing its universalist credentials. It begins to sound parochial. Friedrich Hertz compares national ideologies to coloured glasses which only a very few in the national community are able to take off. Grant belongs to that clear-eyed minority. He has shown, particularly in the last pages of *Lament for a Nation*, that he can see without his Loyalist spectacles. "My lament," he writes, "is not based on philosophy but on tradition. If one can not be sure about the answers to the most important questions, then tradition is the best basis for practical life. Those who loved the older traditions of Canada may be allowed to lament what has been lost, even though they do not know whether or not that loss will lead to some greater political good."[15] In the end the note of compulsive Canadianism dies. Even the destruction of Canadian independence could turn out to have been a blessing in disguise.

Elsewhere in his writing, however, Grant sounds less magnanimous. He leaves the impression that tradition and philosophy are one, and hence that progressivism must be looked upon not as a global idea but as an imperial one; as the idea, in fact, behind United States cultural and economic imperialism in Canada. Grant is fully aware that the worst forms of tyranny in the name of progress are being exercised in the world today outside North America. The KGB and the CIA are simply not in the same class, nor is the treatment of Canadian consumers at the hands of American big business in any way comparable with what is happening to the peoples of Eastern Europe and Soviet Asia who have the misfortune of being neither Marxists nor Great Russians. Even Amnesty International is hard pressed to find prisoners of conscience in the capitalist west. Grant knows all this, but being a loyal Canadian nationalist, he concentrates his published invective on the uncivilizing and anti-communitarian impact of United States imperialism. This is a matter of strategy as well as conviction. He is, after all, as he insists in a footnote to *Philosophy in the Mass Age*, a strong supporter of the idea of a British North America, which must mean being prepared sooner or later to use the weapons of philosophy to combat the idea of a purely American North America. Thus in writing against the mass age, he predictably implies it is the American age.[16] Would not Socrates in the same position have been "guilty" of similar intellectual ethnocentricity, and in any case is not ethnocentricity more often than not a pejorative term for patriotism?

The danger, of course, with patriotic writing is that it gives rise to over-simplification. Kenneth Minogue calls nationalist theories "distortions of reality which allow men to cope with situations which they might otherwise find unbearable." George Grant, faced with the unbearable prospect of *de facto* continental assimilation, slackens his pursuit of undistorted reality. He makes a philosophic virtue out of the patriotic necessity of seeing the world in terms of us and them. Too often Grant's reader is led to believe that the United States is a nation of wicked anti-Canadian contractualists, and that the Marxist interpretation of capitalist imperialism is in fact the correct one. A footnote in *Lament for a Nation* expresses sympathy for Barry Goldwater's brand of conservatism, but it is only a footnote. The text sees no important difference between the 1964 platform of Senator Goldwater and that of Lyndon Johnson. Under the skin, both were American libertarian progressivists, both opposed the organic or British Canadian view of society, both represented an ideology whose exponents were out to get Canada.

No wonder, then, that Grant was taken up by the New Left nationalists in the sixties. They too wanted to see the struggle between right and wrong as a Canadian-U.S. affair, down-trodden Canadian workers victimized by grasping American capitalists. Grant's Loyalist rhetoric could be made to bear out their left-wing demonology. His rumblings against U.S. imperialism added authenticity to their own tired old anti-American sloganeering. A previous generation of Canadian liberal nationalists had dismissed such stereotyping as being clearly symptomatic of paranoia, and a small but hardy band of moderate liberals led by Robert Fulford of *Saturday Night* continues to do so. Explaining why the Canadian nationalist movement turned leftwards in the sixties is not the purpose of this paper. Certainly, it was helped in that direction by George Grant apparently lending support to the rhetoric of leftwing extremists, by his writing, for example, about Vietnam as if the only aggression being carried out in that war-torn country was at the hands of United States airmen in the name of progress dropping bombs made in Hamilton on unoffending villagers.[17] Unwittingly Grant has helped to make such a view part of the current wisdom involved in being Canadian.

But in the end Grant is not a nationalist. He is not after power for a particular class. He does not see national independence as a means of collective self-advancement. Above all he has abided by his own warning that "to want one's thought about the practical to be influential can lead to ... corrupting ambition."[18] He does not hunger and thirst after influence. He is perfectly willing to swim against the tide in obscurity. Hence he and the New Left have long since parted company, and in the seventies he is criticised not only for day-dreaming about the Rosedale of his childhood, but for being at heart just another member of the Ontario bourgeoisie, his thinking having been conditioned through birth in what one critic contemptuously dismissed as a Fine Old Ontario Family. According to this view Grant is pessimistic because he doesn't really *want* the class struggle to succeed.

It is Grant's yearning for a homeland, not his desire for power which is behind his Loyalism. As a Loyalist he is better able to resolve the conservative's terrible dilemma of being a stranger in his own gates. Grant knows that whatever was genuinely conservative about the tradition of his ancestors has long since departed from it. He himself was brought up among the truest and bluest Toronto Loyalists. They were progressivists to a man. He told me that, with them, keeping to the old beliefs was simply good breeding. The idea behind Upper Canada College was to turn stock brokers into gentlemen. Nor, to do justice to that academy, did its sister schools in England entertain any higher objectives. Grant makes clear that the British conservative tradition was dead and buried long before the great American progressivist expansion of the mid-twentieth century. Indeed it is the very impossibility of conservatism which, for Grant, makes it worth being a Loyalist.

Success belongs to progress. Grant seeks after neither success nor progress. This is what distinguishes his anguished conservatism from the purely angry variety espoused by English-Canadian secularists such as Donald Creighton. Grant is a Loyalist because he wants an intellectual country to belong to, outside the modernist establishment. He says: "... it would be lacking in courage to turn one's face to the wall, even if one can find no fulfilment in working or celebrating the dynamo. Equally it would be immoderate and uncourageous and perhaps unwise to live in the midst of our present drive, merely working in it and celebrating it, and not listening or watching or simply waiting for intimations of deprival which might lead us to see the beautiful as the image, in the world, of the good."[19] Adhering to the Loyalist tradition allows him to avoid both alternatives.

George Grant: Liberal, Socialist, or Conservative?
by A. James Reimer

*Such a red tory is George Grant, who has associations with both
the Conservative party and the NDP, and who has recently published
a book which defends Diefenbaker, laments the death of "true"
British conservatism in Canada, attacks the liberals as individual-
ists and Americanizers, and defines socialism as a variant of
conservatism ...*[1]

– Gad Horowitz

The Problem: The Inadequacy of Political Categories

The distinctiveness of the Canadian political tradition lies in the unique
interdependence of its three major parties – Liberal, New Democratic, and
Conservative. Gad Horowitz has convincincly demonstrated how the
strength of socialism in Canada is related to the presence of toryism, how
conservatism shares some crucial ideological views with socialism (an
organic view of society), and how Canadian liberalism, unlike its American
counterpart, is a party of the centre, triumphantly defining itself over
against both the "left" and the "right."[2] In George Grant we find such a
uniquely Canadian interaction between elements of liberalism, socialism,
and conservatism. He is a "red tory," a conservative influenced by
socialism, whose early liberalism has to a large extent determined the
direction of his later thought.

While conservatism is the dominant strand in Grant's work, one
cannot without grave distortion reduce his political and philosophical
thought to that of a particular political tradition, much less a given
political party. In his 1959 book, *Philosophy In The Mass Age*, for
instance, Grant argues for a dialectical balance between conservatism and
radicalism. Here he suggests that the "truth of conservatism," which is its
emphasis on order and limit, must be combined with the "truth of
radicalism," which is its "unlimited hope that evil is not necessary." A
sound political theory needs both a notion of limit and a concept of
history-making. While we all need a "proper conservatism, an order which
gives form to persons, to families, to education, to worship, to politics,
and to the economic system," we must in Canada go beyond a simple
conservatism to avoid justifying the rule of big business, capitalism, and
personal gain.[3]

Despite variations between thinkers and countries, the underlying premise of liberalism, in Grant's view, is the notion of freedom as autonomy — human freedom to shape itself, society, and history without reference to eternal absolutes, to divine law. In his brilliantly argued book, *The Poverty of Liberalism*, American social philosopher Robert Paul Wolff, astutely shows the inherent contradictions within modern liberalism. The poverty of liberalism, for Wolff, as for all nineteenth-century conservatives and radicals alike, is its emphasis of "private interests" at the expense of the common good, a sense of community.

A quick comparison between Grant and Wolff immediately reveals some fundamental differences. They share a common dislike for the poverty of liberalism, and for some of the same reasons. Wolff, however, as a radical, accepts the historicism of the modern age and argues for a more rational, participatory, and communal society in the future. Grant's critique of liberalism and the modern political project goes much deeper at this point: he rejects the underlying historicism of modernity, and lays the blame for this historicism right at the feet of liberalism. Consequently, unlike Wolff, Grant offers us no political vision for the future, for any such political hope would itself depend on the liberal notion of historical freedom.

Liberalism in its broadest sense denotes for Grant "a set of beliefs which proceed from the central assumption that man's essence is his freedom and therefore that what chiefly concerns man in this life is to shape the world as we want it."[4] Western man has one predominant religion, the religion of progress and domination — mastery of human and non-human nature by man. Grant subjects this religion to a profound analysis and critique. His central charge against it is its ironical pursuit of homogeneity. While the modern age pays lip-service to the basic principles of liberalism, such as separation of church and state, and the pluralistic freedom of religious and ethnic minorities, it is in fact committed to the achievement of a monolithic society.

Grant does not, however, limit his critique to liberalism in general. He makes a similar critique of the Canadian Liberal Party. His most popular and most specific treatment of Canadian politics is his somewhat enigmatic defense of John Diefenbaker in *Lament For A Nation*, 1965. Unlike Horowitz, who emphasizes the national distinctiveness of Canadian liberalism, Grant points to the inherent anti-nationalistic sentiments within liberalism. Grant attributes the lamentable defeat of Canadian nationalism and its Conservative champion Diefenbaker to the liberal policy of seeing Canada as "a branch-plant society of American capitalism."[5]

Grant's harsh anti-liberalism may be somewhat mitigated, however, by seeing it in the light of his own intellectual development. Reflecting on his past, Grant attributes the overcoming of the "absolute liberalism" and "secularized Calvinism", in which he was brought up in Toronto, to his experiences in World War Two.[6] In another brief autobiographical allusion, Grant remarks that he recognized "the barrenness of the all-pervading liberalism" early in his life and "spent much of [his] life looking for a more adequate stance."[7] In actuality, Grant did not extricate himself from this early liberalism until much later, as he himself admits.

One of his first major public essays, *The Empire: Yes or No?*, published in 1945, is still dominated by liberal sentiments. There is in this pamphlet a passionate optimism about the perfectibility of man, and a belief in human progress. "Eventually blatant power," he says here, "can be reduced and voluntary law take its place. Human freedom is, in fact, our goal."[8] Even here, however, Grant's stance is not one of unmixed liberalism. His whole essay is in fact a rejection of American rugged individualism and crass capitalism, and an espousal of a balance between individual freedom and an ordered society in a distinctly British-Canadian tradition. His strongly nationalistic sentiments betray an inherent conservatism even at this point.

A similar mixture of liberal values and anti-liberal sentiments is evident in a much later work, *Philosophy In The Mass Age*, 1959. This is by no means a "fiery liberal pamphlet," or a "progressivist tract" to use Lampert's words.[9] Grant has become much more critical of the western notion of progress. His most important category for criticizing liberalism in this work is that of *limit*, a capacity to say "No" to unlimited progress and to evil. Man must regain a belief in absolute transcendence and a belief in God.[10]

Grant's relation to liberalism becomes increasingly more complex after his change of mind in the early 1960s, when he rejects liberalism as such. As late as 1976, in his essay *Abortion and Rights: The Value of Political Freedom*, co-authored by Sheila Grant, he seems to draw heavily on certain aspects of the liberal tradition to refute other modern liberal notions. He argues against abortion and the modern liberal criteria used to justify abortion – convenience, situational ethics, and the rights of the mother in respect to those of the foetus. In doing so, Grant draws on other aspects of the liberal tradition – the political freedom of all Canadians, "the sanctity of the individual," the inalienable God-given rights of every human being to life, including the unborn child.[11] Grant is quite willing to accept some of the wisdom inherent in the liberal political and legal traditions of the west. What he rejects is not every aspect of liberalism, but its dominant assumption; namely, that man is free to shape his life and the world the way he desires.

We have interpreted Grant's view of political liberalism in the light of his relation to liberalism in general. This relation is a complex one. His profound critique of the tradition cannot be reduced to a *simple* rejection. It must be seen in the context of his liberal past, liberal elements in his early writings, and his apparent indebtedness to liberalism in his later thought. Most of all, his own ambiguous relationship to the modern world which is largely founded on liberal principles, must be taken into account. The fact that Grant's own intellectual development has largely been shaped by his struggle against assumptions growing out of liberal society, ironically suggests to what an extent that very tradition has influenced his thought.

The Ambiguity of Socialism

The ambiguity of socialism lies in its equivocal relation to liberalism. On the one hand, growing out of the liberal tradition, socialism was greatly indebted to liberalism, particularly to its notions of scientific reason and historical freedom. Like the liberals, the socialists believed unquestioningly in man's freedom and responsibility to shape history. They assumed that man would be able to overcome the economic contradictions within society, to ameliorate human suffering, and to perfect society. On the other hand, however, socialism saw liberal individualism as one of society's greatest enemies. Here it allied itself with conservatism. It agreed that the social body must be seen in corporate and organic terms, and that social order and control were necessary. This organic notion was characteristic especially of the British evolutionary form of socialism.[12]

This divided loyalty to liberalism evident within the socialist tradition itself largely explains Grant's own rather ambiguous view of Marxism, socialism, and the New Left in America. We have seen how Grant, in the *Philosophy*, strives for a union of conservative order and radical freedom. In this work, Grant gives a remarkably sympathetic account of Marxism, particularly its anti-individualism, its commitment to a "concrete overcoming of evil in the world," and even its "account of science as essentially an ethical, indeed a redemptive activity, the means by which men were to be freed from the evils of pain and work."[13] It is, however, the Marxist's inadequate understanding of the subjective freedom of the human spirit that mitigates Grant's positive portrayal of Marxism at this time.

It was his *Lament*, however, which earned Grant the wide-spread reputation of being a red tory. Here he makes the striking claim that socialism, by using government force to restrain the greedy passions of man for the sake of the common good, appeals "to the conservative idea of social order against the liberal idea of freedom."[14] In Grant's opinion, the confusion of the Canadian socialist movement is the result of its insufficient appreciation for this conservative component in its ideology.

Grant's initial sympathy for the socialist vision becomes increasingly more clouded. His disillusionment with the radical dream of overcoming evil goes hand in hand with his growing aversion to the modern liberal project *in toto*. More and more he sees the task facing the modern world not as the war on poverty or the creation of an organic society, but rather resistance to the technological monolith. It is true that Marxist communism legitimately criticizes the private interests of Western capitalism and its hypocritical espousal of "value-free" science. Nevertheless, the humanism and other virtues of Marxism are ultimately undercut by the socialist commitment to the mastery and domination of nature. Like all the other Western ideologies, Marxism essentially believes that technology is necessary for human progress. While modern Marxism puts technological development into a "corporate framework," it still participates in the modern race towards an homogeneous state.[15]

The mixed feelings Grant has towards socialism come through most clearly in his attitude to the New Left in America. Throughout his work, Grant sees signs of hope in youthful nonconformity, including the radical protests of the 1960s. In a most remarkable dialogue between himself and Horowitz, two Canadian red-tories, Grant declares himself on New Left ideologies.[16] Abbie Hoffman and others like him, Grant says, are reaching for values and categories that transcend the modern Western world — "true being," "the good," "noble deeds." But their thought and action tends to be clouded by utopianism. Marcuse, a "highly intelligent Marxist," is still committed to technology as a way of transcending technology. According to Marcuse, we can enjoy nature by conquering it. It is this domination of nature that Grant believes "will cut men off from nobility and greatness," and leave them with empty freedom.[17]

In the end socialism's affinity to liberalism proves to be stronger than its ties with conservatism. It is Grant's profound realization that both liberalism and socialism lead us down the path to a universally administered homogeneous society that makes him into a conservative. It is this turning from the future to the past, this rejection of any radical vision of a future perfect egalitarian society, that ultimately explains Grant's search for a "true" conservatism.

The Impossibility of Conservatism

The defeat of Napoleon in 1815 marked the beginning of conservative reaction to revolutionary ideology in Europe and its cries of liberty, fraternity, and equality.

Grant argues that at the time when Canada was becoming a nation, there was no longer a true conservatism.[18] Presumably, Grant means that British conservatism had already become historicist and progressivist in its view of man and society. It is true that Burke, while rejecting revolutionary ideology, did accept the notion of progress *per se*. Through careful guidance society could move forward to ever higher degrees of perfection. Grant considers this kind of "progressive" conservatism as being inherently modern. Increasingly, Grant identifies himself with a much more radical form of conservatism — an ancient non-historicist type of conservatism.

It is undeniable, however, that Grant holds many things in common with modern philosophical conservatism. Robert Schuettinger cites five "dispositions", which he feels characterize the conservative mind: belief in 1) divine purpose within history and God-given laws of morality, 2) social order through restraint and respect for tradition, 3) variety rather than uniformity, 4) a qualitatively good life including honor and duty, and 5) limit to man's reason.[19] Interestingly, these very themes keep on recurring in Grant's writings.

Absolutely central to Grant's critique of the modern world, for instance, is his belief in the reality of a " 'higher' divine power," an eternal realm of absolute values, which stands over against the relativities of historical existence. Further, it is clear that Grant is convinced that social order and restraint are necessary to check the rugged individualism that characterizes the Western liberal world. Thirdly, Grant's objection to the universal and homogeneous state puts him *ipso facto* on the side of pluralism and variety. Grant also considers the striving after human excellence to be the most noble goal of man. "Love of the good is man's highest end, but it is of the nature of things that we come to know and to love what is good by first meeting it in that which is our own. ..."[20] Modern society has substituted empty freedom and equality for human excellence and nobility.

Despite these obviously modern conservative elements in Grant's thought, his indictment of contemporary political conservatism is clear. The particular application of Grant's disillusionment with political conservatism is perhaps nowhere better expressed than in his *Lament* of 1965. "Conservatives who attempt to be practical face a dilemma," he asserts. "If they are not committed to a dynamic technology, they cannot hope to make any popular appeal. If they are so committed, they cannot hope to be conservative."[21] In the end, "conservatism must languish as technology increases."[22] All conservatives can do is to use existing institutions to provide a remnant of social order and stem the tide of technological chaos. In such a situation, the danger is that conservatism becomes reactionary, defending law and order on the streets, class and imperial interests, and property rights. In the *Lament*, Grant links the impossibility of conservatism with the impossibility of Canada as a nation. Conservatism and nationalism live together and with the inevitable demise of Canadian nationalism, in the face of growing international business corporations, genuine conservatism also necessarily succumbs.

In his *Philosophy*, 1959, Grant still believes in the political utility of philosophy. He considers a synthesis between the conservative notion of limit and the modern assumption of freedom to be viable and necessary. His loyalty and responsibility lies with the modern world. Theoretically, he is unwilling to take sides between the ancient and the modern view of reality. By 1963, when Grant writes his essay, "Religion and the State," he has become convinced that the classical esteem for "reverence" is more true to reality than the modern obsession with "freedom."[23] But he still assumes that his concerns have an audience in the modern world. Conservatism still is theoretically viable. By 1969, when he writes an introduction to this essay in his *Technology and Empire*, Grant has come to the full realization that theoretical conservatism as an anachronism in modern politics, is futile. While conservatism may be "a noble practical stance," theoretical conservatism has no applicability, no connecting point with the modern mind. In fact, a " 'conservative' hope" tends to cloud the most important questions arising out of our age.[24]

A Meta-political Stance

The impossibility of conservatism becomes for Grant not only the impossibility of one political option, but the impossibility of politics itself — liberal, social, or conservative. The noble art of politics has turned into technocracy and administration. The tragedy is that man is essentially a political being, and by being deprived of politics he is alienated not only from society but from himself. What Grant is left with at the end is a type of meta-political stance, which gives him a clarity of understanding but prevents him from identifying with any given political program. He becomes a type of prophet who "calls us to account for what we have done to the world, in the biblical terms of good and evil."[25] Grant concludes that the ancients, particularly Plato, understood reality, politics, and tyranny better than we do.

The impossibility of politics and radical activity for social change leaves Grant with philosophy, art, and imagination, the only true enemies of modern tyranny. This meditative/contemplative mode of thinking, to use Darrol Bryant's terms,[26] takes place on two levels: re-collection and contemplation. On the first level, one attempts to remember something one has lost. In his *Lament*, this takes the form of "lamenting" the death of Canadian nationalism. It is not so much a lament for the concrete political reality as the "lament for the romanticism of the original dream" that the British had for Canada.[27] It is the re-collection of a past good, of "one's own," of a tradition, of a time before the triumph of the modern age. Ultimately, it is the re-collection of a much more distant past – the truths of Athens and Jerusalem.

Grant's longing for the ancient past is not a simple remembering. It is an affirmation that there in fact exists an eternal realm, which the ancients recognized and which we have lost. The second level, therefore, is a philosophical and religious contemplation of eternal verities, which even now may break through our technological dynamo giving us "intimations of deprival."[28] This realization drives Grant beyond a pure fatalism, pessimism, or even despair. To be "pessimistic", in Grant's words, would be to reject belief in an eternal reality, would be to "believe that our society could go on in its present directions without bringing down upon itself catastrophes."[29] Grant's conclusion is a hopeful one: that nature itself will revolt, that the noble, the great, and the good will ultimately triumph. But this victory will not be brought about by political activity as it is perceived in the modern world.

Grant's disillusionment with all radical activity, his rejection of the modern political project as such, would seem to leave him ethically impotent to contribute to the triumph of the noble, the great, and the good; his meta-political stance would seem to sever him from all concrete social involvement. Grant's actual life demonstrates the contrary. His clear sympathy for many of the protests of the New Left in America in the 1960s, his continuing interest in questions of justice, his strong stand on abortion and the right to life, his opinionated views on Canadian and French nationalism, all betray his ongoing social and political involvement. It is, however, a kind of "rear-guard" political potency which assumes that the best we may be able to do is to keep the worst from happening. To engage actively in trying to bring about the best would simply harden the directions in which society is already going.

We have in this essay followed Grant's writings through various phases. His early writings are strongly liberal in sentiment, committed to notions of human freedom and historical progress. As Grant becomes disillusioned with these liberal assumptions of the modern age, particularly with Western individualism and the rule of big business, he moves into a phase which might be called "red-toryism." He attempts to combine elements of socialism and conservatism, notions of limit and freedom. White Grant never quite loses his socialist tinge, his increasing "pessimism" about the ineluctable drive towards a technocratic, bureaucratic, and homogeneous society leads him into a purer form of conservatism. In the

end he moves beyond all three options to make a radical critique of
modern politics *per se.* While liberalism, socialism, and conservatism have
all undeniably left their mark on Grant's mature thought, his final position
can hardly be identified with any particular party in Canada, including the
Conservative Party. Grant ends up with a meta-political position which
sees philosophy as more important than politics, and classical political
thought as more true to reality than any of the modern political options.
Ironically, it is precisely this radical denial of modern politics which makes
Grant's prophetic message so potent for modern culture and society.

II
INTELLECTUAL BACKGROUND

PART II. INTELLECTUAL BACKGROUND

Conversation

Grant: In speaking on this immodest subject, let me start by stating that biographies are grossly overemphasized in our era. One of our great categories is personality — politics and art are dominated by personalities, and people making their own personalities public. With this goes the attempt to understand everything in a particular dynamic context — psycho-history, etc. But in thought, what matters is truth — not particular personalities. When one does an arithmetical sum right, that is not an expression of personality; one's individuality is far more involved when one does it wrong. Perhaps I have sometimes hit on something true in my thought. That is what matters. By which of many possible paths one gets there is of interest to oneself, but to others what matters is the truth. Indeed I have to fight self-importance as much as the next man. One has to learn (and there is much pain in the learning) not to take one's personality too seriously. Everybody likes to talk about themselves, and I hope that temptation is recognised as I talk about myself.

Question: Could I start out by asking about the influence of Charles Cochrane on you?

Grant: Cochrane wrote a great book of history, *Christianity and Classical Culture*, the greatest scholarly book any Canadian ever wrote. It raises the central question of the relation between Christianity and philosophy in the era between Augustus and Augustine. But Cochrane was long dead before I'd reached any of those subjects, and I only read his book after I'd begun to think about Christianity.

Question: How did Harold Innis influence you?

Grant: The person who educated Innis in his later life was Cochrane, because they went for walks around the University of Toronto. He helped Innis move beyond the fur trade, etc., into deeper subjects. I hardly knew Innis and have only read his books in recent years. The great thing about

Cochrane was that after the war of 1914, he moved quite outside the traditions of positivist history which have dominated North American scholarship. But Cochrane has had little continuing influence in Canada, because since 1950 our universities have been increasingly run by the American model – the inadequacies of which he saw with such great clarity.

Question: You studied with Austin Farrer did you not?

Grant: I went back to Oxford to study philosophy and theology after the 1939 war. Before the war I had studied history and politics and law. But during the war I had been converted, and I wanted to discover what that conversion meant. At Oxford, I found the teaching of philosophy dominated by the narrowest tradition of linguistic analysis – people such as Ryle and A.J. Ayer. They simply saw philosophy as the errand boy of natural science and modern secularism. They were uninterested in the important things I wanted to think about. By accident I went to some lectures by Farrer on Descartes, and I recognized immediately this was what I had come to Europe for. He spoke with marvellous clarity and relevance about what had made the European tradition of philosophy and theology – not the minor logical twitterings which dominated Oxford philosophy when I was there. Farrer wrote books not only on philosophy – but about the Gospels. Once when he asked me to come and have a drink with him, I had the only direct vision I ever had. I saw the eagle of St John descend upon him. What Farrer introduced me to was theological rationalism – the heart of Christian intellectual life. What is strange is that I now do not think him a great theologian – but my debt to him for teaching me that European intellectual clarity (which North America has never had) was very great.

Question: You said you were converted during the war. Can you clarify what you mean by that?

Grant: This must become very self-centred. I had been brought up in Toronto in a species of what I would call secular liberalism – by fine and well-educated people who found themselves in the destiny of not being able to see the Christianity of their pioneering ancestors as true. As a substitute they had taken on the Canadian form of what can best be called English-speaking liberalism. At its shallowest one finds this in American eastern seaboard liberalism. The great experience for me was the war of 1939. The liberalism of my youth simply could not come to terms with it. At the worst stage of the war for me in 1942, I found myself ill, and deserted from the merchant navy, and went into the English countryside to work on a farm. I went to work at five o'clock in the morning on a bicycle. I got off the bicycle to open a gate and when I got back on I accepted God.

Obviously, there is much to think about in such experiences. All the Freudian and Marxian questions (indeed, most: the Nietzschian questions) can be asked. But I have never finally doubted the truth of that experience since that moment thirty-six years ago. If I try to put it into words, I would say it was the recognition that I am not my own. In more academic terms, if modern liberalism is the affirmation that our essence is our freedom, then this experience was the denial of that definition, before the fact that we are not our own.

Question: So the Second World War had the effect on you that the First World War had for many Europeans, such as Tillich, whose whole 19th century world-view was shattered by that war.

Grant: Yes, the war of 1939-1945 was the great primal experience for me — as, for example, the Vietnam war was for many young North Americans. I don't like the comparison with Tillich, however. Tillich has always seemed to me a very shallow theologian. He got on well in the United States because they never have had a theological or philosophical tradition of their own strong enough to see through his shallowness and contradictions.

Question: One of the things I wonder about sometimes is the kind of vision of Canada that would have come down to you through your blood lines — your namesakes, the Reverend George Grant and George Parkin.

Grant: I was brought up in a class which has almost disappeared. Canada, before 1940, was largely a producer of raw materials with a small commercial and industrial fringe. I came from that class of ministers, professors, school teachers, lawyers, and doctors who lived in that essentially agricultural and commercial community. They were the educated professionals of the nineteenth century. Now that class has disappeared all over the world — but it has particularly disappeared in Canada, because it has no real place as capitalism advances. Its heart's core has also disappeared with the decay of Protestantism. Now I was certainly influenced by "the values" of that class in which I grew up. For example, they quite liked the people of the Great Republic, but they took for granted they wanted to be different. Their ancestors had been all thrown out. They assumed the Americans were badly educated; now most of our professors either come from there or are trained there. But I would say that though I got my prejudice from this disappearing class, what influenced me to philosophy was the knowledge that it was disappearing. As I have said, this was a class which had no future as Canada became integrated into American capitalism. Nothing so much can drive one to philosophy as being part of a class which is disappearing.

Question: But who really influenced your life, had enormous personal impact on you?

Grant: Of course, first and foremost and always, my wife, who came from an English tradition of education.

But beyond that I would say James Doull, who teaches classics at Dalhousie University. When I was leaving Oxford in 1947, I was offered a job at the U. of T. But the rich men on the Board withdrew it when they heard I had been a pacifist and a socialist. But it was the luckiest thing that ever happened to me, because it meant going to Dalhousie. I had to teach philosophy when I didn't really know any. Doull, who was my own age and really educated in a way I was not, led me into Kant and Plato. I will never forget once, walking down the street in Halifax, he showed me what the image of the sun in Plato's *Republic* meant. Everything that I had been trying to think came together.

Of course Doull's great teacher has been Hegel, and I am not a Hegelian. That has led Doull and me apart. But that doesn't make one forget one's debt. He was the person who made me really look at western philosophy.

Question: What about your "de-Hegelianization"? I'm interested in the process you went through. I can understand why Hegel would swallow up liberalism. What I don't understand is how you get out of Hegel. Once you jump in, you're sucked in.

Grant: What was always the thorn which kept me from accepting Hegel was those remarks in the philosophy of history, about wars being the winds that stir up the stagnant pools. That is the idea that good can come out of bad in a way that we can understand. To put it in Christian terms, it has always seemed to me that Hegel makes God's providence scrutable, and that is a teaching that offended me then and now at the deepest level. But of course I wouldn't have been able to think that out for myself. It was Leo Strauss who has taught me to think this through.

Question: In particular his criticism of Hegel's understanding of nature?

Grant: As a young man Strauss worked for an Institute of Jewish Studies in Germany, and was asked to write a book about Spinoza's criticism of the Bible. His great discovery was to understand that Spinoza accepted Hobbes' account of nature. From that his work in modern political philosophy proceeded. I learned from that work because it laid before me the reasons why the modern account of human nature and politics is just inadequate compared to the ancient account.

Question: You have sometimes mentioned differences that may be between you and Strauss about Plato. Are there any major positions of Strauss that you would object to?

Grant: Let me answer this with hesitation. Strauss is a very great intellect and was a very wonderful person. He was a learned man in a way I am not. My debt to him is daily. But I would say this. One of the wisest things

Strauss ever said was that in Judaism and Islam revelation is received as law, while in Christianity it is received as the being — Jesus Christ. This difference above all affects the relation between philosophy and revelation in those religions. I think in Christianity, philosophy and revelation must be closer than in Judaism or Islam. I think it is this which leads me in great hesitation to differ with Strauss in the interpretation of Plato. But of course Strauss knew much more about Plato than I do. Nevertheless, I think I would differ with him about the *Symposium*, concerning love and reason.

Question: But you wouldn't differ about the *Republic*?

Grant: I think we would differ about the meaning of the *hyperousia* statement in *Republic* 508; that is, about the Good as beyond being. But now we are getting into very deep waters.

Obviously here I must talk of Simone Weil, who has been the greatest influence in my life of any thinker. She has shown me what it is to hold Christ and Plato together. She has shown to me how sanctity and philosophy can be at one.

Question: How did you get interested in her?

Grant: By accident. I had to earn my living and the CBC sent me one of her books to review.

Question: When was that?

Grant: 1950. Since that date she has been the central influence on my thought about the most important matters.

Question: When did you begin to read Strauss?

Grant: 1960.

Question: So you began to read Strauss after you wrote *Philosophy in the Mass Age*?

Grant: Yes.

Question: Coming back to Simone Weil just for a moment. I have heard it said that she is not respectable in an academic context.

Grant: How ridiculous. Her brother is probably the most famous living mathematician and he takes her seriously, including her writings on mathematics. They both come from that French love of the intellect combined with the Jewish love of the intellect. If you want sheer intellectual elegance, this family had it in a way that has never even been dreamt of in the North American academic community. That level of education, taking place from the earliest days, can do dangerous things to people — but with her it was a means to knowledge of the highest matters.

Question: But she's a mystic.

Grant: That was much later, after her early life in the proletarian movement in France and in the Spanish war. She was taught by a very able Kantian, and then at the end of her short life understood Plato. She had an immediate and direct encounter with the second person of the Trinity. I take her writings as combining the staggering clarity of her French education with divine inspiration. I take them as perhaps occasionally mistaken in detail, and as sometimes beyond me, but as the great teaching concerning the eternal in this era.

Question: In what context did you begin reading Heidegger?

Grant: Largely accident. I started reading Nietzsche because one of my children was greatly influenced by him, and I wanted to know why. Till recently it has been almost impossible for English-speaking people to take Nietzsche seriously. He seemed to be a poet who was somehow related to the ghastliness of the Nazis. In fact he is the great understander of the modern.

Question: Why do you speak about Nietzsche, when you are asked about Heidegger?

Grant: Because the two go together. It is unthinkable that Heidegger would have been without Nietzsche. Why they need to be read is that they are the two thinkers who have most completely thought through the modern western project from within it. To use Marxian language, they are the modern project conscious of itself. As it seems to me that the great task of philosophy now is to think through the modern project to its fundamental assumptions, then we must study those thinkers who can help us. Simply at the level of academic philosophy, what is breathtaking about Heidegger is the way he shows us what is going on in the philosophers and scientists who originated the modern project. Take Heidegger's book on Leibniz, *Der Satz vom Grund*; I think that is the book which has most illuminated for me what technology is. It takes one to the very fundamentals of what is being thought in the western world.

Question: But Heidegger was a National Socialist.

Grant: The modern era is extraordinarily strange, but this is one of its strangest facts. This consummate thinker welcomed Hitlerism, in the early years of its power. Some silly academics have seen this as a kind of regrettable foolishness, as if Heidegger could be interpreted as a political innocent who simply did not know the score in practical matters. But that is a childish view, which makes out that philosophic questions are just games played in useless ivory towers. In the last ten years this fact has become a symbol of what I want to think about. How could this amazing unfolder of the nature of modernity, this person who can illuminate the philosophic past, how could he opt for National Socialism at the political level? This is much more than an historical question about Europe in the 1930s. If one uses it as an oyster knife to open up his brilliance, the whole question of the destiny of modernity can be revealed.

Question: Nietzsche's writings were probably the most comprehensive critique of Christianity and Platonism ever written. How is your study of them related to faith?

Grant: As I have said, Nietzsche and Heidegger are those who have thought through most clearly what is happening in modernity, and thought it within the acceptance of the basic assumptions of that modernity. The negative side of that thinking-through is their assessment of what is wrong about Christianity and Platonism — why human beings thought they were true in the past, but why no sane person should do so now. Somebody such as myself, inescapably bound to Christianity, must try to understand what it is to think at a superlative level, with Christianity put aside root and branch. And I do not mean this rejection as a kind of intellectual abstract game, but including Nietzsche's whole account of how Christianity perverted sexuality, and how this perversion is for him central to Christianity. Therefore, it is not a negative activity to read him, but a positive one, in the sense that through his critique one comes to see what are the essential assertions of Christianity, and what it is to think them true. Moreover, as far as philosophy goes, it is almost impossible for anybody to try to apprehend the whole except in terms of the modern assumptions. If that is the case, how then can one even get near to apprehending what Plato is asserting? One apprehends it through modern eyes, and what Plato is asserting is thought in terms of quite other assumptions. How does one then ever move out of the circle of our present destiny? Seeing modern assumptions laid before me at their most lucid and profound in Nietzsche and Heidegger has allowed me (indeed only slightly) to be able to partake in the alternative assumptions of Plato. It is by looking at modernity in its greatest power that one is perhaps able even slightly to escape its power.

All this, of course, sounds much too academic in the shallow sense of that word. Philosophy must arise from the most immediate and concrete experience of our lives, both public and private. I never forget returning home to Toronto after many years in Halifax. Driving in from the airport, I remember being gripped in the sheer presence of the booming, pulsating place which had arisen since 1945. What did it mean? Where was it going? What had made it? How could there be any stop to its dynamism without disaster, and yet, without a stop, how could there not be disaster? And part of that experience was the knowledge that I had come home to something that never could be my home. Philosophy arises in the wonder of such lived experiences. The study of the great western thinkers has to be co-penetrated with such experiences, if one is to grasp what is in those writings.

Some Influences of Simone Weil on George Grant's Silence
by Edwin B. Heaven and David R. Heaven

Discerning critics of George Grant have suggested that while his writings contain a penetrating analysis of the origins and all-embracing effects of modernity, there is a deficiency on the positive side; that is, his writings point to a "better way" but this is not articulated.[1] This paper presumes to suggest some possible reasons for Dr Grant's reticence to write about the vision of the good which informs his work; and these reasons are grounded in one axiom which is self-evident to the authors of this paper: namely, that the works of Simone Weil have had a continuous and profound effect on Dr Grant since he first encountered them in 1950. To whom or what is he directing his readers when, in those occasional moments in his writings, he turns away from his primary task (which is the destruction of inadequate sources of hope) and points toward a veiled but positive affirmation? It is, of course, Plato and the Gospels to which he points as the grounds for his hope, but from among his contemporaries Grant regards the "modern saint," Simone Weil, as having more fully partaken of these ancient traditions than any other. If she is for him the highest and best that this century has produced, then her person and her vision of the good will have had a more foundational influence on his thought than any other contemporary, even Leo Strauss. Grant has acknowledged a distance between himself and the great thinkers and saints, and since, in his view, she is both, some attention to her life and thought must shed light on why he has not offered to the public any detailed statements about his vision of the good.

Grant's silence bears a direct relation to his understanding of the distance between himself and the great thinkers and the saints. It is in the nature of this distance that his debt to Simone Weil is most apparent. He summarizes his position at the end of *Time as History:*

> Nevertheless, those who cannot live as if time were history are
> called, beyond remembering, to desiring and thinking. But this is
> to say very little. For myself, as probably for most others, remem-
> bering only occasionally can pass over into thinking and loving what
> is good. It is for the great thinkers and the saints to do more.

This quotation identifies the two operations essential to man's highest
end — thinking and loving what is good. For both Grant and Simone Weil
the two operations cannot ultimately be separated because the highest
knowledge is open only to those who love the good; or, only insofar as the
soul loves is it qualified to know and understand. As in what follows, the
attempt can be made to discuss the two operations separately, but their
unity is apparent in the attempt to hold them apart. And while Grant's
reflections on his task as a thinker are discussed first they must be viewed
as part of the continuum from which the primacy of charity cannot be
excluded.

The Operation of Thought

Grant writes more of the importance of thought than he does about love
because he is less distant from the great thinkers than he is from the saints.
He regards himself primarily as a philosopher or a thinker, albeit a lesser
thinker than those whom he regards as great. He has no illusions about the
difficulty of the task he has set for himself as a philosopher. In his Wood
Lectures he says that modern thought can be summed up under three
headings, "analytical logistics, historicist scholarship and rigorous science,"
but points out that when added together they do not equal philosophy.
"When added together they are not capable of producing that thought
which is required if justice is to be taken out of the darkness which
surrounds it in the technological era."[2] However, the obvious insignifi-
cance of philosophy in this modern age, he says, does not lead to the
disappearance of the demand to think.

The primary basis for Grant's statement is the tightening web of
modernity in which "technique is ourselves"[3] and therefore reason as
calculation has replaced thought in the classical sense as "steadfast
attention to the whole."[4] He says that there is a pressing need for thought
in this classical sense, but he also states quite explicitly that he is not the
great thinker to accomplish the thought which is required. As a writer and
a teacher, therefore, he sees it as his vocation to point to the need for
thought and some of the consequences of its neglect, but the acknowledged distance between himself and the great thinkers results primarily in
silence concerning the content of what can be spoken. A few muffled
sounds from Dr Grant break this silence but he knows that his notes are

discordant and in distinct contrast to the harmonies of the great thinkers to whom he would rather direct his readers.

A retreat into thought in the face of the demands of charity is a serious decision by any thinker, but Dr Grant says that such a retreat is necessary because it can lead to a glimmering awareness of the nature of the whole.

> Human excellence can only be appropriated by those who have glimpsed that it is sustained by all that is. Although that sustainment cannot be adequately thought by us because of the fragmentation and complexity of our historical inheritance, this is still no reason not to open ourselves to all those occasions in which the reality of that sustaining makes itself present to us.[5]

In an unpublished paper written in 1973 Dr Grant says that "those who live in hope must attempt more than piecemeal thinking about technical civilization," and "the pragmatic concerns of piecemeal social engineering" are not adequate — there is "the need to think technical civilization as a unified historical event within some dimly comprehended whole." He is saying that he has glimpsed a vision of the whole but he is not a thinker of a sufficiently high order to be able to articulate that vision in the face of the contradictions in thought which arise from grappling with modernity.

Two illustrations will suffice. In the first place, he says that when one accepts the claim of an owed service to a given good, "that service required a congruent and specifiable relation between nature and good," but the highest modern intellectual achievement (non-teleological science) is founded on an explicit denial of any such relation. In one paper, for example, he acknowledges his own inability to think together the classical notion of "being as under the yoke of good" and the modern instrumental view of reason, and in another writing he says that they "cry out to be thought in harmony."[6] The second illustration concerns the most profound difficulty confronting thought about the whole. It occurs when the realization dawns that this thought must attempt to comprehend what good is being served by the historical situation in which the "ontology of the age"[7] (technology) dims any apprehension of the good through eliminating from the public realm any language other than "the pure will to will."[8] In *Time as History* he writes:

> And the turn of the screw is that to love fate must obviously include loving the fate that makes us part of the modern project; it must include that which has made us oblivious of eternity — that eternity without which I cannot understand how it would be possible to love fate.[9]

The need for thought on these matters is of crucial importance for Grant. He raises the questions but is largely silent with respect to their answers because of the limitations of his own thought and because others have contemplated these matters more profoundly than he has. While he expresses the need for more than piecemeal thought, Simone Weil has written extensively from within a vision of the whole. She has, for example, put forward a comprehensive and consistent response to both of Grant's contradictions noted in the preceding paragraph. Simone Weil has thought in depth about the way in which the universe, conceived of as necessity and chance (and therefore in the framework of classical science), can be related to the primal claim of the good. And she has put forward a teaching on providence within which *all that is* (including modernity) must be viewed as the will of God.

Simone Weil's treatment of these key concepts of necessity and providence bears a remarkable resemblance to Grant's articulation of them. But there are also significant differences which dramatize his distance from Simone Weil and thus illuminate his silence.

II. *Necessity and Chance*

Necessity and chance are synonymous in the thought of Simone Weil and George Grant, and both thinkers agree that the necessary and the good can be related but only in such a way as to maintain the infinite distance between them of which Plato first spoke. Necessity is that which is other than the good and, as such, is void of purpose. According to Miss Weil, "the blind necessity which constrains us, and which is revealed in geometry, appears to us as a thing to overcome; for the Greeks it was a thing to love."[10] Grant writes often of the attempt to overcome chance as the central aspiration of modern science and this aspiration is identical to the overcoming of necessity as Simone Weil understands it. For both thinkers "chance never appears except at the same time as necessity."[11]

In an unpublished paper he says: "nature conceived of solely in terms of necessity and chance cannot be related to the primal claim of good."[12] The word "solely" is very important in this sentence since it makes it clear that he does think that the primal claim of good can be related to chance and necessity. In other writings he implies that this relation must be thought but that he cannot think it. At the end of his Wood Lectures he expounds the theoretical difficulty which confronts him because of the achievements of modern science:

> Why the darkness which enshrouds justice is so dense — even for
> those who think that what is given in 'The Republic' concerning
> good stands forth as true — is because that truth cannot be thought
> in unity with what is given in modern science concerning necessity
> and chance.[13]

He makes it clear in both the Wood Lectures and in his Royal Society paper that the effort to think the two together needs to be made, and he alludes to two different ways in which to begin the process. When addressing the Royal Society he implies that only someone deeply within theoretical physics should attempt the thought about the whole which is required, and at the end of the Wood Lectures there is the suggestions that perhaps what needs to be rethought is what is presupposed in the modern science of nature issuing from Kant. In neither case does he judge himself to be competent to proceed beyond this pointing in one of these two possible directions. But a glance at Simone Weil's writings confirms that she has proceeded much further along both these paths than Grant. She was a highly skilled mathematician and she wrote extensively about the theoretical foundations of modern science. Grant is clearly reticent, in a way in which Simone Weil is not, to attempt to place necessity and chance within a vision of the whole.

There is another sense in which Grant is reluctant to go all the way with Simone Weil in her thought on necessity. She speaks of obedience as the other side of necessity, and he, while he would probably agree privately with her on this matter, makes no public statement in support of her position. For Simone Weil one side of necessity is chance or the blind purposelessness which permeates the universe, and about this she and Grant speak an almost identical language. But about the other side he never speaks: he never says, as she does, that "necessity is the obedience of matter to God."[14] Her description of the two sides of necessity is as follows:

> So long as we think in the first person, we see necessity from below, from inside, it encloses us on all sides as the surface of the earth and the arc of the sky. From the time we renounce thinking in the first person, by consent to necessity, we see it from the outside, beneath us for we have passed to God's side. The side which it turned to us before, and still presents to almost the whole of our being, the natural part of ourselves, is brute domination. The side which it presents after this operation, to the fragment of our mind which has passed to the other side, is pure obedience. ... This consent is truly in the first place pure absurdity. Also it is truly supernatural. It is the work of Grace alone.[15]

For both Grant and Simone Weil the idea of necessity is central – it is, says Simone, "the material common to art, science and every kind of labour."[16] Both thinkers assert that the idea of necessity must be attended to very carefully so that what it is may be revealed and then subsequently the right use of necessity becomes very important. Grant says that modern science has misused the idea of necessity by seeking to overcome it. The right way of using necessity, says Simone Weil, is by passing through it by means of either contemplation of the beauty of the world or affliction.

Between the two ways of seeing necessity, between the wrong way and the right way, lies conversion or the Platonic *periagogé*. Grant is unwilling to speak from the other side of the *periagogé* although he is undoubtedly on that other side with Simone Weil.

Several reasons suggest themselves for his unwillingness to speak in Simone Weil's fashion about the other side of necessity. First, and most obviously, he does not wish to alienate his readership. He therefore must communicate in the language of philosophy rather than religion. Significant in this respect is his almost consistent refusal to use the western symbolism "God", preferring to use the Platonic language of goodness; yet the two are identical in the thought of both. His careful distinction between religious language and philosophical language is a strategic one, though like Simone Weil he does not allow any ultimate or final separation. It is neither smart politics nor timely pedagogy to speak publicly of the eternal. As Simone Weil says: "To find a place in the budget for the eternal is not in the spirit of the age. So the majority of the philosophers keep quiet about that eternity which is their privilege."[17] Simone Weil and Grant are at one in affirming that it is primarily in the language of philosophy that thinkers must address the problem of their age. She saw it as her intellectual task that "if the crisis in our age is comparable to that of the fifth century, then there is an obvious duty: to make an effort comparable to that of Eudoxus."[18] She was herself an exception to her generalization about philosophers not speaking out about eternity, but her speaking out took the form (in deed as well as in word) of the loving saintly life. Grant knows himself to be far from this and therefore it is not his fate to speak with her from the other side of the *periagogé*: he says, "happily the eternal can take care of itself."[19] He is the philosopher who is back in the cave where his primary task is "to bring the darkness into light as darkness"[20] and to say nothing about the source of the illumination.

Much more important than a strategic reticence to speak about the other side of necessity for fear of alienating his readership is his unwillingness to speak of love. According to Simone Weil it is impossible to speak of necessity without speaking of love. It was noted, for example, that she calls consent to necessity "truly supernatural" and "the work of Grace alone." Grant knows the truth that Simone is proclaiming when she says: "Necessity, insofar as it is absolutely other than Good, is Good itself."[21] He knows it, but he does not proclaim it. He considers himself unworthy of doing so because he is not a saint. For reasons that will become apparent he is more silent in the presence of love than he is in the presence of thought.

III. *Providence and Fate*

Grant and Simone Weil both reject western interpretations of providence which identify necessity and goodness. "Belief is blasphemy," says Grant, "if it rests on any easy identification of necessity and good. ... It must be possible within the doctrine of providence to distinguish between the necessity of certain happenings and their goodness."[22] Simone Weil says: "The ridiculous conception of Providence as being a personal and particular intervention on the part of God for certain particular ends is incompatible with true faith."[23] From this position Simone Weil was extremely critical of much biblical religion and was led to affirm that the true religions are those which emphasize the absence of God.

Grant's use of the language of fate is strikingly similar to Simone Weil's teaching that providence is the certainty "that the universe in all its totality is in conformity to the will of God."[24] She says that "there is as much conformity to the will of God in a leaf which falls unnoticed as in the Flood."[25] Grant prefers not to use the term "will" in connection with his view of providence because he is aware from his studies of Nietzsche that the language of will is at the heart of modernity. But for both Simone Weil and Grant the language of fate or determinedness is the characteristic way of speaking and is far removed from the modern language of freedom. The use of the language of fate implies, says Grant, that "all human beings come into a world that they did not choose and live their lives within a universe they did not make." And, he continues, "it is quite possible to use the word 'fate' and to think that 'nature' is good and not contradict oneself."[26] His written works demonstrate how the maintaining of the separation between necessity and goodness within a doctrine of providence requires a continuous clearing away of western theological notions of divine intervention. The absence of divine intervention is the silence of God which he understands with Simone to be the truth in religion.

One can detect in Grant's writings a purging of purposive language when speaking about himself. In *Technology and Empire* he speaks of the "accidents of existence" which dragged him out from the pervasiveness of the pragmatic liberalism in which he was raised.[27] When writing about the university curriculum he says that "the criteria by which we could judge it as inadequate can only be reached by those who through some chance have moved outside the society by memory or by thought." Again, he speaks of himself as one of "those who by some elusive chance have broken with the monolith."[28] Referring to his own rejection of the lineaments of liberal justice Grant says that he "somehow" has "been told that some justice is due to all human beings and that its living out is, above all what we are fitted for."[29] Not only are his philosophical insights accidental, but also his brushes with revelation: "for those of us who are lucky enough to know that we have been told that justice is what we are fitted for this is not a practical darkness but simply a theoretical one."[30] It was previously noted that Grant did not regard it as his task to exhort others to believe as he believes: it is apparent now that he thinks with Simone Weil that "to believe in God is not a decision that we can make."[31] Most modern Christians reading these passages from Grant would draw the conclusion that this fatalistic language is blasphemy, whereas in effect he is stating that it is their faith in divine intervention which is the blasphemy.

The reason for his deliberate use of the language of fate is made clear in a passage from *The Need for Roots* where Simone Weil writes of the New Testament as follows:

> Thus it is that blind impartiality characteristic of inert matter, it is that relentless regularity characterizing the order of the world, completely indifferent to men's individual quality, and because of this so frequently accused of injustice — it is that which is held up as a model of perfection in the human soul. It is a conception of so profound a significance that we are not even today capable of grasping it: contemporary Christianity has completely lost touch with it.[32]

Once again it is only by understanding necessity as the absence of good (and in this instance the non-intervention or silence of God), that goodness and necessity can be understood as ultimately related to each other. Grant knows with Simone Weil that ultimately they must be related but he leaves the articulation of this vision to greater minds such as hers. He concentrates his work on the destruction of inadequate sources of hope. One such inadequate source of hope is the prevailing Christian view of providence. Others singled out for special attention by him are belief in progress, contractual justice, pragmatism and Marxism. Simone Weil also writes against all of these "things of this world" which, she says, "are not real goods."[33] Grant's destruction of inadequate sources of hope is not fundamentally different from Simone Weil's leading of her readers beyond "the things of this world." But the real difference that he perceives between himself and Simone Weil lies neither in the subject matter of their writings nor in those to whom they are addressed. It lies rather in their different fates. In his view Simone Weil passed over into thinking and loving what is good more than occasionally. But this passing over was a matter of chance or accident; thus it was her fate to be a great thinker and a saint. He is fully aware that one cannot make oneself a great thinker or a saint. His fate he understands to be that of a lesser thinker. As such he can only wait, pay attention and to a very great extent remain silent.

IV. *The Primacy of Charity*

"Beside Strauss Simone Weil is a flame"[34] says Grant, clearly acknowledging the superiority of the saintly over the theoretical life. "Concerning

... important theoretical questions," he says, "my debt is above all to the writings of Leo Strauss," and, "I count it a high blessing to have been acquainted with this man's thought."[35] Through the writings of Strauss Grant has gained a profound intellectual comprehension of modernity, but "beside Strauss Simone Weil is a flame" because her writings manifest "illuminations of love in the domain of thought."[36] Simone Weil's clearest statement on the primacy of charity is as follows:

> Man cannot exercise his intelligence to the full without charity because the only source of light is God. Therefore the faculty of supernatural love is higher than the intelligence and is its condition. The love of God is the unique source of all certainties.[37]

Grant acknowledges the superiority of the way of love but he cannot say very much about it because he will not speak other than from within a way. Authority to speak is always for him a matter of speaking from within such and such a tradition. Only those who are Christian or Jew or Indian or western should attempt to speak the truth about these things for only they are, by virtue of *what* they are, capable of so doing. When Grant writes that "technique is ourselves" this is asserted with an authority that proceeds from the long contemplation of a western fate. In his paper "Knowing and Making" he clearly lays down the grounds of his authority to speak about the implications of what is occurring in the field of medicine. He is within modern medicine – as a patient. As a patient he is the object of that project and is therefore capable of speaking with authority about that aspect of medicine as it relates to the whole of medical research and experimentation. With respect to the way of love, however, he knows that he is not very much within it and hence the silence he imposes on himself by virtue of his knowledge of his distance from the saints; a knowledge which is borne in upon him whenever he reflects on the difference between what Simone Weil loves and what her commentators love.

It is significant that the one place in his published writings where Grant quotes Simone Weil he calls her "a modern saint"; in the same context he acknowledges that the purpose of existence is far from evident and that to be reconciled in the face of "the unspeakable evils and tragedies" of the twentieth century "is a supernatural gift."[38] He similarly expresses his distance from the saints in *Lament for a Nation* where he points out that "a lament arises from a condition that is common to the majority of men for we are situated between despair and absolute certainty."[39] The saint cannot lament because he knows with certainty that the destruction of good serves a supernatural end. Clearly Grant does not know this with the certainty of the saint. What he does know is that he can speak only very feebly from within love, so he rather defers to the saints in whom the truth has become life. From Plato and Simone Weil he has learned that truth and love form a single mysterious unity, for the "good is one."[40] Thus all great works of art reflect the purity of the lives of their makers, or as Simone Weil expresses it, "a tragedy like King Lear is the direct fruit of the pure spirit of love."[41] Vigny bitterly reproached God, says Miss Weil, for the eternal silence "but Vigny had no right to say how the just man should reply to the silence for he was not one of the just. The just man loves."[42] Similarly, she says, Aristotle was not a lover: "a man who takes the trouble to draw up an apology for slavery cannot be a lover of justice."[43]

Grant is aware that the closer one is to love, the greater the renunciation of the "I", or the less he and his ideas are important. Therefore what Simone Weil says about the anonymity of the love of truth sheds light on his silence:

> Every time that a man rises to a degree of excellence which by
> participation makes of him a divine being, we are aware of some-
> thing impersonal and anonymous about him. His voice is enveloped
> in silence. This is evident in all the great works of art or of thought,
> in the great deeds of saints and in their words.[44]

Grant's reticence to speak is most profound at the level which proceeds from his understanding of what it is to be a saint, as opposed to his own being. He is not a saint; therefore he has neither the authority nor the right to speak. For Grant, as for Simone Weil, obligations come before rights and rights are only valid in relation to the obligations to which they correspond. When Grant says that he has no right to speak, this pertains to the highest obligation, his obligation to the good which is God. The qualitative difference which he perceives between the being of the saint and his own being denies him that right and authority to speak.

Clearly as an author and a teacher Grant sees the fulfillment of his obligation to be the communication of the truth, so far as he is able to perceive it – the truth about man, his world, and his relation to what is beyond these. What is beyond these, infinitely beyond, is the good or God. But though the distance be infinite there is nonetheless a mysterious relation between that good and man. Indeed the relation is fundamental, constituting as it does man's very being. The relation is love in the most powerful and noble sense, a longing, a straining after the good. It is man's destiny or what he is "fitted for." But knowledge of this good is not immediate: it is hidden. And even in those instances when one's memory is quickened to some distant primal glimmering of perfect good, rare are the occasions when one can "pass over into thinking *and loving* what is good." For to love in this way is to love the infinitely distant, the absolutely other, and how can man be moved to such a sustained or continuously repeated love by words alone? Intellectual persuasion is not sufficient but must be complemented by acts of love on the part of the persuader. Communication at this level is surely enough to make any man hesitate. According to Simone Weil the greatest difficulty lies in the fact that knowledge of the good which is absolutely perfect can only be apprehended in two ways; the joy of beauty and the pain of affliction — affliction which is intolerable mental and physical anguish, total reduction of personality to nothingness, and absolute humiliation. In Christianity, the two poles, the two essential truths are the Trinity (the knowledge of which is perfect joy) and the Cross (the knowledge of which is perfect affliction). But, to quote Simone Weil directly, "... the human condition in this world places us infinitely far from the Trinity, at the very foot of the Cross. Our country is the Cross."[45]

Thus loving the good comes down to being prepared to consent not only to endure the worst that a cold brutal metallic necessity can impose, but to continue to love throughout it all. This, it seems, Grant cannot tell people to do. Because he is profoundly aware of his own intellectual and moral limitations, such advice clearly would be a violation of his obligation at the deepest level. For, to return to the question of the preceding paragraph, how can one be moved to seek a good which is totally absent, infinitely other, and seemingly infinitely terrible? Since love has no part in force, and since man's immediate response is to fly from such truths, it seems that the answer can only be some form of enticement or persuasion. If this is so, the question becomes "what or who persuades?" Simone Weil's answer to the first part of the question is: the manifest beauty of this world as it is perceived as an image of eternal perfection. But, secondly, this beauty is manifested not only in nature but in certain rare human beings who are like "shafts" or "pinpoints" of light whose very being is a radiant manifestation of eternal truth.[46] In the matter of persuasion anything less than being whose absolute centre is noble love will have the opposite effect of turning men away from rather than drawing them upward to the good, insofar as their lives belie their words. A refusal is easy in the presence of radiant manifestations of "untruth." Simone Weil says that the more difficult the thing to be done, the more evident the good in the persuader must be.[47] Nothing less than a pure image of perfection is powerful enough to persuade anyone to love that which is absolutely other, and seemingly terrible.

Thus in the face of this love beyond human capability and reason Grant is silent. It is a humble silence imposed on him from without, and born of a certain knowledge that he is distant from that about which he would speak. In this distance, this imperfection, he knows he has not the right. To do so would almost certainly violate his deepest sense of justice.

George P. Grant and Jacques Ellul
On Freedom In Technological Society
by John Badertscher

Introduction

By his own declaration, George Grant's discovery of Jacques Ellul — and in particular his book *The Technological Society* — was a major event in the growth of Grant's understanding of our world. His 1966 introduction to *Philosophy in the Mass Age* (1959) bears witness to the discovery. Grant warns the reader that over the seven intervening years his mind has changed about certain questions in moral philosophy. He points to "the dominance of technique" (p. iii)[1] as a cause of confusion in moral philosophy, and cites Ellul's definition of technique as one which he endorses. At the end of the introduction he points to "two contemporary thinkers of clarity and, indeed, of genius" (p. ix) who have led him to his change of mind. They are Jacques Ellul and Leo Strauss. Grant acknowledges his indebtedness to Strauss concerning "theoretical questions," while Ellul's aid has been received in "practical questions," that is, in understanding "the structure of modern society." While this use of the terms "practical" and "theoretical" might be a bit confusing, it is clear that Grant has substantially accepted Ellul's description of the modern world, and that seeing the world through these new lenses has significantly influenced Grant's moral philosophy.

The direction of that influence is indicated in *Technology and Empire*, perhaps most clearly in the introduction to "Religion and the State." "The folly of this writing," Grant says of his own work, "is that it did not grasp what the technological society really is. Therefore the general principles of political philosophy asserted in it have no possible application in the society to which it is addressed" (p. 43). The essay itself first appeared in 1963. *The Technological Society* was published in English translation in 1965.

The "general principles" to which Grant refers are those of conservatism. Grant's last major publication before confronting Ellul's insight was *Lament For a Nation*. Already in this writing, Grant, influenced by Leo Strauss, had come to an understanding of what genuine conservatism is and, through reflection on the defeat of the Diefenbaker government in 1963, had concluded that it is impossible in our era. He laments the defeat of Canadian nationalism, but sees that its triumph is impossible, because "as Canadians we attempted a ridiculous task in trying to build a conservative nation in the age of progress..." (p. 68). Even those who call themselves conservatives "can be no more than the defenders of whatever structure of power is at any moment necessary to technological change" (p. 67).

Grant's reading of *The Technological Society* did not bring a conversion, it seems, but rather a clarification. The clarity which he found in Ellul's analysis did not so much convince him of error as make clear the reasons why his principles could not now prevail. The problem Grant then faced was how, in such a world, to address problems of moral philosophy in a way neither false nor futile. Yet the discovery of Ellul seems to have meant more to Grant than a counsel of silence or despair. He continues to refer others to Ellul's diagnosis as though it were prerequisite to a cure. Though Grant's most recent writings contain no reference to Ellul, in 1966 he reviewed *The Technological Society* for *Canadian Dimension*. Grant enthusiastically says that this book and another by Ellul (*Propaganda*, 1965) are "the most important of all required reading for anybody who wants to understand what is occurring ... during our era" (p. 59). The book leads, Grant suggests, to more than understanding. "I am certainly freer for having read this book." The only criticism Grant offers is directed at Ellul's grasp of the historical sources of technological society. "To understand the origins of modern technique one must surely look more closely than does Ellul at its intimate relation with Biblical religion." Grant wants to excuse even this flaw on the grounds that it may be "a highly conscious and noble turning away from philosophy toward a sociological realism" (p. 60).

Though Grant has had further thoughts about Ellul's shortcomings, he has never repudiated this evaluation of the importance of Ellul's analysis, at least not in print. It is fair to say, then, that Ellul's writings – especially *The Technological Society* – made a major contribution to Grant's own powerful critique of our social order.

However, the thinking of these two figures is far from harmonious. Indeed, it would be hard to find more sharply divergent views on some major ethical issues. This essay will explore the ways in which Grant and Ellul, while agreeing on the analysis of technological society, differ in some presuppositions which lead to, and some imperatives which are drawn from, that common analysis.

The Transformation of Human Life in Technological Society

The opening chapter of *The Technological Society* is given over to the definition of technique. But the matter of a proper definition is so important to Ellul that in a "Note to the Reader," placed at the very beginning of the book in 1963, the following is presented:

> In our society, technique is the totality of methods rationally arrived at and having absolute efficiency (for a given stage of development) in every field of human activity (p. xxv).

Understood this way, technique goes far beyond machines, though its tendency is to mechanize all that it touches. Technique is to be seen as a form of social organization, and, as such, it integrates all aspects of culture and man himself.

Grant accepts this definition, as we have said, and finds it a useful introduction to his own explorations of contemporary social order. Grant shares Ellul's understanding that the phenomenon to be described and understood is not something outside or over against us. It is our own social order, and we have internalized it. The absolute efficiency of rational methods commands our allegiance, serving as an ideal by which our lives are patterned.

In technological society, the higher human pursuits are transformed, as well as the more mundane. Having shown that machines are not technique, but are rather incorporated into it, Ellul turns to the matter of science. At issue is the commonplace assertion that technique is the application of science. While admitting that the emergence of technological society had to await the appearance of modern science, Ellul points out that, at present, "the border between technical activity and scientific activity is not at all sharply defined" (p. 8). Current scientific research depends upon technique in its procedures, and upon technological society for its support and goals. In fact, "science has become an instrument of technique" (p. 10).

Grant takes up this topic in his address to the Royal Society of Canada on "Knowing and Making" (1974). There is an interdependence between the sciences and the arts, he argues, that is unique to our time. "Technology" names well this co-penetration, for we now have "forms of making that are capable of being penetrated at their very heart by the discoveries of modern science" (p. 62). *Techne* and *logos*, making and knowing, are related in a new way. As this new relationship actualizes itself in our society, we begin to see some of the consequences of a paradigm in which science aspires to "make" a new world, and the arts appropriate to such production are generated. For example, we make new things such as radioactive wastes, which may not be readily or conveniently unmade; and we unmake such things as the peregrine falcon, which cannot be readily remade. The reduction of knowing and making to each other makes it impossible to give rational answers to questions about the limitations of knowledge, and about what we should make or refrain from unmaking. The point is not that science is doing these terrible things, but that because it is integrated into the relationship we call technology, science can no longer answer questions about its own proper end.

The natural sciences, however, are not the only aspect of knowledge and higher education to be transformed in technological society. An examination of the social sciences is perhaps even more revealing, for these are more unambiguously correlated with technological society. The greater part of *The Technological Society* is directed toward such areas as economics, public administration, law, and what Ellul terms "human techniques" – therapeutic and social psychology. Though often justified as ways of "humanizing" technological society, they are in fact, Ellul argues, the means by which human lives are adjusted to technological systems.

Grant takes up this theme in his essay, "The University Curriculum" (*TE*, pp. 113-133). He begins with the observations that technological society has increasingly sought the control of human as well as non-human nature, that the need for such control increases with the complexity of society, and that the "value-free" social sciences have developed to meet that need. He goes on to the subtle and highly significant point that while these sciences sought to be objective and quantification-oriented in order to preserve their scientific integrity and independence, these very characteristics have made them "wonderfully appropriate for serving the tasks of control necessary to a technological society" (p. 119). Social science has understood that by being descriptive rather than normative, science could assist men while allowing a pluralism of values. But by treating judgments of good and bad as beyond reason, the social sciences have in fact given powerful support to the supremacy of the values of instrumental control which they embody. Some of the leading preachers of "the dogmas which legitimize modern liberalism" (p. 11) are social scientists, Grant ironically observes.

The transformation of science in technological society implies a transformation of politics as well. In fact, it is in the political realm that technique produces those consequences which both Grant and Ellul seem to fear most immediately. "From the political, social, and human points of view, this conjunction of state and technique is by far the most important phenomenon of history" (*The Technological Society*, p. 233). Ellul sees the state compelled to accept techniques either in order to master other technological organizations, to control them, or to compete with rival states whose power is growing through technology. In such states politicians are either technologists or their servants, for they have a choice between applying technique to the maximum extent and inserting it into citizens' lives in every area possible, or failing to be efficient and losing their mandate. Thus, even if no one consciously plans or desires it, "technique causes the state to become totalitarian, to absorb the citizens' life completely" (p. 284). This analysis does not apply to individual states alone. The increasing interrelationship of state and technique affects political life on a global level. The ultimate product is a total world civilization (p. 318).

One might object that the technology of mass communication has opened up the possibility of far greater political awareness and participation for many people. The leading technological powers all claim to be democratic in one way or another. Ellul answers this objection in another book, *The Political Illusion* (1967). Even in the democracies, he argues there, people do not control the state. Rather, they control to some extent the selection of the personnel in charge of the apparatus, but the machinery runs by its own rules. People have come to expect politicians to be problem-solvers, and have entrusted ever growing areas of life to their responsibility. But problems are solved by technique, not by politics, so the more intensely politicized a people are, the less control they will have over the state, because they are in effect demanding its further technologization.

Lament for a Nation is, in its entirety, Grant's commentary on the political impact of technological society. The defeat of both Diefenbaker and Canadian nationalism are traced to the growing internalization by Canadians of the social ideals of the technological society whose heartland is the United States. In his 1970 introduction to the book, further implications of his defeat are drawn, reflecting Grant's encounter with Ellul.

> Lying behind the immediate decisions arising from our status within the (American) empire is the deeper question of the fate of any particularity in the technological age. What happens to nationalist strivings when the societies in question are given over, at the very level of faith, to the realization of the technological dream? At the very core of that faith is service to the process of universalization and homogenisation. "The one best means" must after all be the same in Chicago, Hamilton, and Dusseldorf. How much difference can there be between societies whose faith in "the one best means" transcends even communist and capitalist differences? (p. ix.)

In other writings Grant argues that this universal and homogeneous state is not the best social order, but is inherently tyrannical and destructive of humanity because, as an ideal, it substitutes freedom for virtue. That is, the "good life" to which it is proper to aspire in technological society is not a life constrained by moral judgements; but is one in which the needs, desires and "values" of individuals find their greatest possible fulfillment. This quest for freedom divorced from virtue entails the desire to dominate necessity, hence leads to tyranny (*TE*, pp. 81-109). When this ideal is combined with the highest degree of technological power, as in the USA., genuine political life is consistently undone by violence (*TE*, pp. 63-78). In an age dominated by technique, even revolution is an inadequate guide to or hope for political life. In "Tradition and Revolution" Grant points out that modern revolutions are made both necessary and possible by "lags between advances in technology and the realized state of freedom." But modern technique is the realization of "the desire to overcome change." As such, it "involves always the reduction of the different to the same. It requires revolution in its primary sense of again and again and again." Thus, revolution which aims at advancing freedom through technology "becomes as it is realized a freedom lived within a tighter and tighter order of mechanical recurrence." Revolution aims at increasing political freedom, but ends in restricting it. "In this sense, a (genuine) revolution in our society can only be a revolution of nihilism" (*LN*, p. 92).

For both Ellul and Grant, then, technological society transforms scientific and political activity, integrating both into a social order whose primary intention is the domination of the human and non-human environment and the elimination of chance. In that context, science increasingly becomes a process which leads to increasing mastery, while in politics the exercise of power tends to displace rational discussion in both democracies and dictatorships.

Since both Jacques Ellul and George Grant are known to have considerable interest in the study of religion, we might here ask in what way they believe religion to have been transformed by technological society. Although Ellul has written extensively on this elsewhere, he says very little in *The Technological Society*. One passage in the work, however, summarizes his position well. Speaking of nineteenth-century England, Ellul comments:

> Here, too, there was a kind of secularization of religion. Religion is
> no longer the framework of society; it can no longer impose its
> taboos or forms upon it. Rather, it integrates itself into society,
> adjusts to it, and adopts the notion of social utility as criterion and
> justification (p. 56).

Religious institutions go the way of all others. In fact technique itself becomes the locus of the sacred even as it destroys traditional forms of religiosity (p. 143).

Ellul is neither surprised nor particularly alarmed by this fact, for reasons which shall be discussed later. For Grant, who agrees with Ellul's diagnosis, the realization that religious institutions have been absorbed into the technological framework comes as a shock, part of that "change of mind" we noted earlier. He writes:

> ... I hoped for years that our ecclesiastical organizations (being the guardians of the beauty of the gospel) might continue to be able to permeate this society with something nobler than the barrenness of technical dynamism. I hoped for this when every piece of evidence before me was saying that it was not true. I could not face the fact that we were living at the end of western Christianity. I could not believe that the only interpretation of Christianity that technological liberalism would allow to survive publically would be that part of it ... which played the role of flatterer to modernity (*TE*, p. 44).

The fate of the churches, however, may not be the most important aspect of modern religion. Grant and Ellul would agree that the religious situation has been drastically altered by technological society insofar as technique becomes itself the object of the devotion of modern man. Grant appears to regard the religious character of our attachment to technique as self-evident. He uses the terminology of the study of religion to describe aspects of our social order. "Progressive dogma," "worship of technique," "the governing faith of the society" – these are only a few examples. While Grant and Ellul agree that the religious situation has been altered in technological society to the extent that technique has itself become the object of devotion and the ground of norms, their quite different responses to this situation suggest that we are approaching some serious divergences between them. The reason why Ellul can accept the fate of the churches dispassionately is that churches are institutions, and Ellul regards institutions as always a barrier to freedom, the more so in technological society (see, for example, *The Ethics of Freedom*, pp. 289-290). For Grant, the problem is not so much with the institutional aspect of the churches as with their theologies and their impact on the modern worldview. In particular, he regrets the ways in which the churches of the Calvinist tradition have "cut themselves off from pure contemplation" (*TE*, p. 35). This theological tendency supported the emergence of the Puritan ethos, which could make itself quite at home in the secularized social order of British liberalism. With this accommodation of religion to secularism, the churches lost their purchase on technological developments, and are now unable to sustain a critique of the society in which all traditions including the Calvinist are obsolete.

Grant was nurtured by this Calvinist heritage, but has now distanced himself from it. Ellul, however, represents a contemporary appropriation of the theology of the Calvinist Reformation. It would be unlikely, then, to assume, as Grant appears to do, that Ellul's inattention to the contribution of the Biblical religions to the rise of technological society is a mere oversight. In fact, Ellul would argue that the domination of technique is due to the failure of Christians to lay hold of the freedom given by God to man, a gift to which the Bible is our witness. Ellul sees freedom as the key concept of a proper Christian theology and ethics, while Grant sees the absolutization of freedom as a key to the degeneration of modern thought. Thus we have been led to a basic division between Grant and Ellul, one most readily elaborated by examining their respective views on human freedom.

Grant and Ellul on Freedom

Ellul sees technological society as the denial of freedom, while Grant sees it as the perversion of freedom. Ellul believes that beneath the false freedom which technique promises, a true freedom can be found which will break the power of technique (or any other power) over us. Grant hopes that above the falsehood of technological domination a word of truth may yet be heard. Ellul looks to freedom as the answer, while Grant takes freedom to be the chief problem.

One aspect of the problem of freedom is that the word has no univocal meaning. It has different meanings for different people in different contexts. In an article published in *Queen's Quarterly* in 1955, Grant discusses "The Uses of Freedom." Freedom has come to mean power, the ability of man "to get what he wants" (p. 518). This is not an understanding of freedom appropriate to the "... strange blending of the Greek and Hebrew which was the basis of western society ..." (p. 516). Yet the Protestant, and especially the Puritan interpretation of that ancient tradition is implicated in the rise and success of the modern view, because of its "inadequate biblicism" and "false denigration of reason" (p. 519).

Grant does not reject outright the modern quest for freedom. It is a problem rather than an evil. The problem with the modern quest is that it has become absolute, detached from questions of truth or meaning. In his first book, *Philosophy in the Mass Age*, Grant argues that this emphasis on freedom needs to be balanced against the restraints on human autonomy embodied in the tradition of natural law. His more mature analysis differs primarily in its judgement that the hope for such balance cannot be seriously entertained. This analysis is stated most succinctly where Grant says:

> The building of the universal and homogeneous state is not in itself a
> system of meaning in the sense that the older ones were. Even in its

realization, people would still be left with a question, unanswerable in its own terms: How do we know what is worth doing with our freedom? In myth, philosophy and revelation, orders were proclaimed in terms of which freedom was measured and defined. As freedom is the highest term in the modern language, it can no longer be so enfolded. There is no possibility of answering the question: freedom for what purposes? Such may indeed be the true account of the human situation: an unlimited freedom to make the world as we want in a universe indifferent to what purposes we choose. But if our situation is such, then we do not have a system of meaning (*TE*, p. 138).

In spite of this sober estimate, Grant sees resources in the human situation from which a response to the problem of freedom can be fashioned. We can yet nurture other human possibilities – the power of recollection or participation in a living tradition, desiring or loving, and thinking. Taken together, these powers ground the possibility of reverence, the quality most desperately lacking in technological society. The eloquent conclusion to *Time as History* begins to spell out the relationship between these possibilities. "In an age when the primacy of the will, even thinking, destroys the varied forms of reverence, they must come to us, when and if they come, from out of tradition" (p. 50). Our first line of defense against the history-making spirit, which understands man's freedom as his essence, is the memory that it has not always been so. Yet it is not enough simply to try to live out of the past.

As remembering can only be carried on by means of what is handed over to us, and as what is handed over is a confusion of truth and falsity, remembering is clearly not self-sufficient. Any tradition, even if it be the vehicle by which perfection itself is brought to us, leaves us with the task of appropriating from it, by means of loving and thinking, that which it has carried to us (p. 51).

For Ellul, this modern understanding of freedom does not go too far, but rather falls far short of authentic freedom. Technological society uses freedom as a slogan to hide the reality of ever-increasing necessity. As Ellul argues in *The Ethics of Freedom*, freedom is not a part of the natural human situation. Human life is under necessity, including its religious dimensions. Technological society is simply a contemporary and peculiarly intense manifestation of that necessity. Man has the power, within that range of necessities, to make choices; but this is hardly freedom, since both the context and consequences of the choices are part of the web of necessity. Rats in a maze make choices.

Freedom enters the human situation with the revelation of God to whom the Bible bears witness. God, in His radical freedom, confronts man with His gracious Word, which is both a commandment and an invitation to fellowship. The intervention of God in human history through the life, death and resurrection of Jesus Christ breaks the power of necessity and gives all human beings the choice of fellowship with Him.

Note that our freedom is not something we have prior to that choice, and by virtue of which we are able to choose. Rather, it is given to us by God in the very act of calling us to fellowship. We are given freedom in the act of obedience to God's command. We never possess genuine freedom, but we can exercise and express it insofar as we live out of the hope which is a response to God's love. "Freedom is the ethical aspect of hope" (*The Ethics of Freedom*, p. 12).

This freedom does not remove us from the common human situation, but it does give us "some room for maneuver" (p. 14). It does this by virtue of our participation in Christ's victory over death, giving us a real future. Our choices are still made within the context of necessity, but the larger context of Christ's victory gives us the right to hope that our resistance to that necessity is not in vain. That resistance is the acting out of the conviction that "all things are lawful." Our freedom extends even to the most deadly expression of sin and alienation, the Law. The Law, in Ellul's view, is oppressive because we have taken it into our own hands, rather than receiving it as the gift of the gracious God. To be liberated from its power by Jesus Christ is to be opened up to the spontaneity of love for and fellowship with the neighbor. Expressions of concern for our neighbor and for the glory of God provide the only limits to "all things are lawful"; and these are not limitations but rather the fulfilments of freedom.

The freedom we are given is real freedom, because our relationship with Christ is personal, not mechanical or metaphysical. Unless we continue to act out of our freedom, to receive the gift as a gift, that freedom is no longer operative. However, our falling away from freedom would not set aside the impact of the incarnation of Christ on human history. That event has decisively broken the myths by which man maintained an artificial unity between nature, society and the individual. The Biblical revelation has shown these social orders to be forms of bondage, injustice, falsehood and illusion. This realization "has made possible the totality of what men call progress. Christ has desacralized nature and shown how men can effectively use a creation that is still in their hands" (p. 282). But unless men take up the freedom that is offered to them in this situation, the net result of the presence of Christ "makes life completely unlivable, radically vitiates civilization and renders society wholly untenable" (p. 277). Such is, in Ellul's view, exactly the situation towards which the technological society is leading us.

To summarize this contrast between George Grant's interpretation of freedom and that of Jacques Ellul, we can say that Grant seeks an understanding of freedom tempered by the restraint of virtue and a sense of the abidingly true, while Ellul regards morality as an enemy of freedom, and looks for ultimate truth only in the immediate encounter of the individual with Jesus Christ through the witness of Holy Scripture. For Grant, freedom is bound to wisdom; only the wise are truly free. For Ellul, freedom is bound to obedience; man's freedom comes through hearing and obeying the command of God.

Conclusions

We have taken note of only one issue on which Grant takes a view sharply divergent from that of a thinker by whom he has been profoundly informed, yet this issue is so fundamental as to leave students of either thinker puzzled. Does this mixture of convergence and divergence indicate a major inconsistency in the thought of one or both of these men? Was Grant mistaken in his enthusiasm for Ellul's writings on technique? This writer would suggest two other conclusions which may be drawn, one having to do with George Grant and the other with the continuing critique of technological society.

One of the most striking things about George P. Grant is the diversity of his friends and students. From Marxists to true-blue Tories, from Thomists to Calvinists, from the deeply pious to the thoroughly secular the numbers of those who have been illumined by his thought are drawn. Such a phenomenon is not so much to be explained as to be admired. One who has thought his world so relentlessly transcends our easy categorizations. That Grant could draw fruitfully on some of the writings of one whose perspective is so different from his own is only the other side, the learning side, of this intellectual vitality.

This is not to say that Grant is right and Ellul wrong about freedom. It may be that other ways of understanding freedom exist which would be found to be even more helpful in the critique of technological society. But this leads us to a second conclusion. Perhaps it is an error, one of the intellectual prejudices of our age, to assume that an adequate critique of our social order must be based on some alternative system or blueprint for which the critic is merely clearing the ground. Perhaps, especially in the case of technological society, it is not possible to give a deductive critique. If that is the case, we may appreciate fully the achievement of both Grant and Ellul. Both have served us by prodding us to see the truth about our world, and to think what we are doing to ourselves and our neighbors. That kind of truth-telling, without pretence or prescription, may be the best that can be done.

Grant's Critique Of Values Language
by Joseph F. Power

Everybody uses the word 'values' to describe our making of the
world: capitalists and socialists, atheists and avowed believers,
scientists and politicians. The word comes to us so platitudinously
that we take it to belong to the way things are.[1]

Since George Grant made this observation in his 1969 Massey
Lectures, the use of the word "values" has no doubt increased; to his list
of users one might now add psychologists and catechists, business men and
bishops. Grant is especially sensitive to the uncritical use of the term by
religious people, as he indicates in continuing his remarks.

What is comic about the present use of 'values', and the distinction
of them from 'facts', is not that it is employed by modern men who
know what is entailed in so doing; but that it is also used by
'religious' believers who are unaware that in its employment they are
contradicting the very possibility of the reverence they believe they
are espousing in its use.[2]

What is it that Grant sees entailed in the mere use of the term
"value" or in the fact-value distinction? And how is it that an unwitting
use of them by religious believers contradicts what they think they are
defending? To suggest how Grant might answer these questions, and, in so
doing to draw together elements of his critique of values language, is the
prime objective of this paper.

To repeat, what would North American rhetoric be without the
word 'values'? But even those who use the word seriously within
theoretical work seem not to remember that the word was brought
into the centre of western discourse by Nietzsche and into the
discourse of social science through Nietzsche's profound influence
upon Weber. For Nietzsche the fundamental experience for man was
apprehending what is as chaos; values were what we creatively willed
in the face of that chaos by overcoming the impotence of the will
which arises from the recognition of the consequences of
historicism. ... North American social scientists have been able to use
the language of values, fill it with the substantive morality of
liberalism and thereby avoid facing what is assumed in the most
coherent unfolding of this language.[3]

What is assumed in the language itself as it stems from Nietzsche is
an original moral chaos as background for whatever order can be created
by human willing. This "European" meaning has been replaced by
ideologies more congenial to North America, but according to Grant,
"such a position could not last. The languages of historicism and values
which were brought to North America to be the servants of the most
advanced liberalism and pluralism, now turn their corrosive power on our
only indigenous roots — the substance of that practical liberalism itself."[4]

Significantly Grant attributes to the language itself a power to shape subsequent thinking, in this case even after a "transfusion" of meaning. Hence his critique systematically focuses on the language of value. In its contemporary use, this language again implies that only by means of creatively-willed values does human experience or the human race acquire meaning: "Purpose and value are the creations of human will in an essentially purposeless world."[5]

We may note in passing that Grant views the creation of values as an integral aspect of a modern worldview which he contrasts sharply with an earlier one:

> Man makes the world, and there is no overall system which
> determines what he makes. To act is to choose what kind of a world
> we want to make. In our acts we show what things we regard as
> valuable. We create value, we do not participate in a value already
> given. We make what order there is; we are not made by it.[6]

We will return to the contrast between traditional and modern worldviews below, but the point here is that Grant often characterizes modern man as creating his own world: creating not only values and purpose, but history, nature and truth as well.[7] For the moment it is enough to say that for Grant the word "value" is never completely freed from the two assumptions that mark its origin: the assumption of a primordial chaos, and the correlative assumption that man himself must create value in it by his own will.

These assumptions are reflected in many current uses of "value" but one series stands out: the familiar distinction between "facts" and "values," the derived difference between judgements of fact and "value judgements," and the resulting claim of sciences to be "value-free."

> The word "value", as we now use it, is part of the logic of the new
> social sciences, which claim to be the chief way we get information
> about our society. Those sciences have at their theoretical centre the
> proposition that we must sharply distinguish between judgements of
> fact and judgements of value. Any neophyte in social science can tell
> one these days that it is self-evident that we must distinguish
> between facts and values. What is meant by this distinction between
> facts and values? What is meant by this distinction is that there is a
> world of facts which we do not make but which we discover and
> about which we can make objective judgements. On the other hand
> there are values which are made by human beings, which are not part
> of the objective world and about which our judgements are
> subjective, that is, relative to us. Man in his freedom makes
> values — they are what he does with the facts.[8]

In this way the contrast with "facts" enhances and enshrines the nuances already present in "value," nuances of subjectivity and relativity, which remove values from the realm of rational discussion or possible agreement. Hence it is only by excluding values from scientific discourse that an "objective" view of the world can be developed:

> The use of the term "value" and the distinguishing of judgement about values from judgement about facts enables the social scientist to believe that his account of reality is objective, while all previous accounts (which were not based on this distinction) were vitiated by their confusion of normative with factual statements.[9]

Grant himself, however, sees the fact-value distinction as a mixture of questionable assumptions and undesirable consequences:

> It assumes a particular account of moral judgement and a particular account of objectivity. To use the language of value about moral judgement is to assume that what man is doing when he is moral is choosing in his freedom to make the world according to his own values which are not derived from knowledge of the cosmos. To confine the language of objectivity to what is open to quantifiable experiement is to limit purpose to our own subjectivity. As these metaphysical roots of the fact-value distinction are not often evident to those who affirm the method, they are generally inculcated in what can be best described as a religious way; that is, as doctrine beyond question.[10]

Some of the undesirable consequences Grant sees flowing in practice from the distinction may be summarized as follows:

1. The reduction of all moral judgement to subjective preference or personal choice, with the consequent impossibility of reasoned discourse about what is good or bad.[11]

2. The ascription of personal and religious values to the private domain in a way which is supposed to facilitate agreement within a pluralistic society, but which has in fact cleared the way for the values of technology to take over uncontested.[12]

3. A high risk of "value-free" sciences serving the interests of the powerful; for Weber the distinction was to be a means of protecting academia from outside pressures, but it has in fact made it easier for value-free social scientists to serve the purpose of government or big business.[13]

If such are in fact the logical assumptions and practical consequences of adopting the term "values" and the fact-value distinction, then it is easy to see why this usage is open to question, and to see in particular why religious people should be wary of adopting it. Yet one may well remain unconvinced at this point. After all, common sense seems to say that the mere use of a term or of a distinction can hardly have so much significance. Besides, how could this usage continue to find acceptance if it were as pernicious as Grant makes it out to be? The fact is, that however much people today differ as to which values they espouse, almost no one questions the "values" way of thinking and speaking. Why is this?

In response to these common-sense objections, certain immediate replies are easily available in Grant's writings. His critique is by no means a set of semantic scruples which could be eased if substitutes were found for the offending words. "Values" is not a word that is incidental to our culture, but is, on the contrary, one of the words "at the core of what we conceive ourselves to be."[14] Hence "value is not a word which we can talk about in exclusion from our own existence."[15] To account for the continued acceptance of the terminology, Grant has already mentioned an immediate explanation. It is accepted ever more widely because it is "inculcated in what can best be described as a religious way; that is, as doctrine beyond question," indeed, "the fact-value distinction is the most sacred doctrine of our public religion."[16]

But still, no doctrine is totally immune to criticism in our culture and so the question of why so few have challenged this particular one requires a deeper explanation. Briefly put, Grant feels that contemporary culture cannot adequately assess the concept of "values" and their alleged distinction from "facts," because these conceptions arose with modern culture and are so intimately implicated in it that any criticism of them is self-criticism – criticism of "the primal" from which we come.[17] More specifically, Grant holds that within our culture "reason" has been restricted to that particular form of reason which is required for technology, namely the acquisition of knowledge for the sake of mastery or control over nature and human nature. As such, reason is regarded as a neutral instrument that autonomous persons can use as they wish; in other words, the view of reason and its functioning is tailored to the "world-creating" view cited above. This restricted conception of reason can scarcely understand itself let alone transcend its own assumptions to assess ideas which are endemic to it. In general terms this is how Grant accounts for the absence of objection to "values" language.

Another example of the difficulty which our era has in criticizing its own assumptions can be found in a discussion of the means of ethically judging the many concrete possibilities afforded by technology. In this case Grant points out that the science which produced these techniques and the new moral science which is supposed to judge them have come from a common source. In other words, "the moral discourse of 'values' and 'freedom' is not independent of the will to technology, but a language fashioned in the same forge together with the will to technology."[18] A little later Grant sums up the problem in even more sweeping terms: "The difficulty then of those who seek substantive values by which to judge particular techniques is that they must generally think of such values within the massive assumptions of modern thought. Indeed even to think 'values' at all is to be within such assumptions."[19]

How is it possible, then, for anyone to extricate himself from the assumptions of modern thought? How does Grant himself pretend to transcend them in order to criticize the language flowing from them? For in all his efforts to explain why so few criticize the notion of values Grant never disguises the fact that he too, as a modern thinker, shares in the difficulty of working through this particular conception of reason which is our common fate.[20] In a general way Grant would say that it is only by a sense of the history of philosophy that one can identify the assumptions of his own age,[21] and only by some reference point independent of the present that one can gain perspective on contemporary thought.

An historical perspective is necessary, first of all because we have forgotten how new the language of values is: "It is forgotten that before Nietzsche and his immediate predecessors, men did not think about their actions in that language. They did not think they made the world valuable, but that they participated in its goodness."[22] Those who lived through that shift of meaning were largely unaware of it because they assumed that the terms were equivalent. And now as long as we assume that "values" is just a contemporary way of speaking of the good, or conversely that the language of the good and of the excellence of man as man is "just a crude way of talking about values, pretending that they have some status in the nature of things beyond our choosing,"[23] we hardly notice the linguistic substitution. Grant is saying, however, as forcefully as he can, that "values" is not the equivalent of what has been meant by "the good".

To appreciate the vast difference between them requires that we have some notion of what "the good" meant in earlier centuries. Based on his own understanding of what goodness meant traditionally, Grant points out that modern uses of the word are decisively different:

> 'Goodness' is now apprehended in a way which excludes from it all 'owingness'. To generalize this as clearly as I am able: the traditional western view of goodness is that which meets us with an excluding claim and persuades us that in obedience to that claim we will find what we are fitted for. The modern view of goodness is that which is advantageous to our creating richness of life (or, if you like, the popular propagandists' 'quality of life'),
> What is true of the modern conception of goodness ... is that it does not include the assertion of an owed claim which is intrinsic to our desiring. Owing is always provisory upon what we desire to create.[24]

That in this modern view all owing is conditional (every "should" implies an "if"), and that it is conditional upon what *we* choose to *create*, shows how extensively our present speaking of goodness is based upon values thinking. If we value this, then we should do that. Of course, if we have difficulty doing the latter, we can always reconsider the original value; since we chose it in the first place we can modify or even reject it. Or again I may be able to "clarify" the values that are reflected in my actions in order to achieve a greater internal consistency; but if my actions reflect, for example, the high value I put on material comfort and security and I consciously choose that value then no one can suggest that I "should" do anything differently.[25] In the last analysis therefore – and without prejudice to the merit it has from other points of view – such an approach to morality is ultimately "impotent to lead to what was once considered (perhaps and perhaps not naively) the crucial judgement about 'values' – whether they are good or evil."[26]

Since our culture has not yet thought through the notion of value or even recognized its novelty, Grant urges caution in using value language lest we unwittingly espouse the assumptions it embodies. Since "value" remains in many subtle ways Nietzsche's and Weber's word, to use it without being aware of its history and the assumptions it bears is to allow one's thinking to be shaped by those assumptions. We can see then why it is so important for Grant to caution all unsuspecting users of values language; it only remains to suggest why he notes a special irony in its use by religious people. The implicit contradiction would seem to lie in this: on the one hand religious believers affirm a God who by his very existence constitutes some limit to human self-creation and to the autonomous creation of values; on the other hand they would be trying to express such limits in a language which, as a matter of fact, was developed to assert that all value is a result of human willing – a language which is thus incapable of expressing any value that is "absolute" or independent of human making.[27] By adopting that language believers would unconsciously undercut the possibility of expressing a God-given moral goodness which they actually accept. After making that point in the context that served as our starting point, Grant added, "The reading of Nietzsche would make that clear to them."[28]

A few final comments may be helpful in order to preclude possible misunderstandings of Grant's position, especially such as may arise from a brief look at one facet of his unique and complex stance toward modernity. First of all it might seem from our summary that Grant is simply opposed to any use of values terminology in serious moral discourse. Now it is true that underlying Grant's criticism of value and of other key modern terms there is an unspoken premise which would state in part: the words we use shape the way we think. That premise runs counter to some widespread assumptions about language, but just as Grant denies that reason and computers are merely neutral instruments waiting for autonomous persons to use them in any way they will, so too would he deny that words are inert instruments exercising no influence on the thought of those who use them. No doubt Grant would allow that thought in its turn also influences and shapes words at least to the extent that the latter are used critically, and that is the crucial difference. Grant's critique is directed specifically and solely against a use of value terms which is *unaware* of their history and assumptions, and which, for that reason, is liable to be influenced unknowingly.

From this clarification it follows that Grant is not simply opposed to every use of values terminology. Its occasional or even frequent use does not automatically vitiate ethical thinking. Thus it is possible to point to authors who have used it without being taken in by its Nietzschean assumptions, because they have written in full awareness of those assumptions and of the limitations of that language. Far from lessening the general timeliness of Grant's critique, such exceptions actually prove the general rule of its necessity.

The practical conclusion to be drawn from all of this, then, is not a simplistic ban on words, but rather a sensitized awareness that will examine every use of values language beginning with one's own and that will continue by testing the awareness of others who use it, and by interpreting accordingly.

A second possible misinterpretation: since Grant often refers to the classical understanding of goodness in contrast to values, some readers may assume that he favours a return to a "morality of the good" as a present possibility. Grant realizes that in trying to offset several centuries' criticism of the older morality[29] he does make statements about perfection and the good "from out of an ancient way of thinking".[30] Yet he is painfully aware that such statements can hardly be appropriated today: they are, in his terms, an instance of remembering but not yet one of thinking the good in our day. Simply remembering or reviving the past is not sufficient:

> Nor (to repeat) should any dim apprehensions of what was meant by perfection before the age of progress be used simply as means to negate what may have been given us of truth and goodness in this age. The present darkness is a real darkness. ... [But] we must not forget that new potentialities of reasoning and making happen have been actualized ... and therefore must be thought as having been actualized, in relation to what is remembered. The conception of time as history is not to be discarded as if it had never been.[31]

Nor, we would add, is the conception of value as humanly created good to be discarded as if it had never been. It must be brought into relation with what is remembered of a good which made claims on us, although just how that is to be done is presently a matter of real darkness.

Even now, however, remembering the good leads to the realization that our present use of value is not at all its equivalent, and thus Grant persists in calling attention to the divergence between these notions and to the grave difficulty it poses. In this sense, far from being an antiquarian seeking the security of past solutions, Grant is rather a prophet fated to decry as false "the most sacred doctrine of our public religion", or indeed a modern social critic seeking to raise the consciousness of a people by exposing the "false consciousness" which simply identifies value with the good.

Beyond proclaiming this non-equivalence of values and the good, Grant does not say what positive doctrine should replace the conventional assumptions, or what "true consciousness" would mean. To do so would be beyond the role of prophet or critic. Yet his very silence at this point may give rise to additional misunderstandings, especially when it en-counters expectations which will not accept that silence for what it is. In many cases it is presumed that an author must have some "ideology" in light of which he criticizes, and that his silence must therefore be concealing that ideology. Such expectations cannot accept silence as an answer even when the reason given for it is that the writer just does not know a positive answer to the problem he poses. For his part Grant freely acknowledges that he is unable to find or to formulate a credible language capable of spanning the gap between what is given us to think in the modern experience and what we are able to remember of a good that is not of our making; he admits that he is rarely able to proceed from remembering to thinking and loving the good in our present.[32]

Unfashionable as such a frank avowal may be, it forces us to face the way Grant sees our present and his own role in it. His view is vividly expressed in a cluster of related images which haunt the final paragraphs of recent writings. For example:

> Our present is like being lost in the wilderness, when every pine and rock and bay appears to us as both known and unknown, and therefore as uncertain pointers on the way back to human habitation. The sun is hidden by the clouds and the usefulness of our ancient compasses has been put in question.[33]

In this situation the philosopher's essential task is to call attention to the fact that we are lost, that landmarks which seem familiar are not in fact what we once knew, that we inhabit a "new found land which is so obviously a 'terra incognita' "[34] – in short, that we live in a darkness that is no less real for being rarely recognized. "Thinkers who deny the fact of that darkness are no help in illuminating a finely tempered practice for the public realm. The job of thought at our time is to bring into the light that darkness as darkness."[35] Part of that darkness is the assumption that "values" are the equivalent of "the good", and so in his critique of values language George Grant is exposing that darkness for what it is. Considered within its temporal and personal context this task is not simply negative, nor is it negligible. It is the most positive and illuminating task possible in our present. With a candor which reflects both humility and hope Grant adds: "It is for the great thinkers and the saints to do more."[36]

III
THEOLOGY AND HISTORY

PART III. THEOLOGY AND HISTORY

Conversation

Question: In what you do I note two things of methodological interest. You continually say "well, not on this level, not on that level." And you do it so often that I sometimes feel you are essentially speaking things that are contradictory, but don't have to admit it, because you say, "well this is on a popular or vulgar level, but really, on the higher level, etc., etc." You distinguish a kind of esoteric in-group level, where we know certain things that we dare not talk about to those outside. This is philosophy. Politics is something else, where we tell, as in Plato, helpful and truthful lies. There's also Christian eschatology, which contradicts everything in philosophy, but is absolutely true.

Grant: Some of that criticism I agree with, some not. You talk of speaking things that are contradictory. Isn't it necessary to distinguish between contradictions which arise from sloppiness, and contradictions the presence of which are the very stuff of life? To live in the face of these contradictions is to be human. Don't serious people have to live in the presence of the contradiction between the perfection of God and the affliction of human beings? Christianity flashes its light into that contradiction – but also makes it a deeper contradiction. The light does not overcome the contradiction between perfection and affliction – except perhaps for the greatest saints. Christianity is only a kind of beacon flashing into darkness. That beacon does not overcome the necessity of philosophy in the way that certain theologians seem to think it does. And immediately there is the attempt to seek knowledge of the whole – that is, philosophy – different levels are present in themselves, and for different sorts of people.

At all times and places human beings have had to talk at different levels of intelligible discourse, not only because of the difference of the people they are talking with, but also because of the strange situation of knowing and not knowing. Different levels are forced on us by our gnosticism and our agnosticism. But in our era, the levels have become amazingly complex, because we live in a civilization which has lost its originating assumptions, and can't find any others. We live in a time when everybody is in darkness about the most important matters, unless they delude themselves. The only clarity is in certain of the positive sciences, but they do not provide us clarity about the most important matters. How can anybody deny that the western world lives today in intellectual darkness, and that it affects anybody who is serious? This involves talking at many levels to different people at different times.

Question: You often speak about your dependence on the traditions of Athens and Jerusalem. Obviously the tradition of Athens, and of Plato in particular, is present in everything you say. But what is less obvious is what you incorporate from the tradition of Jerusalem. I can see the New Testament there – but I wonder to what extent the Old Testament, the so-called Hebrew Bible, and the whole Hebraic background of Christian faith, is of vital importance in your thought?

Grant: Let me say first that I do not like talking in public these days of the differences between Judaism and Christianity. I don't think any political good is served by talking of such differences, because it would be taken in the basest and most vulgar way. But that does not mean there aren't grave intellectual differences between Christianity and Judaism. Clearly, for myself, I'm on the side of Christianity that is farthest away from Judaism, and nearest to the account of Christianity that is close to Hinduism in its philosophic expression. I would accept what Clement of Alexandria said: some were led to the Gospel by the Old Testament, many were led by Greek philosophy. This same applies today when there are many ways into the apprehension of what is universal about Christ. What I object to in many modern theologians (particularly the Germans) is that they make Christianity depend on the religious history of a particular people, as told in the Old Testament. They make Christianity such an "historical" religion that its universal teaching about perfection and affliction is lost.

Question: It seems to me your use of the term "tradition of Jerusalem" is really an empty use. If you take the Hebrew element out of the religion, what you have left is a pale Hellenism.

Grant: Obviously there are wonderful and true things in the Old Testament. There are also the exclusivist parts. What I want to insist is that the universal truth of Christ is not tied too clearly to the religious life of a particular nation, and that Christianity is not tied to an account of God's dynamic activity in the world, which appears to me to be unthinkable and

to lead directly to atheism. Both western accounts of Christianity —
Protestant and Catholic — have emphasized the arbitrary power of God in
a way which seems to me fundamentally wrong and which has produced a
picture of a God whom one should not worship. I think those emphases on
the power of God are related to that exclusivity and dynamism which have
led to some of the worst sides of western civilization. We in the West are
called to rethink all this, which started somewhere close to St Augustine.
What seems to me sad is that just when this rethinking is so necessary,
many theologians are reemphasizing this God of dynamism in the name of
the Bible.

Question: Let me go back to the religious implications of what you were
saying in the discussion of politics. You defended nationalism as the love
of one's own, and said that we move from love of one's own to love of the
good — God. I'm asking you what keeps human society unified, rather
than simply falling apart into a multiplicity of diverse groups, all of which
glory in that which is particular to them? What are our obligations to the
universal community? You talk about the universal and homogeneous
state, and speak against it. But there is another universal community — the
one holy Catholic Church.

Grant: I am sure that the world-wide universal state would be a tyranny.
To whom am I asked to give loyalty in this world-wide community? When
it comes down to it, I am asked to give loyalty to one of the great empires.
That I won't do. They should be balanced off, one against the other.
Beyond that, about the Church; it seems to me you have a central point. It
makes some claims to universality, however much it has failed in detail.
How does one put together the love of one's own in a particular century,
with the love of universality? How would you express your loyalty to the
universal human community?

Question: Well, I express my loyalty to the universal human community
by refusing to acknowledge any part of it as my own. That is to say, there
is nothing human that is alien to me. It seems to me the height of idolatry
to talk about a movement from love of one's own to love of the good,
finding God through one's own particularity, rather than in the repentant
turning away from that which belongs to me, and seeking to find God in
the face of a stranger. It's been hard for me to realize that my mother and
my wife and my children are just people, and in the plan of God no closer
to me than any person in this room or any person elsewhere in the world.

Grant: You're talking as if people didn't have bodies.

Response: I am a Platonist.

Grant: That's not Platonism. Plato always recognized that people had
bodies.

Response: I would say this about the body: we are created by God for eternal life. There will be no bodies, at least as we know them. The body, therefore, is not essential.

Grant: It's a transitory dispensation; that I grant completely.

Response: It's purely pedagogical. It's like a canteen on a pilgrimage. When you get to the end you put it aside. The primacy of the body, especially in Heidegger and contemporary philosophy, is part of the very modernity which is the source of so many problems. In the Kingdom of Heaven there is neither marriage nor giving in marriage, and before the face of God, therefore, marriage and parenthood fall away as we are incorporated within one family of God, and we have only one father and one mother.

The debate within Christian theology is about the degree to which these eschatological realities are susceptible of realization in the order of space and time. Are they merely prefigures sacramentally, or are they factors that begin to fill space and time and reshape political life here and now?

Grant: Most of what you have said I accept as true, except some of the remarks about eschatology, which I have never thought through, and therefore simply do not understand. I would make some qualifications, however. To say that the body is pedagogical is to say a lot. In the dispensation we live in now, the body is our infallible judge. What we do to our own bodies and to other peoples' bodies, is our partaking in justice here and now. We can't learn anything about justice apart from bodies.

Also I've spent much of my life having to learn not to hate myself as a body. And I think that since I have not hated myself as a body, I have been better able to love the universal good (though of course not well) than when I did hate myself as a body. There was a side of North American Protestantism that was around me in a secular form that wanted one to learn to love good out of neglect of the body, or even hatred. All it made was a kind of resentment and a pretended love of the good. The present erotomania in North America may be foolish and degrading, but it is a reaction to that torture of the body in North American Protestantism. Just because we must dislike that reaction, it does not mean that we should go back to what it is a reaction against. I may emphasize this too much just because my life has required that I overcome that neglect of the body which could be such a cause of phony love of the good.

I'm sure you're right to say that the body is a temporary dispensation, and must not be taken too seriously. That is the fundamental thing to say. I'm also sure that the Catholic tradition was wiser about this than certain forms of English-speaking Protestantism. One can see this in so many Catholic priests and sisters. They took on the religious life, not because they hated the body, but because they saw it as a passing dispensation.

Comment: I would like to hear something about the role of the universal visible community and the good which transcends love of our own, and the place that they play in political philosophy. That's what I haven't heard when you speak about nationalism.

Question: What do you mean by the universal community?

Response: Everybody on earth. There's a sense in which what is my own is everybody's on earth.

Comment: How do you get at this "everybody on earth"? It seems to me such an abstraction. I thought that what Grant was arguing about nationalism is that the route to this broader community is through your own. There can be no authentic international horizon unless you start with your own social and human collectivity. The acceptance of imperialism and a type of colonialised mentality prevents you from having any real contact with an international community.

Grant: I agree with the last point. In Canadian terms, when one is asked to serve the international community, it comes down to doing what IBM or the American government wants. That is our difficulty in specifying the international community in Canada. Internationalism generally means just being a servant of English-speaking capitalism. At the university it is often said "science and scholarship are international." What that means generally is "let's hire a lot more professors from Cal. Tech. or Harvard." I have heard the ruling class in Canada say "let's take on atomic bombs in the name of international commitments." That is just liberal nonsense.

But beyond that is the question of how one comes to love the universal good, except in terms of first loving what is near and close to one. If faith is the experience that the intelligence is illuminated by love, then how can human beings learn to love if the beginning of love is not love of one's own? It is in this sense that I think love of one's own is connected to love of the good. It is not the element of possession or of extension of self, which makes one's "own" so important, but rather its availability for being known by us, and known as good.

Question: Isn't it true that in the modern world the notion of freedom and will have changed? In the Bible, true freedom is perfect obedience to God, and justice is therefore the structuring principle of our actions. Whereas in the modern world, freedom has been separated off from the structures of justice, and is identified now with creativity. In the university the idolatry of the sciences is technology, and the idolatry of the humanities is aestheticism and the worship of beauty as coming out of human creativity. Is it not this transformation of the notion of freedom and will which you oppose?

Grant: Yes, this is what I have been trying to say. I would add to what you say about the Bible, that Plato also is very close to what you are saying. The union of happiness and justice is almost the same as the union of freedom and obedience. Clearly, the union of happiness and justice cannot be thought of in any purely immanent sense. What seems to me central to the whole modern experiment is the exaltation of freedom and will outside any given structure of justice. The given — what the scientists call data — is chaos; we create within that chaos. One of the central moments in the arrival of that view of will occurred when Kant affirmed the autonomy of the will. Freedom had never meant that we made our own laws before that.

Of course the whole matter is confused, because the words "freedom" and "will" have come to have so many differing and unclear meanings. When we talk of political freedom, what sane human being could be against that? The word only becomes dangerous when it is tied to will, and it comes to mean man's power to make the world as he wants, outside any received structure of justice.

What you say about the modern exaltation of human creativity seems to me essential. Just recently I sat on a panel with two famous physicists. They both said that the only things that give meaning to the world are scientific and artistic "creativity." This is an idolatry which excludes meaning from most people's lives. The possibility of thinking that our lives are concerned with the opening up of structures of justice, in which we can partake, was excluded for these very clever men by what they took to be the consequences of modern thought. This is just one example of what one hears everywhere — namely that the English-speaking elites are fast becoming Nietzschians, whether they have ever heard of him or not. What a terrifying vision of justice is going to arise from that! This is what scares one about the modern enterprise.

Question: Is the problem that the use of the will *per se* is wrong, so that everything that belongs to the order of will is, if not bad, at least a deviation from the primary purpose of life, which is contemplation? There are things you've said in certain of your writings about contemplation that lead us to believe that you hold the view of Augustine, who never found a way to will anything in this world which was not marred by concupiscence. Or is the problem not in the use of the word "will" *per se*, but in the disordered use of the will?

Grant: That raises a whole series of complicated and interrelated questions. First let me speak of contemplation. It is a word I like less and less. It is so tied to the notion of the thinker as living the highest life — the account of the philosopher which one finds in Aristotle, and which is to me so distasteful. The vision of human life which sees it producing at its height great thinkers seems a kind of blasphemy. If that is the way the universe is, then I simply say "no" to it. The supreme acts seem to me open to any human being, and do not depend on the degree of our intelligence. There may be good arguments against equality at a political or natural level, but if one is a Christian, there can be none at the supernatural level. That seems to me to take one to the very core of Christianity. Anybody whose life is given over to philosophy needs to read the thirteenth chapter of First Corinthians regularly. Anybody is open to love, and that is the supreme act. As I have said, faith is the experience that the intelligence is illuminated by love. I mean by love, attention to otherness, receptivity of otherness, consent to otherness. If contemplation means at its centre, love, then I don't mind the word; but if it carries the implication of the thinker as the height of human existence, then it seems to me a dangerous word. This is above all why I would call myself philosophically a Platonist, and why I so fear the Aristotelian tradition. Plato proclaims the dependence of intelligence upon love in a much clearer way than Aristotle.

What I don't like about the modern apprehension of will is that it implies that we stand over against love. I recently heard a very practical bureaucrat describe human beings as "mobile, electronic command centres." Such a description takes one close to what is now meant by will.

Question: What then is sin?

Grant: I find much of the language of western theology very opaque at this point — the language of sin and fall, of choice and will. This may simply be my lack of understanding and perception. What seems to me given in the Gospels is that the highest is to give your will away. But this does not seem to be a matter of choice, but of being chosen. There is a low level of life — in which most of us live — where will operates. Moral evil or sin is there the liberty of indifference. We can talk about sin as being indifferent to loving that which is truly loveable. To think this way necessarily implies the doctrine that evil is not the opposite of good, but its absence, and that moral evil is finally an indifference to good, to otherness. I think here once again Kant was of great significance in turning around the tradition. He taught that evil was radical, and not simply an absence of good. This was another way in which the wills of human beings were exalted and turned into the first cause of events.

Response: I do not think there is such agreement between your opinions and Christian theology as you make out. In the Bible, freedom is perfect obedience, and what is at stake is that the will expresses itself in a distorted manner. I sense that you are saying that the expression of the will itself is evil.

Grant: No. I am simply saying that the height is to get rid of the will.

Response: But that's not Biblical, that's Platonic.

Grant: Everybody is always saying that something is not Biblical. The question is what is in the Gospels, and this is what I find. At the height Christ surrenders his will. We certainly seem to see that the saints have no love of their own, and what is more one's own than one's will? People such as myself have no direct experience of that. But we see it in the saints, and all of us have dim intimations of what it is to give ourselves away.

Comment: I'd like to pick up some of the historical implications of what you're saying. There is no doubt that our modern emphasis on will arose through a thinking about will that took place within the western Christian tradition. It is only in the early Middle Ages that voluntarism begins. A lot of this reflection on will was influenced by the scriptural accounts. The medieval reflection on will had to do with God's will, and with man's conformity to it. Then somehow thought about God's will got transferred to thought about man's will, and so you come to the emphasis on autonomy. For the medievals, God's will created the good, whereas modern men began to talk of their will as if it created values.

Grant: I agree with you entirely, and also about how difficult it is to sort this out. Let me ask you a question, because you know much more about this than I do. Do you think it wise these days to attribute "will" to Deity? I prefer the word "love." Indeed in the modern world the word "love" has been sentimentalised, but the word "will" has been brutalised. How much is it necessary to use the word "will" about Deity?

Response: The question is how much you associate "love" with "will." I must say that I have experienced some of the same opaqueness about the word "will," even in reading within the Patristic and Scholastic traditions. I have a very great difficulty in understanding what they mean by will because of the confusion with the modern notion.

Grant: I have the same difficulty. Also I am lost with the theological and metaphysical questions when they reach a high level. Yet I am sure they are the most important questions, despite all the modern contempt and indifference to them. They are indeed essential if we are to come to any clear vision of what technology portends. One thing I am sure about is that if you carry the language of "will" about Deity too far, you are led into all the language of miracle which has plagued and confused the West. You use language which implies that God interferes with secondary causes in an arbitrary way. Then any sane person asks, why is the torture not stopped that is going on this minute? I do not mean by this that events which we call miracles have not happened. Obviously they have. But we must not carry the talk of God's arbitrariness so far that these events become absurd. All I am saying is that these events should not be talked about in the arbitrary language of power. On the other hand, one can get into a kind of shallow rationalism which is just the modern attempt to try to make the ways of God scrutable. This seems to me to lead to saying that good is evil and evil is good. But how we are to think the truth of theology in the face of the coming-to-be of technology is the great question.

The Barren Twilight: History And Faith In Grant's Lament
by M. Darrol Bryant

In 1965 George Grant published an elegant meditation entitled *Lament for a Nation*, and with that publication resurrected a long-forgotten form of political commentary: the meditative lament. The aptness of the form was as striking as the content and claims of the work, which centred on the fate of Canada. That the subject of our present and future should take the form of a lament was not accidental; rather, for Grant, such a form was necessary since he felt that Canada was dying. With its republication in the Carleton Library Series, the work has attained the status of a (minor?) Canadian classic, and perhaps there is something dangerous about this: classics are often more admired than understood. *Lament*, however, deserves a better fate.

The year 1965 also saw the publication of Harvey Cox's *Secular City*. The coincidence of the year of publication is the only similarity between the two works. While Cox was enthralled by modernity as exemplified in the secular metropolis, Grant lamented the devastating effect of modernity on the Canadian nation. For Cox, modernity freed man from the restrictive bonds of small town provinciality. For Grant, modernity spelled the end of a political society which sought "to build, along with the French, a more ordered and stable society than the liberal experiment in the United States."[1] The contrast of sensibilities is also reflected in the differences of style. Cox's work proceeds in a bright, crisp, journalistic way, inviting his readers to embrace the secular world. Grant's work, on the other hand, is dark and argumentative, challenging its readers to consider the devastating impact of the age of progress on the things we love (or at least should have loved).

The result of Grant's reconnaissance of the contemporary landscape is the image of the "barren twilight."[2] Cox, on the other hand, presents us with the "secular metropolis" as the "pattern of our life together and the symbol of our view of the world."[3] These contrasting images emerge in part from differing judgements concerning the relationship of Christian faith to the modern age. Cox argues that modern secularization grows from biblical roots, and thus recommends that we embrace this secular age; Grant's judgement in *Lament for a Nation* is rooted in its genre more than in any explicit argument. However, in another context, Grant does insist that "to partake even dimly in the riches of Athens or Jerusalem should be to know that one is outside the public realm of the age of progress."[4] These divergent judgements of the relationship of Christianity to the age of progress bear closer examination.

What is *Lament for a Nation*? That the answer to this question is not self-evident is clear from the variety of critical responses to the work. A. Brady, writing in the *University of Toronto Quarterly*, insisted that the *Lament* was "mainly concerned to express indignation with what we have."[5] Kenneth McNaught, the noted Canadian historian, acknowledged the importance of Grant's analysis, but hoped that his conclusions "were exaggerated."[6] The *Canadian Banker* concluded that "Grant's tale [was] fundamentally wrong due to its extremely superficial and naive view of the evolution and exercise of economic power."[7] Another critic, R.K. Crook, saw Grant's work as important, but marred by its tendency to nostalgia.[8] From the range of accounts one could assume that *Lament for a Nation* is either a self-indulgent exercise in personal annoyance, or a work of history, or an economic analysis, or a nostalgic longing for the past. What is the *Lament*?

As a way into this question let us ask about the mode of speech appropriate to the exploration of the present and the articulation of the future. In social-scientific circles, it is commonly assumed that this is the language of analysis and prediction. Many critics, as indicated above, have approached Grant's work on this assumption. One may, then, dissent from his work in several ways. One could disagree with his prognosis by claiming that Grant's analysis of economic institutions is inadequate. Like McNaught, one could find discontinuity between the analysis and the conclusions, or, like Brady and Cook, one could reject his description of the present state of affairs. But is Grant's *Lament* an analysis and prediction?

Although Grant employs some social-scientific terms, e.g., "class," his work falls outside the categories and canons of the social sciences. The reasons for this are complex, but they revolve around Grant's assumption that such language forms are inadequate to the task at hand. In part, the *Lament* is a critique of technological civilization as inimical to the "good" and hence the languages of technological civilization are inadequate to that criticism. Grant calls his work a meditation.[9] Hence we must look outside the context of the social sciences in order to get our bearings.

Since the meditative form is apparently unfamiliar to Grant's critics it is important to recall that a meditation is a "mental prayer in its discursive form."[10] We are, then, dealing with a religious genre. Moreover, it is a religious form which is essentially reflective and reflexive. The *Oxford Dictionary of the Christian Church* reminds us that the meditative method is one of "devout reflection on a chosen theme, with a view to deepening spiritual insight and stimulating the will and affections."[11] Hence, Grant's work presupposes a specific relationship to his subject: a relationship of affection and care. Moreover, by selecting this meditative mode, Grant aims primarily at an inward movement in the soul of his readers, a movement which will deepen spiritual insight.

Grant further informs us that his is a special form of meditation: a lament. In the first pages of *Lament for a Nation* Grant is very explicit and tells readers unfamiliar with the form, that "to lament is to cry out at the death or at the dying of something loved." Thus he clearly places his work outside the context of social scientific analysis and prediction. For Grant, "the end of Canada as a sovereign state' is not a conclusion of an analysis, but the presupposition of his meditation. Thus in the very form of Grant's work is signaled his distance from the assumptions of the age of progress.

Grant is aware, moreover, that the form he has chosen is highly unusual. "Political laments," Grant writes, "are not usual in the age of progress, because most people think that society always moves forward to better things." This is not Grant's assumption. Nor, as some of his critics assume, would Grant ascribe to the converse. The point here is that it is the form, the meditative-lament, which gives Grant his starting point, a starting point that dissociates, that provides the necessary distance.

When Grant turns his attention – and ours – to his chosen theme it is not on the basis of a dispassionate analysis of a current state of affairs, but on the basis of a memory of something loved. For Grant, personal biography and the story of Canada are inextricably intertwined, since "some form of political loyalty is part of the good life." Hence the question of Canada's demise is not something to be considered at arms' length, but requires a more personal mode. Indeed, it requires the ritual form of a lament. Consequently, the reasons articulated and the arguments mustered are not predicated on empirical inquiry, but attempt to give form and meaning to the anguish felt at the death of something loved. Since Grant dissents from the prevalent view that "society always moves forward to better things" it is necessary to find a form appropriate to his message. In his *Lament for a Nation* Grant employs the lament as a form of political commentary, a form appropriate to his message. Indeed, the form is the message.

The occasion for Grant's meditation is a specific political event: the defeat of Diefenbaker in 1963. The structure of Grant's meditation is, as one would expect, a spiral, a movement from the more particular to the more general. First Grant turns to the ambiguities of Diefenbaker's own version of Canadian nationalism, a version flawed by its confusion of the American emphasis on the "rights of individuals" with the Canadian emphasis on the "rights of communities." Then Grant moves to the larger forces of Liberalism and Continentalism, forces which, since the era of Mackenzie King, have identified Canada's future with the aims of corporate capitalism. And, finally, Grant turns to the assumptions of the age of progress, assumptions within which Canada's disappearance was inevitable.

Although we have argued that Grant's meditation is articulated outside the context of prediction it does participate in the tradition of prophecy.[12] One must, however, distinguish two modalities within the prophetic traditions. The first mode may be characterized as activist, the second as meditative. Behind each mode of prophecy lies a particular view of history. For the activist mode of prophecy, history is the creation of the human will. Thus the language in which prophecy is articulated is the language of decision. However, for the meditative mode, history is something suffered. Thus, the language in which prophecy is articulated is the language of the meaning of events.

Given this distinction, we can understand why Grant has selected the meditative form: it corresponds to his sense of history. For the meditative tradition, history is the given context of human life; when that history becomes unendurable we are driven to scrutinize events for meaning, to cry out to our fellows and to God. Such a cry is not for the sake of urging a specific action, but to give voice to one's suffering, a suffering that is also the suffering of a people. It is the meditation itself which gives form to that suffering, which allows the search for meaning to proceed by "standing under" the events in order to understand.

Such meditation is noble when it respects the ambiguities of historical events and when it acknowledges the limitations of our ability to know. The paradox of meditation is that it is a mode possible only for those who do not know. The meditation exists for the sake of wresting some meaning from things which seem devoid of meaning, of wrestling with the spirits in order to discern their origin. The activist tradition, on the other hand, rests on another presupposition, namely, that the events are so clear in their meaning that they call out for a decision.

This distinction between the meditative and activist modes of prophecy is, I suggest, crucial to the right understanding of Grant's *Lament for a Nation*. In the light of this distinction we can better understand what Grant is doing, as well as how he is doing what he is doing. Moreover, this distinction allows us to answer the usual questions about Grant's prophetic powers, questions predicated on a misunderstanding of the nature and mode of the *Lament*. It is not a piece of social science, nor is it a call to decision. Its truth does not rest on its validity as a prediction, but on its capacity to move us to deepened insight into the forces that we suffer, to create a community of shared attention through participation in the meditative lament.

One of the forces we suffer, according to the *Lament*, is history itself. Grant challenges readers who are infected with the notion that history is the will writ large and that they are its masters; his dissent from the religion of progress disturbs many of our preoccupations. However, when this dissent is developed within the context of the meditative-lament, we can understand that the identification of historical necessity with goodness is a demon which Grant seeks to exorcise.

The meditative tradition of prophecy is primarily oriented towards the mind; hence the meditative mode seeks to free the mind from entrapment. It is this idolatrous identification of the "good" with "necessity" that has bewitched the modern mind and thwarted the development of genuinely political society. Without a certain amount of openness around the question of the "good" it is not possible to have the kind of public discussion necessary for genuinely political society. Grant suggests that as long as this identification of the good with what happens persists, an articulation of Canada's destiny in terms consistent with its historical origins remains closed. Grant however respects the limitations of the meditative mode by leaving the question of the good open. Rather, it is raised indirectly through his evocation of two theological/literary antecedents: the writer of *Lamentations* and Richard Hooker. The first forerunner is evoked through a formal association, the second through a direct quotation.

The formal association is contained in the very title of Grant's work: *Lament for a Nation*. Grant's lament falls in the tradition of the writer of the book of Lamentations. This work, ascribed by tradition to the prophet Jeremiah, is written in the context of exile. The writer laments the fall of Israel. In the midst of captivity he writes that

Jerusalem remembers
in the days of her affliction and bitterness
all the precious things
that were hers from days of old.[13]

Grant is sufficiently modest not to belabour the identification. However, Grant's literary as well as his religious knowledge would make it highly unlikely that he is unaware of the formal parallel. Indeed, he writes that "those who write laments may have heard the propositions of the saints, but they do not know that they are true."[14] Nevertheless, Grant does know that the form is appropriate, even if the specific claims may be doubted; it is the mode of the saints that Grant employs.

Moreover, the formal parallel is important because of what it reveals about the exiled situation of the writer. Exile is crucial to Grant's lament also. The exile Grant takes upon himself is intellectual; it offers him a vantage point outside the assumptions of the age of progress. It is only outside those assumptions that one can even imagine lamenting the demise of the "old" Canada. Within the assumptions of the age of progress, Canada's demise is both necessary and good.

The second forerunner of Grant's work is the 16th century English theologian Richard Hooker. The identification of this work with Hooker's is made explicitly. Grant quotes Hooker in stating his purpose: "posterity may know we have not loosely through silence permitted things to pass away as in a dream."[15] Hooker too was a champion of lost causes. In his major work, *The Laws of Ecclesiastical Polity*, we find a prescient critique of Puritanism, a critique that went largely unheeded. By evoking Hooker, Grant identifies his work with a voice which speaks what it sees, even though the tides of history may be against him. Grant, again like Hooker, is aware that the currents of history are more powerful, but not necessarily more right or humane, than can be dammed by a single voice.

What is one to think when the life-giving web of a people's life has been broken? By choosing a meditative form, Grant invites his readers to engage in reflection and self-examination concerning our public life. Moreover, like the forerunners evoked, Grant invites us to a situation of exile, a place outside the "age of progress" where we can "wonder whether modern assumptions may be basically inhuman."[16] Such an excursion necessarily requires that we set aside, as Grant does, any desire for "practical proposals for our survival as a nation."[17] The prophetic tradition in which Grant stands asks whether or not we have sold our birthright for a mess of pottage.[18]

This excursion outside the assumptions of the age of progress presupposes, moreover, some tradition of faith and wisdom which can sustain the excursion. By arguing for some fundamental consistency between the Biblical tradition and the secular world, Cox undercuts the possibility of a fundamental critique of the age of progress. Grant, on the other hand, presupposes a fundamental discontinuity, and thus is able to articulate a critique of modernity. In another context Grant bluntly states his judgement concerning the option which Cox takes: "... secularized, or perhaps better, immanentized Biblical religion is nonsense."[19] Without an awareness of an alternate tradition which would sustain dissent from the age of progress (and its implicit religion), one courts, as Grant is aware, nihilism.

Given Grant's "conservative" stance, such a consequence would be unacceptable. The alternative tradition of faith and wisdom which Grant invokes, through his genre, is the Christian tradition.

The dark meditation on the forces that have resulted in the demise of Canada as a sovereign nation is possible, it seems to me, precisely because of Grant's tacit understanding of a sustaining tradition of faith. The dialectic of faith and history is what rescues Grant's lament from the charge that the *Lament* is simply an expression of "indignation with what we have."[20] For readers who know only the modern world, Grant's meditation opens onto an abyss; for readers who know, however dimly, "the riches of Athens or Jerusalem,"[21] Grant's meditation can at least be endured, since those traditions know something of man's dual citizenship in eternity as well as in history.[22] Although Grant disavows certitude about such metaphysical citizenship, his work does presuppose an awareness of that possibility.

Hence it is Grant's fidelity to an ancient tradition of faith and wisdom which allows his meditative lament and consequent descent into the darkside of the age of progress. Such a descent, lit by the perhaps frail lights of the ancients and sustained by its forms, is necessary in order to wrestle with the confusion of the "good" with the "necessary." Implied here is also a critique of the "secular theologians" – those who give theological comfort to this "easy identification." For Grant, "belief is blasphemy if it rests on any easy identification of necessity and good."[23] But that criticism does not obviate the need for Grant to articulate an understanding of the relationship of "necessity" and "good" which would overcome this blasphemy.

Moreover, it is this identification of the "good" with "necessity" which blinds the modern mind to the consequences of its own assumptions. In Grant's view the modern era is in principle inimical to the preservation of national political communities. Modernity is characterized by the notions of freedom from the restraints of tradition, by progress, and by the inevitable tendency towards homogenization. These larger forces of the modern age make the nation redundant, an obstacle in the fateful march of modernity. One element, then, of the solution to this blasphemous belief must surely lie in the fact that we have access to other traditions of faith and wisdom in which we can at least think our situation. This implication is hidden in Grant's *Lament*. As Grant's genre makes clear, we have access to traditions which have lived through more than one historical or cultural epoch. Such traditions may thereby provide us with some insight or pointers or ways of thinking which are crucial to survival in our "barren twilight." Unfortunately, Grant does not develop this implication of his work. Nevertheless, it does appear that we must regard the story of humankind in a much more differentiated way than the age of progress assumes.

Even though the more ancient traditions of faith and wisdom may not have practical solutions to offer, they may enable us – and in this case, have enabled us – to understand theoretically some dimensions of our discontent. It is important that such discontent fall prey neither to repetitive rebellion nor sterile nihilism, but be reconnected with older traditions of intellectual life and perhaps even practical necessity. Even the conservative tradition knows about the great refusal – witness Hooker and the Writer of Lamentations. Yet such a refusal must not leave us in the air, but rather reground us in traditions that can inspire and sustain a new reading of our present situation. The point here is not nostalgia, but the demonstrated capacity of other than modern traditions to illumine the modern landscape.

Indeed, one must finally regard *Lament for a Nation* with a certain amount of irony. The irony is that Grant's work has, in many instances, given birth to a renewed, even intelligent, love of Canada: a determination not to allow Canada to "pass away as in a dream."[24] Although that possibility is bleak, it is, nevertheless, one of the ironic results of Grant's impact on many of his readers.

Be that as it may, there are some implications and questions which, while rooted in the text, take us beyond the text. Here I have especially in mind the end – a more appropriate term than conclusion – of Grant's *Lament*. To quote Grant's ambiguous ending:

> Beyond courage, it is also possible to live in the ancient faith, which
> asserts that changes in the world, even if they be recognized more as
> a loss than a gain, take place within an eternal order that is not
> affected by their taking place. Whatever the difficulty of philosophy,
> the religious man has been told that process is not all.
> 'Tendebantque manus ripae ulterioris amore.'[25]

How are we to take Grant at this point? What is "the further shore" to which our arms are outstretched? In a meditative-lament the purgative effect is central. And the *Lament* does purge us of the idolatrous confusion of goodness with necessity. However, beyond that effect lies the question of the proper object of loyalty and longing. In one sense the ambiguity of Grant's ending is an echo of the writer of Lamentations who closes with these words:

> But thou, O Lord, doest reign forever;
> > thy throne endures to all generations.
> Why dost thou forget us for ever,
> > why dost thou so long forsake us?
> Restore us to thyself, O Lord, that we
> > may be restored![26]

Here the future is left suspended in the hands of God. Is this "the further shore" evoked at the end of Grant's *Lament*? If so, then there is an implicit promise in Grant's ending that is yet to be fulfilled: namely, an articulation of the orienting power of faith and the objects appropriate to our love.

The occasions of Grant's meditation – the loss of that political society in which one came to apprehend the good – has precedents which have led others to a rearticulation of the relationship between faith and history. We have already alluded to the writer of Lamentations and to Richard Hooker. Hooker, however, may not be a sufficient guide here. What is at stake is a critical issue which underlies Grant's work: the relationship of religion to political society, of Christian faith to political community. More relevant than Hooker is St Augustine, who was confronted with a similar dilemma in the disintegration of Roman society. For Augustine, the solution is a doctrine of "rightly ordered loves" which grows out of an analysis of human nature and a specification of the limits of loyalty owed to the various communities in which we participate. In other words, the problem of the relationship of faith to history arises because of a confusion of the temporal order with the eternal order, of political society with the communion of saints. The theoretical solution is the disentangling of our confused passions on this point. The simplicity of the theoretical solution should not, however, obscure the existential difficulty of attaining to a right ordering of our loves. The point is not to recommend Augustine's solution, but to remind us of sources for dealing with the problem posed by Grant's *Lament*.

Grant, however, makes an important contribution to the present discussion of the relationship of religion and political society, although it is a contribution outside the currently fashionable boundaries of that discussion. Grant has not only displayed the relevance of religious forms – in this case the meditative-lament – to political commentary and critique, but has also reminded us that the first question is not the relationship of traditional religious communities to the political order, but rather the *religious assumptions of modernity itself*. For example, Grant exposes the fateful confusion of "goodness" and "necessity," a confusion that leads to the idolizing of whatever is. When we begin with the religious assumptions of the age of progress, then we are not led, willy-nilly, to see the issue as a reinterpretation of Christian faith in the modern age, but to a critique of the age's religious assumptions. Such a critique, I would suggest, is essential to the recovery of theology.

Grant's contribution needs, however, a fuller articulation of the understanding of faith and history implicit in *Lament for a Nation*. In Grant's subsequent writings he has continued to develop his critique of technological culture. In part that critique is dependent, as we have seen, upon elements within the Christian tradition; but that dependence requires more explicit development. While it is surely right and important to eschew the confusion of whatever happens historically with Providence, it is surely also necessary to articulate one's understanding of that relationship. Otherwise the critics of Grant, albeit often for the wrong reasons, may be justified in sensing in Grant an unrequited pessimism. Here the issue is not, it seems to me, optimism versus pessimism, but rather the nature of Christian hope. In the Christian tradition, hope incorporates the experience of suffering in its understanding of resurrection.[27] Thus it is a category outside the dubious alternatives of optimism and pessimism.

For Grant, history tends to overwhelm faith. But faith, at least within the Christian tradition, is precisely the power which leads us through, as well as sustains us during, the dark night of the soul and the dark times of history. For Grant, the present age is so constituted by the forces of modernization that the future is foreclosed. One often has the impression that even a theoretical analysis, let alone the posing of any practical alternatives, is so much whistling in the dark. Though the future does not automatically remain open, it is a conviction of Christian faith that, in the words of Rosenstock-Huessy, the future may be "re-opened by our own inward death and renewal."[28] A lament without the awareness of the "resurrection of the dead" is despair; a lament cradled by the Christian doctrine of the resurrection is a ritual of renewal. This renewal is not optimism since it passes through the crucible of our own "inward death and renewal." Although one might agree with Grant that "the kindest of all God's dispensations is that individuals cannot predict the future in detail,"[29] it is equally important to remember the corollary, namely, that the future is always something other than the present.

While one must heed Grant's public proclamation, his prophecy, one cannot rest there content. In the Christian tradition which Grant shares it is finally a matter of faith, that power and longing of the soul for orientation, which is at stake. The bittersweet image of the "barren twilight" contains a fortunate ambiguity. The twilight is as well the light before a new dawn as the light before the full dark. Even if the light that Grant spies is barren, it is at least light. Grant, I would suggest, must give expression to the light he sees as well as to the suffering he endures.

The Significance of Grant's Cultural
Analysis for Christian Theology in North America
by Douglas John Hall

It is not the purpose of this essay to discuss George Grant's cultural analysis as such. That has been touched upon in most of the papers in this collection, and it must be assumed that readers already have sufficient awareness of Grant's reflections on our culture to be able to recognize its broad outlines in the present statement. My intention is rather to consider the significance for Christian Theology of Professor Grant's thought about us as a people.

My reason for pursuing this topic is only incidentally related to Grant's own Christianity. It stems rather from the conviction that he has thought through the meaning of our identity as North Americans in general, and Canadians in particular, in a way that is both profound and unique. I believe that Christian theology, to be faithful to its roots, must always be *contextual*, and my thesis here, to state it very broadly, is that Grant's analysis of our culture can contribute to the contextualization of theology on this Continent – a quality which it has consistently lacked. Beyond that, I think it is equally possible that a theology which had sufficiently immersed itself in its own milieu might serve, in turn, to provide some incentive and direction for the very "search" Grant believes necessary for us as a people to undertake: the search for "new meaning" and a way into the future.[1]

One qualifying remark is required with respect to the use of the term 'Christian theology'. Although I believe that the substance of the final section of the essay applies to all forms of Christian theology today, the critical analysis of theology in the first part of the essay particularly refers in a more restrictive sense to Protestantism. This is partly because I do not feel qualified to speak for the Roman Catholic or the Orthodox traditions as they have manifested themselves in our history; and it is partly because of the conviction, which I share with Grant, that the most decisive form of

Christian influence in the formation of this society has been from the side of the Reformation, more specifically, from Calvinism which "provided the determined and organized men and women who could rule the mastered world."[2]

Theology as an Unamerican Activity

There is a statement in Grant's essay, "In Defence of North America," which goes straight to the heart of the problem of Christian theology on this Continent. He writes:

> In a field as unamerican as theology, the continually changing ripples of thought by which the professionals hope to revive a dying faith, originate from some stone dropped by a European thinker.[3]

There are obvious exceptions to this generalization. One thinks of the Social Gospel in Canada and of Reinhold Niebuhr, whose thought (not incidentally) parallels Grant's at many points. Yet it is indisputable that the general character of theological work on this Continent has been consistently informed by European patterns and movements. The extent to which this is so has been underscored for some of us today by the emergence of theological groupings which explicitly reject the European adherence. In an issue of *Christianity and Crisis*, Black theologian C. Eric Lincoln complained of the practice of sending theologians off to Europe for indoctrination: there, he said, they cannot find "light for *our* darkness."[4]

While this adherence to European authority can be noted in many fields of human endeavour, as Grant has maintained,[5] theology suffers from this practice in a special manner. I am not referring to the mere subservience the habit betokens; that would be a superficial reason for concern. The real problem consists in the fact that our self-consciously European orientation as churchmen has inhibited us from entering deeply into our own experience as North Americans. And that is a very serious charge, for it is tantamount to saying that it has inhibited us from becoming a genuine theological community. For theology can only occur at the point where the Christian tradition meets the spirit that informs a culture — what the Germans call the *zeitgeist*.

If one asks why theology in a genuinely dialogical sense has not occurred significantly amongst us, it is possible to answer at different levels of analysis. One type of answer has already been suggested: the abiding authority of the European 'Mother' churches. In Canada this factor has been stronger than in the United States, especially in Protestant and Anglican churches. Until very recently, for example, it was simply taken for granted that theological colleges should be staffed, if possible, by British teachers. The preaching of the gospel might be entrusted to locals (though "important pulpits" were normally reserved for those possessing stained-glass accents of a markedly Scottish or English flavour!); but the indoctrination of the locals was another matter. Another type of explanation is the strong conviction that theological truth is in any case above all the vicissitudes of time and place. This conviction still characterizes most religion in the Western world, and there are few who perceive what Marx knew perfectly well: how this very attitude hides within itself the sure and certain capacity for legitimizing the *status quo*, and so endears itself to the ruling classes.

Such explanations as these should not be neglected by anyone who ponders why Christian theology is such an "unamerican" activity. However, I find it necessary to go beyond them. If it is true that we have been able to exist as an important theological community for three centuries (!), surely the explanation must be more specific than Marx's and more rudimentary than the observation concerning the abiding authority of the parental European churches. It is no doubt more closely related to the phenomenon of Establishment; but that is a universal phenomenon of Western Christianity and does not provide a satisfactory answer to the problem of theology in North America as such.

Here I would pass beyond Grant's generalization. In a real sense, what is interesting about North American theology is not that it borrows from Europe but simply that it borrows. In fact recent tendencies in theological circles on this Continent support this contention. I refer to the latest "ripples of thought", which do not emerge from European sources but from South American and other Third World theological movements which provide us with our current slogan, "Liberation!" This propensity to borrow from anyone who appears to have an exciting idea gives, I think, the necessary clue to the deeper explanation of why theology in the best sense has not been an "american" activity. It has to do with what is regularly and superficially labelled 'the question of identity.'

Heretofore we as a people have been able to exist without raising that question. Never before have we been in grave doubt about the identity the parental culture gave (and in many ways still wants to give) us. Never before have we questioned the destiny first envisaged for us by those real 'discoverers' of America, i.e. those European intellectuals who saw in this Continent the stage on which the new man they heralded would enact his enlightened role. We have accepted that destiny, and have embellished it with messianic significance of our own devising. Until now, we have not been driven to ask whether the vision upon which we were founded could be wrong or deluded; and so the sense of moral ambiguity, of the tragic, and of an ending, which have all been powerful stimuli behind all dynamic theological reflection, have been conspicuously absent from our experience.

We have known how to ask critically about Europe, some of us; but heretofore we have not been caused to ask critically about the dream European intellectuals once dreamt and generations of immigrants made lively, the dream called 'America'. Content with the role assigned us, we could do no more at the level of philosophical and theological thought than tinker with variations on the theme. At least in theology, there can be no depth of thought about the "things eternal" if there is no deep dis-ease with "things temporal". To ask 'Who is God?' is nothing but a sophomoric prank if it does not emerge out of the existential pain of not knowing how to answer the question 'Who am I?' This is as true for communities as for individuals. And until very recent times the North American community has not had the occasion to anguish over its identity.

II. *The Owl of Minerva*

It is especially as a chronicler of this "occasion" that George Grant's thought seems to me significant for Christian theology. Probably the most direct statement of his feeling for the "occasion" is to be found in the opening pages of *Philosophy in the Mass Age*. The possibility of depth of thought is given in North America today, Grant argues, precisely because the problematic of modern Man is more conspicuous here than elsewhere. Other societies are "moving in the same direction", including the Soviet Union;[6] but amongst us the modern experiment has been able to proceed virtually unimpeded, just because there were no alternative visions of society to inhibit it – except, as he will say later, that of the French, which however has been consistently swept aside.

Grant immediately qualifies himself: he does not want such a possibility to be understood in the facile sense of "liberalism", *viz.* the faith that "the forms of society can be easily changed." "Philosophical faith", he says, "is something rather different. Its hope is more indirect." What "philosophical faith" hopes for and believes possible is that there is a residual power of imagination and memory in Man which renders him capable of questioning what happens to him.

> As we live in these conditions of mass culture, we come to recognize them as profoundly new and this newness forces us to try to understand what they mean. We ask what it is that man has created in this new society. And as we try to see what we are, there arises an ultimate question about human nature and destiny.

To ask after the meaning of human nature and destiny in such a society as ours is a highly original undertaking; for, as we have observed in the first part of the essay, North Americans have been able heretofore to accept, as given, the definition of Man refined for us by Enlightenment Europe. But since we have carried *that* definition to its furthest limits and have sensed something of the darkness into which it is leading us, we are driven to ask the question again. What *are* our purposes, our boundaries, our "fixed points of meaning?"[7] We were taught to expect only light, and that it should grow ever brighter! Instead, we perceive "the terrifying darkness."[8]

At least at this point in his life, what Grant finds he can entertain as one who has membership in such a society is the possibility of a search for *new* meaning. Being a "conservative", he has been accused of reaction; but he has never been an advocate of return to some "golden age", though he loves above all the "tradition of Athens". Even in later works, where he has obviously become less enthusiastic about the search he echoes the same sentiment expressed at this juncture in *Philosophy in the Mass Age* concerning all attempts at returning: "Such reactionary experiments are always vain."[24] The search for new meaning must entail a disciplined return to the roots of our civilization, for even if remembrance and hope are not quite "the same thing" (Ricoeur) there can be no authentic hope which is not first a remembering. On the other hand, there can be no thought of a simple return for those who have gone as far as we along the road of modernity.

The theological enterprise on this Continent can become *contextual* today (i.e. it can become in an authentic way *theology*) because the doctrinal *ideology* that we inherited has been shown up as incapable of explaining, or even relating to, the life we actually experience. Either we should abandon our Faith because of this incapacity, or else we must rethink it in an original way, i.e. in dialogue with actual experience. The *occasion* is: we may rethink it.

III. *The Tradition of Jerusalem*

Grant's statement of the opportunity of our historical moment is accompanied from the start by the fear that it will not, and perhaps can not, be taken up by us. This fear sometimes verges on skepticism and worldly despair, and in at least one of his writings he seems almost to have lost the gift of hope, at least so far as this world is concerned. I refer to *Lament for a Nation*, where a particular aspect of the 'occasion' given us in these times, viz. the development of a genuine (Canadian) alternative to the "universal homogeneous state", is treated as an opportunity that has already passed away.

This tendency to regard the occasion *ex post facto* is not confined to his thought about Canada, however. The character of "lament" is present in all his works. He no sooner introduces the prospect of original thought and moral reflection in *Philosophy in the Mass Age* than he cautions that such a mode of existence is so foreign to our experience that it is almost inconceivable for anyone to entertain it as a real possibility. Grant shows that our very preconception of the meaning of thought (the instrumentalist view of reason) prevents us from taking seriously the *kind* of thought to which the moment beckons us. We are so immersed in the modern vision that to question "the religion of progress" is to court total alienation from our society. While the search for new meaning is given us as opportunity, then, it can be grasped only by those who consciously prepare themselves to swim against the stream: "We ... must admit that our very society exerts a terrible pressure to hold us from that search."[9]

It would seem that this note of skepticism about the prospect of our actually taking up the search has come to qualify Grant's statement of the 'occasion'. In the 1966 "Introduction" to *Philosophy in the Mass Age*, he has become even more distrustful of the "liberal" concept of change because in the meantime he has realized more fully than he had been able to do in 1959 that the technocratic *imago hominis* is not merely an external construct by which the society at large is determined but something by which our very souls are shaped. Or, as he put it bluntly in "A Platitude": "We are technique."[10] To quote the "Introduction":

> So pervasive and deep-rooted is the faith that all human problems will
> be solved by unlimited technological development that it is a terrible
> moment for the individual when he crosses the rubicon and puts
> that faith into question. To do so implies that unlimited technologi-
> cal development presents an undoubted threat to the possibility of
> human excellence. One can thereafter only approach modern society
> with fear and perhaps trembling and, above all, with caution.[11]

The consequence of the technocratic captivity of the soul is that we have lost any vantage-point from which to make a discerning assessment of what is happening to us. Thus while we may be given a moment in which to make good the human potentiality for "excellence", we are kept from it by the lack of any real alternative to the capitalist-liberal ideology "which seems to many a splendid vision of human existence."[12] Like the generations of children in our society who have learned their aesthetics from the same machine that entertains them, we have lost whatever criteria we might once have had access to, to help us determine who we are. And ... "how can we think deprivation unless the good which we lack is somehow remembered?"[13]

The final sentence of the essay "In Defence of North America", which I find one of the most devastating of Grant's "laments", puts the matter bluntly. Having held out the prospect that, being the most fully realized technological society yet to have been, we might be best suited to comprehend what that means, Grant takes back the hope with the observation:

> Yet the very substance of our existing which has made us the leaders
> in technique, stands as a barrier to any thinking which might be able
> to comprehend technique from beyond its own dynamism.[14]

It is far from my mind merely to contradict this profound expression of doubt, or the fundamental uncertainty and incipient despair of which it is an articulation. To ignore that, or minimize the seriousness of it for any human endeavour today, is to court superficiality. And yet as a Christian and a theologian I find that I must contend with it. That is, I choose to regard it more as a summons to the most serious intellectual and spiritual wrestling than as a final assessment of the human prospect. Not to contend with it in this way would mean to capitulate. And some of Grant's own self-consciously Christian affirmations – those especially which make their appearance at the endings of his books and essays – do seem to me, on occasion, a form of capitulation: The historical situation fails, Canada fails, Man fails ... but there is always eternity! That is a too simple statement of Grant's own Christian faith, which is after all not so fastened upon "things eternal" as these statements sometimes would lead one to believe, or so disdainful of "things temporal". No one really laments who does not believe in the first place that this world, or even some tiny part of it like "Canada", is worth tears – God's tears!

All the same, there is enough capitulation in these "in conclusion" statements of George Grant that I find it necessary to remind him that the attitude of resignation belongs more clearly to the tradition of Athens than to the tradition of Jerusalem. For all its flirtation and entanglement with Athens, the tradition of Jerusalem still represents something distinctive and rudimentary for a Christianity which tries to rethink itself. It is to that tradition in particular that I turn in order to contend with the wordly despair and heavenly resignation that I detect in Grant ... and in myself.

What I would argue is that in spite of the complicity of Christianity in the predicament of our society (a thing to which I have already devoted considerable attention), there are resources still in this ancient Faith for providing a certain incentive and direction for the search for meaning and a way into the future. If this is not possible – if through a thoughtful faith in Jesus as the Christ it is not possible to discern a Way that at the same time antedates modernity and opens one to a future beyond the impasse of the technological society, – then it is high time to abandon this religion. I believe that it *is* possible to discern such a Way; and so that this will not be taken as a mere boast, another instance of Christian triumphalism, I would advance the following reasons:

First, *the emergence of a form of faith and theology which is conscious of being "post Christian".* To elaborate: It happens that at the same time as we are experiencing a crisis of modernity and of the form of Christianity implicit in it, sensitive Christians throughout the world have become conscious of living at "the last days of the Constantinian era."

In such an atmosphere, it is possible that a significant segment within the churches and on their periphery may discover a way back to a more authentic version of the tradition of Jerusalem than what the Constantinian Church has found it convenient to preserve. As the Church becomes what it was originally – a *Diaspora*, a *communio viatorum* – as distinct from the official religious dimension of Establishment, it is opened again to the present. If, as Grant believes, the search for an alternative system of meaning must involve the searchers in a return to the origins of our civilization in the traditions of Athens and Jerusalem, it is altogether pertinent to this search that a Christian community is coming to be throughout the world today which in one way and another attempts to do precisely that.

Second, within the churches today as well as in the culture at large are *various minorities which aid the process of Christian re-thinking* by insisting that Christianity is distorted and inauthentic when it is used to support reigning powers and institutions. Amongst these are the Blacks, Christian Marxists, various liberation movements and representatives of the poor, the oppressed, the young, the old, etc. Using aspects of the tradition which have been neglected by the regnant orthodoxies, these minorities have brought to bear on the cultural religion a judgment which cannot be ignored. Their influence has been felt even in well-fortified bastions of bourgeois Christianity. In consequence, it is again possible to call upon that prophetic tradition of Biblical faith which assumes that criticism of existing structures of power belongs to the essence of faith. The captivity of the Faith by the powers-that-be can thus no longer be easily assumed.

Third, *the ecumenical nature of the Church*, in spite of the fact that it is still more rhetorical than real, at least makes possible today a situation which may be unique in history: Christians of those parts of the world which suffer most from the domination of the "Christian" nations make their presence felt in the *Oekumene* as communities of faith which refuse to identify the substance of the Faith with the 'positive Christianity' of the First World peoples. They, too, have brought to bear upon Western Christians the need to re-examine their belief radically—specifically to determine whether much of it is not just a subtle cloak for Western imperialism.

The ecumenical nature of the Church today also makes possible and mandatory a meeting of Protestants, Catholics and Orthodox traditions. This has obvious implications for Christian reflection on Grant's analysis of our culture. If it is true, as he has maintained, that the North American experience has been molded in a particular way by "the meeting of the alien yet conquerable land with English-speaking Protestants" (our "primal", as Grant calls this);[15] and that Catholicism has always been representative of medieval and other views of the world which did not find the modern vision appealing, then it follows that an encounter between Protestant and Catholic today must have consequences, especially for the Protestants, who have been able heretofore to assume that their version of the faith was superior because it could seem to be on the wave of the future. In Quebec, moreover, the meeting in question is not only with Catholics but with French-speaking Catholics, who bring to the dialogue assumptions and hopes which were never taken seriously on this Continent but which today can no longer be sloughed off.

Fourth, because of such encounters and because the old ideology of progressive neo-Protestantism is more and more obviously irrelevant, there are here and there on this Continent *attempts to find a theology indigenous to our experience as a people.* Here and there we give strong evidence of wanting to cease being borrowers of other peoples' theological struggles. What is being discovered by many in and on the fringes of the churches today is that what we have been living on is a particular version of Christianity. Ours has been a special, truncated, sentimentalized variation of that strident, triumphant, world-conquering Western religion which Luther summed up in the slogan: *theologia gloriae* (the theology of glory). It presents a world in which the Night has been forever banished. It is no accident that Calvin, amongst the Protestants, triumphed on these shores. His theology was not a triumphalism of the medieval sort, which based itself on natural theology. But — certainly compared with Luther's — it had no room for an abiding darkness; for the Resurrection ended all that.

But in a time when the Night will not bow to human banishments (including theological banishments!), it is necessary either to eschew such a religion as pure theory or else find a more credible version of it. In the line of a faith which is more willing than historic Christendom has been to learn from the Jews; and in keeping with that concentration on the real *humanity* of Jesus which Paul clung to over against docetic and gnostic elements ("Jesus Christ and him crucified!"); and in the line of Luther's alternative to the theology of glory, which he named *theologia crucis*, it may be possible to discover a strand of the "tradition of Jerusalem" which could equip us to enter the darkness of our own epoch without dishonesty, surprise, or ultimate anxiety.[16] And at a time when the characteristic experience of Man is such that systems of meaning which make no place for the "terrifying darkness" must be dismissed as dreams or lies, such a strand is by no means irrelevant to those who search for a *new* system of meaning.

It is not a foregone conclusion that such a search will succeed, or that the Christians will have something to contribute to it. But it is at least possible, and in human life and history nothing is ... necessary. The tradition of Jerusalem may still have its greatest part to play. Not in the usual sense "greatest" ("He who would be great amongst you must be servant"), and not alone. But in a sense more consistent with the love which dies to its own glory in order to glorify God and the Neighbour, the faith of the Crucified may yet help to provide a point of vantage from which, in this most problematic of human societies, men may gain the courage to confront their failure and find light in the darkness.

George Grant and the Problem of History
by Larry Schmidt

In the Massey Lectures of 1969,[1] when George Grant sets out to enucleate "time as history," he makes it clear that he intends "to write about the word history as it is used about existence in time, not as it is used to describe a particular academic study."[2] When history is understood as existence in time, Grant explains, time is understood as "that in which human accomplishments [will] be unfolded; that is, in the language of [their] ideology, as progress."[3] When men see time as history, they are not concerned with the past as much as the future, and this concern manifests itself in a desire to determine the future by mastering human and nonhuman nature through technology. Grant elaborates what this means in the course of his lectures by performing a careful exegesis of Nietzsche's philosophical writings. His purpose is neither to inoculate men against the modern conception of time nor to convert men to it. One cannot be inoculated against the air one breathes nor does one need a conversion to begin breathing. His purpose is to let men know where they are. Having done so, however, Grant declares that time as history is not a conception that man is fitted for.

As an alternative to conceiving time as history Grant makes "a call to remembering, to loving, and to thinking."[4] Because the modern age, in its preoccupation with the future and with technical mastery, "has destroyed as living options all other traditions but itself, people must turn back to the past in the hope of finding there what has been lost in the dynamic present."[5] Remembering is the only way out of the wasteland of the present:

> Those of us who at certain times look to grasp something beyond
> history must search for it as the remembering of a negated tradition
> and not as the direct thinking of our present. Perhaps reverence
> belongs to man qua man and is indeed the matrix of human nobility.

But those several conceptions, being denied in our present public thought, can be asserted only after they have been sought for through the remembrance of the thought of those who thought them.[6]

It is not my intention in this paper to disagree either with Grant's analysis of modern man's understanding of time as history or with his criticism of the culture that such a conception has spawned. I would, however, like to ponder the ironic fact that the alternative (to conceiving time as history) which he suggests has been made possible (at least in part) because of the historical scholarship whose methods were developed in the modern era. The modern age which gave birth to the scientific method also brought forth "critical history." "We see the enormous interest in the last two hundred years in the study of man's past from the way that resources have been poured into those studies."[7] Modern scholarship, Grant admits, if it holds itself above the great gulf of progressivist assumptions, can aid a man to enter into the human past "not simply as an antiquarian interest but as a search for the good which can be appropriated to the present."[8]

Grant has acknowledged his debt to modern scholarship particularly as it has enabled him to enter into the thought of Plato and the classical political philosophers. He has specifically expressed his gratitude to Leo Strauss[9] whose "writings are devoted by and large to the interpretation of the great thinkers of the past."[10] For Strauss, as for Grant, "historical studies are intended no less than the dialogues of Plato or the treatises of Aristotle, to contribute to political philosophy as a non-historical pursuit."[11] Through modern scholarship, "what the wisest men have written about the most important questions"[12] can be appropriated to the present and the question of the good can be raised. Somewhat paradoxically, then, modern scholarship or "critical history" which has been developed in a society dominated by the account of "time as history" which Grant rejects, helps him to explore the meaning of Plato's conception of time as "the moving image of eternity."

Nevertheless, Grant has insisted that "the conception of time as history is not to be discarded as if it had never been."[13] And this means to me that a deeper *theoretical* understanding of history must be developed by thinking through the *philosophical* implications of the critical historical method that forms the basis of modern scholarship. This task is particularly important for those of us who agree with Grant that "we live in a civilization the fate of which is to conceive time as history,"[14] and who know that the working out of the present understanding of that conception must lead to destruction.

In his discussion of time as history Grant explains that two common conceptions are merged in the modern world. The first conception is assumed by those (particularly English thinkers) who "have insisted that we apply the word history to stones and birds as well as to man;"[15] the second is proposed by those (particularly continental writers) who have maintained that man alone is a historical being. To simplify matters, I shall call the first conception the evolutionary-positivist, and the second, the historicist-hermeneutical. Regardless of the differences between the evolutionary-positivist and the historicist-hermeneutical conceptions of history, Grant maintains that they are both uniquely modern and their

> languages come together as man is seen not only as part of evolution
> but as its spearhead who can consciously direct the very process
> from which he came. In such speaking man is seen as the creator
> who rose from accidental evolution, or if evolution is conceived
> within a terminology about the divine, man is then viewed as a
> cooperator or co-creator with God. The latter language is very popu-
> lar in the United States, particularly among those who wish to
> include Christian or Jewish theology within the liberal ideology of
> their society.[16]

The reference here, though unstated, is to "process" philosophy or theology, and perhaps more specifically to the thought of Teilhard de Chardin. The Jesuit author of *The Phenomenon of Man* is (elsewhere) referred to as a "flatterer to modernity"[17] because his work leads naturally to "the identification of technology with evolution, and the identification of evolution with the movement of the race to higher and higher morality."[18]

While I concur with Grant's negative judgement about the evolutionary-positivist and historicist-hermeneutical conceptions of history, I would like to suggest that, as theoretical accounts of history, they are incompatible with each other; and that though they are both facets of modernity, they serve to legitimate different aspects of it. It seems clear that the evolutionary-positivist conception legitimates the progressivism of the modern age while the historicist-hermeneutical conception legitimates the relativism and the pluralism which, as Grant has demonstrated,[19] opens modern society to unlimited technological expansion. Be that as it may, I would like to compare the two conceptions of history and demonstrate their mutual incompatibility and intrinsic inconsistency. This will be a prelude to suggesting a more adequate theoretical understanding of history.

The historicist-hermeneutical understanding of man (as a historical being in a way that no other being is) is based on a phenomenological analysis of existence or of perception such as that performed by Heidegger, Merleau-Ponty or Ortega. Such an analysis leads to the conclusion that *Dasein* or human existence is always being-in-the-world,[20] or that every object of perception is (in part) the product of human perception. Further, all perception is from a point of view, and perspective is part of reality. This means that time is in man rather than that man is in time. Heidegger expresses this by saying that "man is temporality." The conclusion I would like to draw from all this is a simple one: *phenomenal* being does not exist without the participation of human consciousness. There are no "objective" phenomena independent of the human perception which objectifies them. The phenomenal world is the correlative of consciousness.

But this has implications for our understanding of evolution, implications which have been ignored by scientists like Teilhard. The term evolution cannot refer to the evolution of phenomena independent of human consciousness. If evolution refers to anything, it must refer to consciousness and the correlative phenomena. This evolution can be understood in different ways depending upon how one conceives man's changing participation in the phenomenal world. For example, one can talk of man moving from a mythical to a historical self-understanding,[21] or from compact to differentiated symbolic forms,[22] or from original to final participation.[23] But in any case, the evolution of consciousness refers to the evolution of man's manner of participating in being.

What are the implications of this for our understanding of history? First, it means that the events of pre-history as they are commonly described by both scientists and historians, never took place. If pre-history is understood as the development of the cosmos, as it took place prior to the emergence of man, it cannot be imaginatively reconstructed as if human beings with scientific or historical minds such as those of modern men, were there to witness it. The evolution of the cosmos, as described by Teilhard de Chardin or H.G. Wells, could not have taken place because human consciousness was not there to objectify it in the way described.

Awareness of man's participation in the phenomena of his perception enables us, therefore, to dismiss the notion that the cosmos has a history prior to man's appearance within the cosmos. It also allows us to criticize the common understanding of man's development prior to the emergence of historical consciousness. Precisely because the humans who participated in being did not understand their participation in terms of history-making as we moderns may, the reality of human pre-history cannot be understood as a historical process. The evolution of man which is thought to have taken place between the emergence of consciousness and the development of historical consciousness cannot be understood as a *historical* development.

In retrospect, we can see that these misconceptions about evolution and history have their origins in positivism. In the nineteenth century, when the positivist movement was at the height of its influence, scientific interest was directed at the phenomena in the belief that they could be known objectively, that is, independently of the consciousness that knew them. That was bad enough. What was worse, positivistic science became the model upon which all knowledge, including knowledge of history, was understood. In some circles, it remains so. Nevertheless, in the twentieth century, we are aware of the illusory nature of positivism's quest for categorical objectivity in both science and history.

In the realm of science, Heisenberg's indeterminacy principle may be viewed as the symbolic expression of the "inadequacy of mechanical causality and of categorical objectivity."[24] The examination of sub-atomic particles, it was acknowledged, changes them. In the realm of history, we have come to see that the past, not being objective, cannot be understood objectively, though it can be reconstructed critically on the basis of historical evidence. An objective understanding of history is *not* an ideally desirable goal which cannot, in practice, be attained. It is the case rather that the quest for an objective understanding of history distorts the reality of history because it presupposes that history is made up of a course of objective events which the historical observer represents to himself. But because historical events are of the order of conscious events, they are participated events. They cannot be known from the outside, though we can imaginatively reconstruct the experience of those who participated in them.

This is the basis of George Grant's criticism of the research industry that has been developed in our universities. It has taken the methods developed in the sciences and transposed them to the humanities.

> The very procedure of research means that the past is represented
> as object. But anything, insofar as it is an object, only has the
> meaning of an object for us. That is why it is quite accurate to use
> the metaphor of the mausoleum about our humanities' research.
> Moreover, when we represent something to ourselves as object, we
> stand above it as subject — the transcending summoners. We there-
> fore guarantee that the meaning of what is discovered in such
> research is under us, and therefore in a very real way dead for us
> in the sense that its meaning cannot teach us anything greater than
> ourselves.[25]

Research, thus understood, is based on a distorted notion of history. Because history is something we make, not something we participate in, the past becomes something we can learn about, not something we can learn from. The evolutionary-positivist conception of history, then, is clearly inadequate.

The historicist-hermeneutical conception of man thus forms the basis of a critique of the evolutionary-positivist notion which does not acknowledge man's participation in history. But ironically enough, the historicist-hermeneutical concept shows the same inadequacy and can be shown to be intrinsically inconsistent. The distinction between *Historie* and *Geschichte* is commonly accepted in historicist philosophical circles which derive from Heidegger. As Grant points out, the term *Historie* is generally used to describe the "scientific study of the past"[26] while *Geschichte* is used to designate the "course of human existence in time"[27] or the actual flow of past events. But this distinction is misleading insofar as it creates the impression that there is some actual flow of past events that has objective reality *(Geschichte)* which can be studied scientifically *(Historie)*. The actual flow of past events does not exist now, except in the minds of living human beings who imaginatively reconstruct the events. The events that are said to have flowed in the past had a historical reality only insofar as they were part of the experience (the perception and the interpretation) of those who participated in them in the past.

But if we take the notion of participation seriously, the matter cannot be left there. It is even more complex. Not all human beings who have existed in the past or who are living today have understood themselves or do understand themselves to be participating in history. Mythical consciousness has been (and perhaps still is) much more widespread on the face of the globe than historical consciousness. As Eric Voegelin says in *Order and History*, historical consciousness has only emerged "because of the epochal differentiating events, 'the leaps in being' which engendered the consciousness of a Before and After, and in their respective societies motivated a symbolism of a historical 'course' that was meaningfully structured by the event of the leap."[28] This means that unilinear history must be understood as a cosmological symbolism which "has remained a millenial constant in continuity with its origins in the Sumerian and Egyptian societies through the cultivation by Israelites and Christians, right into the philosophers of history of the nineteenth century."[29] The notion of a historical event, historical interpretation, and historical consciousness emerges only in a society which participates in that symbolism.

It is not within the scope of this paper or within the capacity of its author to elaborate the process whereby the historical symbolism was developed, the intra-cosmic gods were removed from the cosmos and a dedivinized nature was set free to be explored by science. But it is important to note that the differentiated symbolism of history, whereby the "time dimension in the flux of divine presence is brought to attention,"[30] fulfills the same function as the compact symbolism of "timeless" myth. Both symbolisms attempt to illuminate the reality of existence in the In-between (to use Voegelin's expression) or in the *metaxy* (to use Plato's term).

And so any understanding of history, historical events, historical interpretation or historical consciousness which ignores or denies the symbolic character of history or the In-between nature of consciousness (as does the historicist-hermeneutical concept of history) is clearly inadequate. A conception which begins by ignoring or denying the symbolic character of history must end with the oblivion of eternity and the reduction of Being to the temporal. Is this awareness not at the heart of Grant's criticism of Nietzsche and Heidegger?

In *Time as History*, we have seen, George Grant rejects the evolutionary-positivist and the historicist-hermeneutical conceptions of history. Time as history is not a conception man is suited for. But we are left with the question: What is a suitable conception of history? Grant does not give us an answer. Recently he has suggested that history does not exist at all: the modern philosophical distinction between nature and history is a false one. Further, Grant will argue that Christianity is a non-historical religion.[31] While there is a sense in which Grant's statements are true, I do not think that we can avoid the task of reconceptualizing history by denying that it exists. It seems more apposite to me, therefore, to delineate a third conception of history. In the course of my analysis such a conception has emerged, and I shall call it a symbo-theological conception of history. This conception which has been worked out most carefully by Eric Voegelin, is, I believe, one which men are suited for.

According to Voegelin, historical symbolism emerges when the compact symbolism of myth is differentiated into the realms of human existence and history. This differentiation does not, however, abolish the cosmos. Nor does the historical symbolism do away with the need for an aggregate symbolism which "must provide for the experience of divine presence not only in the soul but in the cosmos in its spatio-temporal existence and order."[32] Christian theology, for example, has provided such an aggregate Symbolism by relating the creation of the world, the Incarnation and the Parousia to the Logos, the second person of the triune Godhead. The passage from the beginning to the end of time, and from the birth to the death of the individual, is understood as the "history of salvation." History is understood as providence.

Such differentiated symbolism can be understood literally as knowledge about the beginning and end of history (understood as intra-worldly events). The aggregate nature of the symbolism is lost and, as Grant has shown, "the Christian idea of history as the divinely ordained process of salvation, culminating in the Kingdom of God, passes over into the idea of history as progress culminating in the Kingdom of Man."[33] As this new conception of history prevails, new historiogenetic constructions emerge whose purpose is no longer that of the aggregate symbolism. Their purpose is to justify a type of imperialist expansion and to rationalize the will of power, not to attune man to the order of the cosmos or the truth of human existence.[34]

Nevertheless, Voegelin explains, understanding history as a progressive course from a known beginning to an appointed end, whether this takes the form of Hegel's philosophy of history or of enlightened progressivism, does not make it such. History remains a symbolism by which human beings express their participation in the mystery of being. In this sense, history does not "exist" any more than does myth. Neither history nor myth can be examined from some vantage point outside the In-between of consciousness. And the distinction between nature and history is a false one devised to legitimate the progressivism of modern society. One can speak of the distinction between nature and myth as intelligibly as the distinction between nature and history. History and myth are both symbolic forms. And one can say that Christianity is not a historical religion if history is understood as a flow of intra-wordly events. Christianity is nothing if its revelation is not concerned with the relationship between time and eternity. All that notwithstanding, time may be understood as history, if history is understood in Voegelin's terms as "the process of man's participation in the flux of divine presence that has eschatological direction."[35]

Let me conclude by suggesting some of the implications of the symbo-theological conception of history that has emerged in the course of this article. If history is the symbolic expression of man's participation in being or the cosmos, it is clear that man cannot "make history" any more than he can make the cosmos. And insofar as modern man pretends to a knowledge of the end of history or a knowledge of the whole, he is guilty of *hubris*. Philosophy teaches that knowledge of the whole is impossible for him who participates in the whole. The truth of man's situation is no different for modern man than it was for Socrates, though the probability of modern man denying it may seem greater.

> Knowledge of the whole would have to combine somehow political knowledge in the highest sense with knowledge of homogeneity. And this combination is not at our disposal. Men are constantly tempted to force the issue by imposing unity on the phenomena, by absolutizing either knowledge of homogeneity or knowledge of ends. Men are constantly attracted and deluded by two opposite charms: the charms of competence which is engendered by mathematics and everything akin to mathematics, and the charm of humble awe, which is engendered by meditation on the human soul and its experiences. Philosophy is characterized by the gentle, if firm, refusal to succumb to either charm.[36]

From a theological perspective, modern history-making must be viewed as a form of idolatry and loss of faith. When a human being dies, he does not leave behind him a life that he has made. When history is ended, mankind will not leave behind a history that it has made. Death is the irrevocable end of time and history. This is the human condition and is as true for the believer as for the unbeliever. Nonetheless, the religious man believes that time and history *already* participate in the eternity of God. But he knows that he can only participate in the eternity of God by faith. Insofar as modern man seeks an illusory immortality in the making of history, he removes himself further and further from the Word Who was with God at the beginning of time and Who brings eternal life today. With George Grant, the religious man will acknowledge the present darkness as a real darkness, but he will also assert that the Light continues to shine in the darkness which can neither comprehend nor extinguish it.

IV
PHILOSOPHY

PART IV. PHILOSOPHY

Conversation

Question: What exactly do you mean by modernity?

Grant: I mean by modernity the society that has come to be in the western world and which has arisen since western people have concentrated on what is best called "technology." I used to think that the continental European use of the word "technique" was better than the word "technology", because "technology" was a poor neologism made by putting together the two Greek words *techne* and *logos*. But I changed my mind for the following reason. Technology puts together what the Greeks could not possibly have put together, making and knowing. It expresses a new union between the arts and sciences – a union of the greatest complexity. It seems to me that modernity comes forth, above all, from this new union of the arts and sciences, and what it portends for us.

I was led into thinking about modernity through political philosophy and theology, and certainly modernity involves enormous changes in how we look at political things and the possibility of theology – but at its heart is this new interdependence of the arts and sciences – "technology." This is obvious at every lived moment. The deepest account of modernity is found in the writings of Heidegger. He is a genius on this subject, however fearful one may be of his political and moral stance.

Question: I am very interested in what you said about Heidegger and that you've learned a great deal from Heidegger concerning modernity. I'd be very interested in some of the particulars in which you are fearful of Heidegger.

Grant: Let's not go into his political opinions in detail. We could discuss their complexity all day. Let's say no more than two things. Anybody who in 1953 could publish his *Introduction to Metaphysics*, which he had written in 1935, and say that all errors were corrected, yet nevertheless include the phrase, "the inner truth and greatness of National Socialism," is saying something that makes one fearful. But second, the greatest book for understanding Heidegger is in my opinion his first volume on Nietzsche – an amazing book. What he declares about justice in that volume is, it seems to me, the modern view of justice taken much further than what we find in American liberalism or Marxism. It is a turning away from what is given about justice in Platonism or in Christianity and Judaism, a turning away which in my opinion bodes ill for the future.

What seems to me true is the connection between this new view of justice and historicism. It seems to me that Heidegger is the most perfectly thought historicist that I have ever read. There is a debate about that – whether he is or not – but I am sure that he is. And that that historicism is, above anything else, responsible for the undermining of the older tradition of justice which I hope many people in this room would accept as true.

Question: May I interrupt to ask about a connection here? The first thing that you said about modernity is that it's that kind of society that has emerged from this new integration or understanding of the relationship between the arts and the sciences.

Grant: Which we call technology.

Question: Yes, and that seems to suggest that you're offering an analysis and description in your work, of this social phenomenon. Then you move from there to speaking about Heidegger as a primary example ...

Grant: As an illuminator of what modernity is. In his book on Leibniz he just lays down what technology is, as I have never read elsewhere.

Question: Is modernity, then, another way of speaking about historicism?

Grant: Historicism is surely a principle of method, which is the profoundest principle governing not only the social sciences but the natural sciences. There is clearly a profound relation between historicism and Heisenbergian physics.

Now I am not competent to think about that relation. I just don't know enough. But I do begin to grasp in talking to physicists that there is something of historicism in their work. As a physicist said to me the other day, "what quantum physics is saying is that being is never still." The science of the modern world in its most serious form, physics, and in biological and social sciences, is dominated by this central affirmation – historicism. Historicism is the intellectual end-product of modern western European society, and dominates what is most important about any society – its conception of knowledge.

Let me add, modern historicism seems to me rooted in a primal affirmation about will which lies behind that historicism. That affirmation about will has something to do with western Christianity. Here you are faced with the simple fact that the chief historical event which came between the greatest of modern thinkers, for example, Kant, and the greatest of ancient thinkers, Plato, was the rise of Christianity – I mean Western Christianity. Therefore it seems to me if one wants to see the difference between ancient knowledge and modern knowledge (call it, if you will, science or even philosophy), it is of crucial importance to understand the influence of Christianity in making that difference. This is of particular importance for those of us who are Christians. And for Christians this also raises the whole question of what is Christianity, and is it to be identified with a particular manifestation of it, Western Christianity?

Let me also say, as strongly as I can, that I do not know what modernity is or what it tells us about the whole. For example, I do not want to say that I simply reject modernity. People have often said that I do. They do so because their faith is so completely given to the modern enterprise that when they hear somebody speak against it, they like to see it as simple reaction – as a simple rejection. But that is not the point. The point is to try to understand what the coming-to-be of modernity means in terms of the whole.

Western technological society, which is now world-wide, has come to be. What does that coming-to-be mean? That seems to me the great modern philosophical task. And the prodigious difficulty of that task of judgement is that we who have to do it are all moderns, and are therefore held by the modern account of knowledge, and can only judge modernity in its own terms, and that is just not good enough.

Question: You've accepted then the word "technology", it seems to me, as really capsulizing what modernity is. Would you also accept the notion of "technocracy" as an expression of what has happened to politics within modernity?

Grant: I would prefer to put it that there is a tendency in all modern societies to overcome politics and turn it into administration. Horkheimer, of the Frankfurt school, a Marxist, had the view that in the coming-to-be of technology there are all kinds of revolts of nature going on – a wonderful conception – and there are revolts of people who want to return to politics, as a natural form of human activity.

I think in this modern world everything moves towards politics becoming administration (I would rather use this expression than technocracy, because administration is a substitute for politics as Plato or Aristotle meant it). All kinds of revolts against administration are going on. How long those revolts will last, no one can predict. We are living in one now, in Canada. There is much to be said about what is happening in Quebec – but doesn't one feel triumphant that administrative efficiency in the North American context wasn't able to win – wasn't able to make them want to give up their language? Dr Laurin is in politics because he found out in his psychiatry that taking away any people's language meant taking away their womanhood and their manhood, taking away their nature.

If you say there is such a thing as human nature (and I am not saying that it is easy to think that, in terms of modern knowledge), then there are going to be revolts against administration in the name of politics. I am sure that we can say there is such a thing as eternal justice. There are therefore going to be those revolts, and I think one should rejoice in them. There are going to be revolts against the tendency towards the universal and homogeneous state which is run by administration.

Question: Are you saying that even before we get to the union of *techne* and *logos*, there is a development in the west of the primacy of the will that will not endure eternal justice, that revolts against eternal justice?

Grant: An extremely difficult question. First, the word "will" has meant so many different things to so many different people through the ages. What does it mean in the modern world where it has become the dominant affirmation of reality – as human will?

Secondly, how and why does it enter the western world as a new affirmation? By the time of Kant, it is right out into the open. When Kant says that human beings are autonomous, the makers of their own law, the idea of will is right out into the open, proclaiming something about reality and humanness which is quite new in the world and quite easy to see. But before that, how is that idea coming to be? For example, when Leibniz says the monads are *appetitus et perceptio*, I know that something new is being said about reality – but what it is that is being said is too difficult for me. These final ontological questions which lie at the heart of what technology is are beyond my capacity.

Question: You have sometimes described the heresy of modernity as liberalism, the notion that man's essence is his freedom – a different way of putting it than the combination of *techne* and *logos*.

Grant: But surely both these propositions are saying the same thing. Isn't the question to understand exactly how the affirmation that man's essence is his freedom lies at the heart of technology, and how technology as something new leads human beings to define their essence as freedom? What has to be understood is that primal apprehension of being, out of which both liberalism and technology come. It is this which is so difficult.

Question: I myself feel more at home in trying to locate the origins of what you mean by modernity in this line of thought: the notion of man's essence being his freedom, beginning in the late Renaissance or probably earlier, provided the indispensable condition for the development of a variety of things including technology and the kind of society we have, because it seems to me that saying man's essence is his freedom means you can no longer speak about justice.

Grant: Yes, I agree with that. You can either say that you can no longer speak of justice, or you can say that when you start to think in this way, justice comes to mean something quite different from what it did in the traditions of the Greeks and the Bible. This is why I think Nietzsche and Heidegger are so important. They affirm that with the coming-to-be of technology, justice becomes something new. This is what Nietzsche means by the transvaluation of all values. Before them, thinkers such as Rousseau and Kant had accepted the coming-to-be of the new technological science, but thought that would go with the great tradition of western justice, rendering each human being his due.

Question: But Nietzsche says outright that justice now means something new. It is human, creating and annihilating. You can't talk of justice or hang on to the ancient conception of justice — as rendering each human being his due.

Grant: Perhaps you can in a way, except that under the new conception of justice some human beings have no due. I think this is both the greatness and the terror of Nietzsche and Heidegger; they recognise that the new affirmation of reality in technology brings a new account of justice. I think the English-speaking world is only beginning to see this; namely, that the new affirmation of reality in technology means a new conception of justice. This will be a terrible realisation in the English-speaking world. It is to this new account of justice as a human creation that I fundamentally say no. And it is because this new account of justice goes with the technological society that that society is terrifying for Christians.

Of course in all this there are the intellectual questions that we as philosophers have to think out. Very difficult. One of them is the enormous difference between ancient materialism and modern materialism. Why is it that in the ancient world the materialists were the private apolitical thinkers, while the Platonists were interested in the public realm, whereas in the modern world the nationalists are so politically directed? Right at the centre of modern materialism is this idea of man's essence being his freedom.

If you try to see the difference between the two you always come back to this fact: Biblical religion came between the two outbreaks of philosophy. To say man's essence is his freedom is to say something new about will.

Question: Jacques Ellul is a person who has written at great length about technological society. What do you think of his account of modernity?

Grant: When I first read Ellul's *The Technological Society*, it seemed to me a wonderful account of what was going on — the illustrations of the central fact that the unfolding of technology was determinative in the modern world. That dominance was a destiny which transcended all else and to which all else in the modern world had to be related. One gets so sick of the liberal and Marxist ideologists and their accounts of technology as a means at the disposal of human freedom. When they speak that way they forget that both capitalism and communism are but predicates of the subject, technology. Ellul's description of technology was quite outside such a shallow account, and he faced what was actually happening with his lucid French and Christian common sense. He just seemed to state the score. But then I began to read his other books and to think more carefully about what he was saying about technology, and it has become clearer and clearer to me that he does not get to the heart of the matter of what is happening in the modern world.

Question: Is it that his account of technology is tied to the kind of Calvinist tradition that seems to have fallen so easily into the acceptance of secularism?

Grant: Ellul's account of modernity seems to me to fail because it comes out of a type of Christianity which scorns the discipline of philosophy. Obviously there has been a side of Protestantism — what one might call positivist Protestantism — which tries to cut off Christianity from philosophy. It seems to me Ellul's writings about technology exactly show the failure of such a position. It fails to understand what technology truly is, because it refuses to come to terms with reason, except as a human instrument.

Question: It is remarkable, however, that somebody, coming as he does out of the self-conscious reappropriation of the Calvinist tradition, should see so clearly what is going on in technological society.

Grant: Yes, he sees it with great clarity at an immediate level. But our need is to think through modernity to its very foundations. What is being said about reason in the modern enterprise? I am grateful for his hard-minded common sense; but I am sad that his positivist Christianity prevents him from going deeper. His failure to take that step is intimately bound up with his particular type of Christianity. It prevents him from asking the basic question: to what extent is modern technological society connected to, and a product of, the western interpretation of Christianity? This is very hard for Christians to ask, because it may seem to bring into question our fundamental loyalty to Christianity itself. It was an easy question to face when western society appeared an unequivocal triumph. Then one could simply say: look at what Christianity is responsible for. But now that modernity appears, not only in the greatness of its achievements but in its ambiguities, it is a more difficult question to face. We may easily refuse to try to fathom the relation between modernity and western Christianity, because we may think such a fathoming may put in question what is most dear. But that is not the point. What we are called to do is to think through how the western interpretation of the Bible was responsible not only for the greatness of modernity, but also for what is frightening in it. This kind of questioning cannot be faced by a Christianity that envisages reason simply as a human instrument, and therefore cuts itself off from philosophy. To understand technology requires that we try to understand what is the true relation between love and reason. Did western Christianity go wrong in its understanding of that relation? The whole attempt to understand modernity cannot be cut off from the attempt to understand both philosophy and Christianity and their relation. The temptation is always to try to understand technology from within technology.

Philosophy, Revelation and Modernity:
Crossroads in the Thought of George Grant
by Bernard Zylstra

Greek philosophy, Christian revelation, and secular modernity are central themes in the thought of George Grant. In this article I will attempt to explain the relationships between these themes in his later writings. My thesis is threefold. In the first place, I will attempt to show that for Grant the proper foundation for western civilization consists in a synthesis between Greek philosophy and Christian revelation. In the second place, I will argue that in Grant's thought the break-up of this synthesis has led to secular modernity. Finally, I will conclude by showing that in Grant's thought secular modernity is implicit in the religion of the Bible, notably the Old Testament.

From the outset it should be clear that Grant is deeply suspicious of modernity. One of the numerous ways in which he has described the modern project can be found at the end of *Time as History:* "the mastery of human and non-human nature in experimental science and technique, the primacy of the will, man as the creator of his own values, the finality of becoming, the assertion that potentiality is higher than actuality, that motion is nobler than rest, that dynamism rather than peace is the height."[1] Grant's simultaneous repudiation of modernity and his acceptance of a link between the religion of the Bible and that same modernity reveal a fundamental ambiguity in his thought. For Grant writes as a Christian, who accepts the revelation that lies at the basis of Christianity. I will try to explain the nature of that ambiguity.

Greek philosophy and Christian revelation

Grant insists that modernity entails a repudiation of the essence of both the Greek and the Christian view of man. For this reason those who reject the modern account of man must begin by remembering "the core of what has been handed over to us from Athens and Jerusalem," namely, the "language of good and evil ... a language which belongs to man as man."[2]

One of the very first questions to be addressed to Grant is this: do Greek philosophy and Christian revelation speak the same language? This question is nearly as old as Christianity itself but today it receives a new significance in the confrontation with modernity. The critics of modernity who look to the classical heritage of the West as the criterion for judgment do not agree on what part of that heritage maintains validity. Hannah Arendt builds her thought primarily on Greek and Roman foundations. Leo Strauss, though he does not for a moment "forget what Jerusalem stands for," focuses our attention mainly on Athens where political philosophy first came to light.[3] Eric Voegelin, though not overlooking differences, speaks of "agreement between Plato and Paul on the fundamental structure of reality."[4] Though Grant has been highly influenced by Leo Strauss, his position on this issue is closer to that of Voegelin. Basically he holds that the elements which Greek philosophy — especially Plato's — and Christian revelation have in common together constitute the criterion by which we can properly judge modernity. This means that Grant, though he does not neglect differences, proceeds from the assumption of an agreement on central matters in Greek philosophy and Christian revelation. He has formulated this assumption as follows:

> ... central to my affirmations ... are the propositions: the core of our
> lives is the desire for perfection, and only that desire can make us less
> imperfect. ... The attempt to argue for my propositions would require
> a very close historical analysis of how the use of such words as
> 'desire' and 'reason' have changed over the last centuries. It would
> require, for example, what the ancients meant by 'passion'. What-
> ever the differences between what has come to us from Plato and
> from Christianity, on this central point there is commonness. The
> height for man could only come forth out of a 'passion'.[5]

I interpret Grant to say that because of this commonness, Greek philosophy and Christian revelation could provide a stable foundation for western civilization. In his view they were "the chief compasses of the western past," though he fully realizes that "the proper relation between them was considered an extremely complex question and was at the root of many controversies of the preprogressive era."[6] The controversies dealt with the content of the height for man, the object of the passion or the desire, as well as the language which informs man of that content. What are the respective languages and what do they say?

While Christianity speaks the language of revelation, Greek culture speaks the language of philosophy. Grant warns us that the language of philosophy is not always lucid, that "philosophy has always been problematic to itself."[7] Nevertheless, he is certain that this language, as articulated by its greatest representatives — Plato and Aristotle — is plain. It says that contemplation is the height for man, that "in thinking ... men find their fullest satisfaction," that the "highest good for man is wisdom."[8] There is a hierarchy in the activities of mankind which reaches from labour and work through moral and political action to the height of thought. This height is reached in the life of the philosopher who "contemplates the divine order and takes part in its eternity."[9]

Christianity's language of revelation again is not always lucid. Grant warns us that "Biblical religion is not an easily definable entity, either for those who conduct their life of worship within its terms or for those outside it."[10] Nevertheless, as with the matter of philosophy, Grant has expressed himself about Christianity, though one wishes that he had said more. He answers the "central question of Christianity" affirmatively — "whether revelation of a decisive nature has once and for all been given."[11] The core of that revelation is this: that love is the height for man. Love is attention to otherness, an "obedient giving oneself away."[12]

Grant considers contemplation and love as the two primals of European civilization. The relation between these primals brings to the fore two questions, a formal one and a material one. The formal question concerns the structural connection between philosophy and revelation. Grant holds, with the older tradition, "that philosophy and religion fulfil different (albeit related) roles in the lives of human beings and that the practice of both are [sic] necessary to the healthy life of a society."[13] He acknowledges that the older political philosophers such as Plato, the Jewish Aristotelians, and Aquinas, asserted that *unassisted* reason could arrive at valid conclusions about society, but within limits outside of which divine revelation was deemed necessary.[14] Greek philosophy can therefore be described as "thought not determined by revelation."[15]

But does the philosopher who accepts revelation enjoy a similar autonomy of contemplation, namely, the thinking of "thought not determined by revelation"? Grant asked this question of Leo Strauss, in these words: "whether he thinks there is in the Bible an authority of revelation which has a claim over the philosopher as much as over other men."[16] While Strauss never answered that question clearly in his writings, Grant willingly subjects philosophy to "the magistery of revelation."[17]

If the formal relation of Biblical revelation and philosophy entails the subjection of the one to the other, what are the consequences materially? What is the juxtaposition of thought and love? It is one thing to say that western civilization presupposes two primals, but it is a contradiction to accord primacy to both. Here Grant sides with what he considers to be the revelation of the Bible, within which "charity was the height and therefore contemplation was finally a means to that obedient giving oneself away."[18] What did premodern western civilization do with its two primals? I sense an ambiguity in Grant's answers. On the one hand he seems to say that the West fused thought and love together in harmony because contemplation had been brought under the magistery of revelation. But on the other hand Grant is fully aware that the premodern West was in tension precisely because of its dual primals. "Many of the deepest controversies in which western men defined what they are have been centred around the proper ways of relating or distinguishing what was given to them from Athens and Jerusalem."[19] The public expression of the presuppositions of Athens and Jerusalem had led to a "strange blending in western Europe."[20] In fact, Grant admits that the reciprocal misinterpretations of the traditions of thought and love as well as their antithetical interrelations "formed the chief tension out of which Europe was shaped."[21] Its civilization was new and expressed neither thought in its fullness nor love in its fullness. In short, I interpret Grant to say that the tension between the traditions of thought and love was creative because it made possible a society in which men could live as men, within good and evil and not beyond good and evil. No matter how great the tensions between these two traditions were, premodern society maintained an inner unity. A healthy society requires the practice of both philosophy and religion. It is better to risk tension between them than to eliminate either or both of them.

Christianity and modernity
This brings us directly to the second facet of my theme, namely, the relation between Christianity and modernity. It is helpful here to compare Grant's treatment of this relation in his earlier writings with that in his later writings. In the first phase of his development — before the radical repudiation of modernity — Grant dealt with this matter quite explicitly, and in two ways. In the first place, he argued that the Thomist synthesis of Greek philosophy (with its natural realm of human reason) and Christianity (with its revealed realm of God's mighty acts in history) was unable "to hold the minds of western Europeans after the fifteenth century. And in the four hundred years since the breakdown of that balance, there has gradually arisen our world-wide scientific civilization."[22] In other words, at that time Grant interpreted the medieval synthesis as a union of *irreconcilable* primals which would break down sooner or later. In the second place, Grant assumed that there was a positive link between Christianity and the foundation of modern civilization. He found this link in the notion of history as progress and in the view of man as the maker of that history. "The most important cause of this change to man seen as the maker of history," he then wrote, "seems to me without a doubt to be Christianity."[23] One might combine these two avenues of interpretation by saying that the breakdown of the medieval synthesis entailed the

abandonment of a static, Aristotelian view of nature (which had been combined with the history of salvation in the supernatural reality of the church) and the unfolding of a dynamic, future-oriented history (which gradually assumed the form of a purely natural, inner-worldly progress). In his first phase, Grant accepted the Hegelian account of the synthesis between the Greek world and Christianity and the later synthesis between Christianity and modernity.[24] But when Grant later rejected that account, he still had to explain "the connection between the religion of western Europe and the dynamic civilization which first arose there."[25]

In unravelling that connection, we are confronted with a strange ambiguity in Grant's thought. On the one hand he cannot deny that there are positive elements within modernity that are rooted in Christianity. On the other hand he asserts that there are negative elements within modernity that are also rooted in Christianity. So there are both negative and positive links between Christianity and modernity. One of these positive links is the modern belief in equality which, Grant argues, cannot be understood apart from the change of emphasis concerning man's highest activity from contemplation to love. The realm of contemplation is accessible only to the few; the realm of love is accessible to all. The universal character of the Christian religion contributed to the equality of the modern age. But Grant is willing to go beyond this. He acknowledges the existence of a link between technology, i.e., the systematic interference with chance which is embedded in the heart of modernity, and Christian love. For technology was not undertaken simply for its own sake, nor merely for the realization of freedom or as an expression of the will to mastery: "indeed it was undertaken partly in the name of that charity which was held as the height in one of these ancient systems of meaning."[26] The realization of love may well require technology. At any rate, no writing about technological progress and the rightness of imposing limits upon it should avoid expressing the fact that the poor, the diseased, the hungry and the tired can hardly be expected to contemplate any such limitation with the equanimity of the philosopher.[27]

I have found no adequate explanation of this positive link between love and technology in Grant's later writings. This link contradicts Grant's more encompassing assumption that love and technology are at odds with each other since love restrains the human passions while technology emancipates them. Technology leads to the homogeneous society, which is oriented to the universal satisfaction of passions but which excludes love of the particular, love of one's own. Since technology is the foremost societal expression of modernity, one would expect Grant to assert the discontinuity between Christianity and modernity. However, the enigma of his thought consists in his insistence on a second link of continuity between Christianity and modernity. Grant holds that the negative, indeed destructive, elements of modernity cannot be understood apart from Christianity. This theme can best be discussed in terms of the nature of secularization. Grant interprets modernity as a secularization of Christianity. Secularization in his thought is not the gradual elimination of all "supernatural" restraints imposed upon the human condition by the Christian religion so that man can realize himself in autonomous freedom. The latter interpretation of secularization would consider the Italian Renaissance a major avenue toward the liberal, rational and intramundane culture of the modern age. But the Italian Renaissance hardly figures in Grant's view of the roots of modernity. This is due, I think, to the fact that for him secularization has little connection with the elimination of the "supernatural" or the rejection of revelation. It is my thesis that for Grant the secularization of Christianity – and thus the appearance of modernity in world history – depends upon elements inherent in the Christian religion itself.

Modernity as secular Christianity "is penetrated by an acceptance of certain aspects of that which is being criticised." An understanding of what is accepted and what is criticised in Christianity by modernity will present the clue to the problem at hand. The relation between acceptance and critique is very close; it is comparable to the relation of parents and children, in which there is "at one and the same time a critical turning away from our origins and also a carrying along of some essential aspects of them."[28] In other words, secularization is as normal and apparently also as inevitable as the growing up of a child. But when the child grows up, what does he carry along and what does he leave behind? Or, when does the child grow up and when does he decide to leave behind the childish things? In struggling with these questions, Grant seems to give a variety of answers in which the moment of secularization of Christianity is pushed ever further back into history. Upon first reading "In Defence of North America" and "Canadian Fate and Imperialism" in *Technology and Empire* one gets the impression that the real break occurred within Anglo-Saxon Protestantism in North America. For in these essays Grant expresses his profound concern about how much his spiritual ancestors left behind in Europe and how little they took along. Hence these essays at first glance look like a new version of Marx's or Weber's thesis about the relation between Puritanism and capitalism, a version passionately pro-pounded because Grant himself daily experiences the mastery of a continent under the aupices of the Protestant American empire. But that would be a far too superficial comparison. Precisely because Marx and Weber were only concentrating on the practical relation between religion and society, Grant contends, neither was concerned with the deeper level of the matter, namely, the inherent connection between Protestant theology and modern science. There was something within Protestant theology itself which secularized Christianity. Protestant theology was a vital link in the process of secularization, not because it was less "biblical" than Roman Catholic theology but because it was less Greek!

As I indicated above, in Grant's view western civilization was founded on two primals, Greek contemplation and Christian love. The peculiarity of Protestantism lies in its break with the Greek primal. Here is the fundamental element of discontinuity in the history of the West. But of course this break occurred before Protestants set foot on North American soil. "Calvinist Protestantism was itself a break in Europe – a turning away from the Greeks in the name of what was found in the Bible. We brought to the meeting with the North American land a particular non-Mediterranean Europeanness of the seventeenth century which was itself the beginning of something new."[29] Protestant religion proved to be so eminently suited for the empty spaces of a new continent because its Europeanness was de-Hellenized. The Protestants' break with the Greeks meant that they had not cut themselves off from the primal of love but that they had cut the cord with contemplation. For this reason they were spiritually uprooted, without autochthony, individualized, and thus well prepared for the task of mastering a continent, of performing unparalleled industrial conquests:

> Greece lay behind Europeans as a first presence; it has not so lain for us. It was for them primal in the sense that in its perfected state-ments educated Europeans found the way that things are. The Greek writings bared a knowledge of the human and nonhuman things which could be grasped as firmness by the Europeans for the making of their own lives and cities. Most important, Plato and Aristotle presented contemplation as the height for man.[30]

Here it seems as if Grant's argument is against Protestantism. But if Protestantism as de-Hellenized Christianity is a link to secular modernity, then there must be an element within Christianity itself that is the root of modernity. What is that element? What within Christianity led to the break with the Greek primal of contemplation? In answering this question, Grant goes beyond Protestantism to the wider context of the development of theology in the Latin countries of the mediterranean basin. In that theology he sees the gradual appearance of the primacy of the will. It was St Augustine who already exclaimed: *Quid sumus nisi voluntates?* "What are we but wills?"[31]

Grant defines willing, not as the conscious expression of the soul in each of its earthly dimension, but as "one type of agent in a total process of good purposes."[32] Willing is related to one activity (doing) in distinction from other activities (thinking and desiring or loving). In other words, Grant locates willing at a particular level in the hierarchy of human nature, below thinking and desiring. While desiring is an expression of dependence and thinking a contemplation of the whole, willing is the determination to do, to make things happen.

> Willing is that power of determining by which we put our stamp on events (including ourselves) and in which we do some violence to the world. In willing to do or not to do we close down on the openness of deliberation and decide that as far as we are concerned, this will happen rather than that. Indeed, one strange ambiguity among human beings is that what seems required for the greatest thought is opposite to what is required for the greatest doing.[33]

Willing is undoubtedly one of the necessities of being, but Grant argues that in western Christianity the will as primal has absorbed love and thought, so that the will's peculiar activity of making things happen has become the core of our civilization.

At this point I think we can arrive at a provisional conclusion concerning Grant's argument about the relation of Christianity to modernity. That relation is not the success of one of Christianity's sectarian expressions – Calvinism or Puritanism. Western Christianity itself articulated the will as primal. But how can that be when the height for man in Christian revelation is love? Did Christianity absorb the primacy of the will from some non-Christian religion in the mediterranean basin? No! The essence of modernity was potentially present within the religion of the Old Testament. Within Old Testament religion, in Grant's view, there is a fundamental ambiguity as to what is primal, love or will.

So here we are confronted with three primals: contemplation, love, and will. A healthy society presupposes the practice of both contemplation and love because the passions of the will can only be checked by love aided by contemplation. Modernity is the emancipation of the passions, of the will. Modernity could not have arisen out of Greek culture because that culture was not ambiguous about its primal. But modernity could – and did – arise out of the religion of the Bible. Grant is radically consistent here. In 1964 he asked the question, "whether the Machiavellian and Hobbesian politics are at least in part a result of the Biblical orientation of western society."[34] In 1971 this was his answer, again at least in part:

> If we were searching for the origins of our present, we would first try to state what was given to men in Judaism or Christianity, and then seek out how this intermingled with the claims of universal understanding which were found in the heights of Greek civilization. As Christianity was the majoritarian locus in which that intermingling

occurred, we would have to examine how it was that Christianity so opened men to a particular consciousness of time, by opening them to anxiety and charity; how willing was exalted through the stamping proclamations of the creating Will; how time was raised up by redemption in time, and the future by the exaltation of the 'eschaton'.[35]

This passage clearly indicates Grant's conception of the origin of the primacy of the will: "willing was exalted through the stamping proclamations of the creating Will." The primacy of the human will is founded on a conception of a God who wills – who wills a creation. The fundamental source of Grant's ambiguity in understanding the relation of philosophy, revelation, and modernity appears to be his discovery of two deities in the religion of the Bible. There is the God of perfection, who as the eternally lovable is the object of human contemplation and the end of man's desiring. This deity bears a remarkable resemblance to the God of Greek philosophy. And then there is also the God who wills, who creates, who commands. He accepts the God who *is* love while he hesitates before a God who *wills* love, and who has the sovereign right to command love because he is the maker and redeemer of man.

This depreciation of creation in Grant's thought is, I suggest, largely dependent upon his Platonic conception of man, in which we find a hierarchy of passion, labour, work, political *praxis*, and contemplation. Grant accepts this hierarchy, but adds the dimension of love. In this juxtaposition, he relates will to the lower dimensions in the ladder of being. He does not understand that *the will to love* must direct every dimension of the human hierarchy, and that therefore neither will nor love can be "located" at a particular level within that hierarchy. Grant cannot speak of a properly directed will in distinction from a misdirected will. The will itself appears to be misdirected unless love or contemplation subdues it. In this light Grant depreciates whatever might possibly hint at will, in human nature and in the divine nature. This is the basis for his repudiation of modernity. But in rejecting modernity in this manner, Grant experiences great difficulty in giving a proper account of human subjectivity, of obedient creatureliness in history, of man's tilling and keeping the earth, of science whose mastery is limited by reverence for the Creator and the creation. In relating philosophy, revelation and modernity, Grant accepts only the redemptive *omega* of revelation but has no place for the creational *alpha* of revelation. In this *alpha* of revelation we learn that it is the created nature of the will to be a servant of love, an avenue through which "Thy will be done." The promethean rejection of that creaturely status of the will lies at the foundation of modernity.

The Technological Regime:
George Grant's Analysis of Modernity
by William Mathie

The following remarks examine the account George Grant has given of our own world. The central term of that account and the subject of these remarks is "technology." To grasp the nature and implications of this novel activity, brought into the world by certain western European thinkers some few centuries past and now constituting the power of North America to dominate and shape the globe is the task to which Grant's writings have been increasingly devoted. To understand the modern world that informs our actions and thought is above all to think what technology is and how it has come to be our comprehensive destiny. Few now deny that technology is a pervasive fact of our world, more and more wonder if technology can continue to contribute to the relief of man's estate without higher and ultimately prohibitive costs to the environment, and many express the vague fear that the products of developing technology threaten our freedom; none of these hesitations and fears begin to reflect what Grant intends when he calls technology a comprehensive destiny within which our politics, lives, and even thought is to be worked out or to glimpse the difficulty "of thinking a position in which technique is beheld within a horizon greater than itself."[1]

A language, and framework, that may aid us to see the significance of Grant's claim is furnished by pre-modern political science. For Aristotle, and traditional political science in general, the fundamental political phenomenon is the *politeia* or regime. When it spoke of the regime, traditional political science referred at once to the way of life and to the rulers of a community. These are two sides of the same coin for that political science — oligarchy is a regime within which a life devoted to the appropriation of wealth is seen as the best kind of human activity and within oligarchy it is the wealthy who rule, directly or indirectly. To understand any political community is to grasp the deliberate choice of a way of life which informs that community. For several reasons the founders of modern political science chose to separate "state" and "society", to treat the way, or ways, of life of men as if these were simply matters of individual choice, and to assess alternative forms of political order as these were more or less convenient to the private pursuit of privately defined ends. However we may judge the practical consequences of this new political science, it does not furnish the basis for an adequate analysis of our situation precisely because it denies or obscures the relation between how men live and how they are governed. When Grant remarks that "communism and contractual capitalism are predicates of the subject technology,... ways in which our more comprehensive destiny is worked out," he surely suggests that technology defines a regime for us.[2]

The claim that technology constitutes our regime becomes plausible when we reflect that most of most men's lives within our world is directed by the needs and assumptions of technology, and that the chief qualification for a share in rule is competence within, or in relation to, the technological sphere.[3] If, as Aristotle supposed, a regime is above all preserved by an education in the habits suited to that regime, further evidence for the identification of our world as a technological regime is found in the aims and content of education within our societies. The contemporary university both trains those who must run technological society at its various levels and promotes general support for the assumptions upon which it is founded; indeed, as Grant has said, "the university curriculum, by the very studies it incorporates, guarantees that there should be no serious criticism of itself or of the society it is shaped to serve."[4] That technology constitutes a regime for us is also suggested by the fact that activities outside the assumptions of technology are directed away from the public sphere; even madness acquires specifically technological forms.[5]

The comprehensiveness of technology for our politics and the fact that western society increasingly constitutes an expanding regime defined by technology become apparent as it is seen that those who dissent from the aims and character of this society must themselves argue within the assumptions of technology or become powerless. The fate of Canadian nationalism in the Diefenbaker years shows the impotence of a politics that seriously questions those assumptions.[6] Conservatives who attempt to preserve the good as known to them in their own societies must lack popular support or seek the preservation of the power and culture of their societies through policies ultimately inconsistent with that good they had sought to defend. When the majority equate their own material well-being with technological progress it becomes impossible to preserve any remnant of tradition. In our society, right and left come to express their

disagreement with the policies of the technological elite within technological assumptions. If the right hesitates to embrace all of the consequences of technology, it still praises free enterprise as the vehicle of
technological advance. If the left seeks a more radical liberation, the
liberation it demands entails an ever greater control over nature through
technology.[7]

Nor does Marxism constitute an effective political alternative to the
technological regime. In the first place, the Marxist dream of overcoming
oppression as constituted by scarcity and the division of labour commits
Marxist society to continued technological progress; indeed, Marxists must
hope against reason for a result from that progress contrary to its manifest
tendency.[8] At the same time, Marxism expresses the technological
principle less completely than capitalism because Marx retained a notion
of man's good that "predates the age of progress."[9] Only thus can Marx
identify human alienation as such. Nevertheless to retain such a notion of
man's good is to contradict the definition of man as freedom central to the
technological principle; that definition is more fully realized in the
thought of the most sophisticated in western society – "they recognize
that no appeal to human good ... must be allowed to limit their freedom to
make the world as they choose."[10] Marxism as it presupposes a conception
of man's good that entails limits on human freedom sees technology still as
an instrument rather than as an end in itself. The "value neutrality" of
Western social science more precisely realizes the technologists' own
self-understanding. Finally, Marxism reveals itself as guilty of unwarranted
optimism, or confusion, in its belief that the elimination of scarcity can
mean at once the elimination of oppression through greed and the
emancipation of all human desires. In fact, all Marxist and socialist regimes
have found it necessary "to use government to restrain greed in the name
of social good" and Marxist and socialist parties have had limited success
in Western societies already committed to a more thorough emancipation
of the passions.[11] Marxism is for Grant, then, a less progressive force than
the technological regime to be found in the capitalist West because
Marxism entails a notion of limits and must in practice oppose the
complete emancipation of the passions.

Though capitalism is, for Grant, a mode and conception of human
activity more completely in accord with the needs and assumptions of
technology than is communism, both capitalist and communist societies
are more and more committed to technological expansion as an end in
itself. "Technological progress is now being pursued not first and foremost
to free all men from work and disease [as capitalists and communists might
differently argue it is, or must be], but for the investigation and conquest
of the infinite spaces around us" and the extent of this task means "that

modern society is committed to unlimited technological progress *for its own sake.*"[12] Grant has cited the space programme as one illustration of this commitment. Grant's claim is not merely that capitalist and communist societies, and indeed all significant opposition within or to these regimes, are committed to technological progress but that this commitment especially in our own regime, less and less regards technology as a means to some intelligible human purpose apart from technology itself. Technology becomes our comprehensive destiny as the prevalent modes of thinking our existence either preclude any conception of a human end that could direct or limit technological development or declare a human purpose that is contained and actualized in technological development itself.

This analysis may be supposed to document an increasing unity in the western world, and elsewhere as the balance of the globe is westernized, without demonstrating that technology names the essential character of this unity. In recent years many have spoken of a convergence of the societies of the east and west but they have supposed that this tendency was one of "liberalization." Many hold that it is neither capitalism nor technology but rather liberalism that defines our regime. Liberty – political liberty and the liberty of individuals – was the intention of those who founded this regime in the seventeenth and eighteenth centuries and continues to be the good realized through the institutions those men devised and the way of life those institutions support. It is true as Grant says, that a serious concern for what human life and excellence are is foreign to public deliberation in our society; yet, it may be held, this only preserves the principled refusal to treat that question which distinguished the modern regime directed to liberty from its predecessors. The notion of "the end of ideology" and even the fact/value distinction are only vulgar expressions of what the founders of liberalism believed, that a decent and moderate government could only arise when men gave up the effort to identify a greatest good or final end of human action that could obtain public recognition.[13] It is true that liberalism as classically expressed endorsed, if it did not invent, capitalism, but the liberal claim that "the first object of government is to protect men's unequal faculties of acquiring property" did not deny the priority of liberty; rather liberty in acquiring property was urged as something that would secure a broader liberty of the individual as well as greater prosperity for all.[14] If, further, liberalism welcomed technological progress, this was only because a more complete mastery over non-human nature could obviate the ancient dependence of the liberty of some upon the slavery of others.[15] Technology remains in principle, an instrument of human good amenable to our judgement and control because it still operates within the moral and political framework of liberalism.

Grant's most complete consideration of these claims for liberalism is to be found in his Wood Lectures of 1974 on *English-speaking Justice.* Here Grant acknowledges that for us at any rate, "liberalism is the only political language that can sound a convincing moral note in our public realm," but he notes the growing evidence that "modern liberalism and technology, although they have been interdependent, may not necessarily be mutually sustaining, and that their identity may not be given in the nature of reason itself."[16] Liberalism has claimed, and still claims, that "the good which is liberal society" is to be accomplished through technological advance. However, as technology is increasingly directed towards the mastery of human beings through such means as "behaviour modification, genetic engineering, and population control by abortion," it becomes necessary to ask whether the human good in equal liberty under law is advanced by technological progress, and to reconsider the basis of the liberal vision of that good. One must ask how and whether liberalism sustains a justice that can protect the liberty and even lives of those most vulnerable to the dictates of "technological reason."

The incapacity of liberalism in contemporary form to sustain justice against the new claims for convenience raised within technological society is most clearly revealed, as Grant shows, in the majority decision of the U.S. Supreme Court that no state may enact legislation preventing a citizen from receiving an abortion in the first six months of pregnancy.[17] According to that decision the rights at issue must take precedence over any account of what is good and thus the Court need not consider that account of the good which may have led a state legislature to pass restrictive legislation. The Court confines itself to the question of individual rights as these arise under the American constitution supposing that rights are prior to any account of the good within the Constitution and, indeed, that the Constitution was based on the acceptance of an unlimited moral pluralism. The Court decides in favour of the right of the mother to control her own body because it denies the status of *person* to the foetus. Called upon to judge the conflicting claims of two members of the same species the Court determines that a mother is, and a foetus is not, a person. To reach this verdict the Court must distinguish ontologically between mother and foetus and so open up the larger question of what constitutes our species and connects membership in it to the possession of a claim to equal justice:

> What is it about any members of our species which makes the liberal
> rights of justice their due? The judge unwittingly looses the terrible
> question: has the long tradition of liberal right any support in what
> human beings in fact are?[18]

As Grant shows, the majority decision in Roe v. Wade exhibits a fatal inability of contemporary liberalism to sustain justice against new kinds of claims on behalf of convenience.[19] What must still be asked is whether liberalism *simpliciter* collapses here along with its contemporary form?

Clearly there is a difference between liberalism as classically expressed by Hobbes and Locke, or Kant, and the form of liberalism expressed academically and judicially in our era. A great gulf separates the account of natural and inalienable rights given by Hobbes, Locke, or Jefferson from J.S. Mill's definition of a right as "something which society ought to defend me in the possession of" for "no other reason than general utility".[20] As Grant says, much is lost of Locke's "comprehensiveness, subtlety, and depth" in Mill and his followers. If John Rawls rightly recognizes the inadequacy of utilitarian justice measured against our ordinary moral judgements, and therefore returns to the contractarian tradition, his return is far from complete; while the state of nature is for Hobbes and Locke the fundamental account of our true situation, Rawls' original position is a knowing abstraction conceived within the denial that there can be any true account of the way things are.

While for Hobbes and Locke we know what constitutes our highest or most urgent self-interest and that knowledge leads to our recognizing the need for justice, Rawls separates the calculating of self-interest and derivation of justice from any such knowledge:

> What must be asked then about Rawls' theory is not only (1) whether justice as liberty and equality can arise from a social contract reached from a calculation of self-interest in general; but also (2) whether it can be derived from a calculation in which the interests are self-evidently independent of any account of the way things are as a whole.[21]

The first of these questions addresses the liberalism of Hobbes and Locke as well as Rawls; the second addresses the attempt to express contractualism within the prohibition known as the "naturalistic fallacy." The two must be kept distinct; the vulnerability of justice within a liberalism that denies the possibility of our knowing the way things are may *not* be shared by the justice of a liberalism that does claim such knowledge of our fundamental condition.

One could also argue that there is a difference between earlier and contemporary judicial expressions of liberalism. As Grant notes, in Roe v. Wade Mr. Justice Blackmun quotes Holmes who had done much to support "the principle that the constitution was based on the acceptance of moral pluralism in society".[22] Holmes had been responsible for a revised opinion of the Constitution; he had advanced "a purely contractual interpretation" of the Constitution. A telling and appropriate measure of the movement of liberal justice under the Constitution might consist in the comparison of Mr. Justice Blackmun's decision in Roe v. Wade with the speeches of Abraham Lincoln in opposition to the Supreme Court's Dred Scott decision and the interpretation of the Constitution given by Chief Justice Taney in that case.[23] Admittedly, Lincoln refuted Taney's denial of standing to a negro slave by arguing that the Constitution must be read in the light of the claim of the Declaration of Independence that "all men are created equal" and so possess "certain inalienable rights, among which are life, liberty, and the pursuit of happiness," but his refutation remains a claim for equal justice basing itself upon a statement of classic liberalism. One might even find in Lincoln's precise account of the equality affirmed by the Declaration, against Taney's "proof" that equality could not possibly extend to negro slaves, the basis for a response to Blackmun's demonstration that foetuses had never been "persons in the whole sense" in law.[24] If the earlier liberalism of Lincoln and the Declaration could stoutly oppose powerful claims of convenience in a context remarkably like that of Roe v. Wade, what should we make of the current development of liberal opinion?

What is at issue here may be expressed in the language of regimes if we recur to the account of the defective regimes furnished by Socrates in the *Republic*. In his analysis of the deterioration of political order from aristocracy to tyranny Socrates suggests we may distinguish two kinds of corruption. While aristocracy and timocracy collapse because of the difficulty of preserving the principles of these regimes, oligarchy is ultimately undermined by the operation of the very principle that defines it as a regime.[25] Is the failure of liberalism in Roe v. Wade a corruption or extension of the principle defining our regime? Grant sees the movement from the liberalism of Lincoln and the Declaration to the decision of Roe v. Wade, as a movement towards theoretical clarity or purity. The purely contractual interpretation of the constitution is true to the original intentions of liberalism. From the beginning, liberalism had at its heart a fundamental political vacuum; precisely on the liberal view that avoidance of violent death is our highest end it could neither explain why anyone should make sacrifices for the common good that entailed risk of life or should value "the reign of justice more than their life."[26] What disguised this vacuum for generations and provided the "moral cement" consistent liberal contractualism or utilitarianism could never provide was the fact that so many of those who adopted the teaching of Locke were also held by Protestantism. As that belief has been eroded by liberalism itself, the status and substance of justice within our regime has lost its only foundation. Is the true nature of liberalism spoken in the decision of Roe

v. Wade, as Grant argues? Could a more adequate liberalism sustain justice against the claims of convenience issuing out of our technology?

I have suggested that Lincoln's dissent from the Dred Scott decision might show the possibility of finding a justice beyond the dictates of convenience within the liberal tradition. If, however, one may describe the depth and wisdom of the liberal statesman Lincoln as standing in relation to that of Mr. Justice Blackmun as does the liberalism of Locke to that of John Rawls, the case of Lincoln does not unambiguously manifest the capacity of liberalism itself to sustain equal justice under law against convenience. Though Lincoln demonstrates the possibility of a justice beyond bargains it is not clear that the foundation for that justice lies within liberalism. The Declaration of Independence, to which Lincoln appeals, based equality of right upon the fact that men were "created" equal and endowed with certain rights by their divine creator. Lincoln's argument may only demonstrate that "the moral bite" of this compound of liberalism and Protestantism is now dissolved. The hard question remains: Is there in classical liberalism, in the thought of Hobbes or Locke, a solid basis for a justice that can overrule the kind of convenience urged in Roe v. Wade?

Justice for Hobbes consists almost exclusively in the keeping of covenants.[27] Though the obligation to keep covenants is not itself a product of covenanting but rather a law of nature, that obligation is the product of a calculation. Recognizing our vulnerability to violent death in the natural condition where each has right to everything, we can calculate the need for peace if it is obtainable, the need to relinquish by covenant our right to everything in order to obtain peace, and the need to undertake the obligation to keep those covenants in order that this may be accomplished. Whether Hobbes succeeds in showing the necessity of justice for peace does not, however, settle the question raised by Grant's analysis inasmuch as justice for Hobbes is confined to the keeping of covenants. One must turn to what is more fundamental than justice for Hobbes, what he calls equity or the acknowledgement of natural equality, for justice itself is "a kind of equality." One must ask whether equity has an impervious foundation in that philosophy. As the basis of justice, equity could then sustain such rights of the individual as are attacked in Roe v. Wade.

Two reasons for the requirement that we acknowledge natural human equality are furnished by Hobbes. That acknowledgement has, in the first place, a natural basis in the passionate fear of violent death; to be moved by that fear is to acknowledge our equality. Secondly, Hobbes says natural equality must be acknowledged, whether in truth it exists or not, because that acknowledgement is a necessary condition for peace. By the latter statement equity itself becomes a product of calculation and so no basis for a justice that can resist strong urgings of convenience. One is left then with the identification of equity with the fear of violent death. Yet if Hobbes rightly regards that passion as a reliable motive for justice as the keeping of our covenants, it is no basis for demanding that the rights of others be secured. Modest or equitable men will claim no unequal right for themselves but they need not concern themselves that others actually enjoy equality of right.

Equity, which was for Hobbes a virtue in relation to civil law that corresponded to charity in relation to the laws of nature, is no firm basis of a justice demanding the protection of the rights of all. If such a justice has been pursued within the regime founded upon the teaching of Hobbes and Locke this can only be because those seeking this justice have continued to acknowledge the claims of a Biblical religion or preserved a few remnants of an older notion of a justice chosen for its own sake. The present failure of "liberal justice" to stand firm against technological convenience must, then, be understood as the dissolution of this fragile combination and, in particular, of "the central Protestant vision ... under the influence of ideas elucidated by [thinkers] incomparably deeper and more consistent" than so many of those they influenced.[28]

The collapse of liberal justice, or, more exactly, the discovery that our regime is not informed by a liberalism that guarantees equality of right, constitutes the falling of a "terrifying darkness ... upon modern justice."[29] I have so far employed the traditional language of regimes in discussing Grant's political analysis. Precisely because modern political science erects a set of distinctions that obscure the ultimate authority of the political – church and state, politics and economics, private and public – and disguises the political intention realized in the very making of these distinctions, the traditional political science of regimes seemed better suited to an examination of Grant's analysis. Finally, however, it must also be doubted whether traditional political science is fully able to express the character of our present darkness.

Though the political science of regimes always maintained that "there is everywhere one regime that is best by nature" the realization of the best regime remained for it a matter for prayer; in fact, that political science looked to the continued existence of a number of conflicting claims to rule reflecting a variety of notions as to how men should live. If it sought to ameliorate the conflict among these claims and even to urge a reconciliation within which human excellence might be advanced, it did not look to a theoretical restructuring of the political community. Thus even if we ignore its ironic character, Socrates' proposal that philosophers should rule preserved the difference between philosophic and political activity. If the political problem might be largely solved by the rule of those who live in full awareness of the difference between what is and what seems to be, it remains the case that the basis of the political community is opinion. For traditional political science the best political order is not a community whose members live in the light of a complete theoretical account of the whole; it is rather an order within which the contemplation of the whole (by a few) may occur without endangering that opinion. To the extent that ancient political philosophy shook the loyalty of some men to the city of their birth, it did so on behalf of an activity beyond politics; that activity, contemplation, was indeed the refutation or antidote to tyranny and imperialism.[30]

The crisis Grant explores cannot be understood simply as the corruption of one particular regime in traditional terms because of the universal and theoretical character of the principle that animates our world. This principle has pointed towards a universal and homogeneous state that actualizes what is held to be the true theoretical account of the whole and of man's relation to that whole. If liberty, or better freedom, has seemed to name this principle, the movement towards its realization in a universal order has been welcomed by most, for that freedom has been understood within a persisting commitment to justice. It has for this reason been supposed that the freedom of each will entail the freedom of all in this new order. Now, however, as the universal and homogeneous order is increasingly actualized while the security and content of justice become increasingly questionable we are forced to rethink the character of that principle upon which this order is based. Grant's analysis of modernity and of the failure of liberal justice within the technological regime leads us finally to the imperative task of laying bare the identity of that "primal affirmation" which was at once the foundation of technology and contractual liberalism.

George Grant And The Terrifying Darkness
by William Christian

Like poor Queen Anne western civilization has been a long time a-dying. It is by no means an easy task to understand why its obituary has been written so many times by serious philosophers, historians and social critics. Yet this phenomenon is by no means irrelevant to a discussion of the thought of George Grant, since so much of his writings is coloured by a tone of mournful regret at what has passed and at what might yet be lost.

One powerful theme that has run throughout western reflection, at times dominant and at other times recessive, has been the notion that there are forces active in the world that are leading remorselessly to deterioration and decline. Sometimes this decay is attributed to powers external to the human personality or human mind, such as Providence or Fortune; at other times it is attributed to the unforeseen outcome of the choices made by a multitude of men. The cyclical theories of social and historical change advanced in the writings of Plato and of certain Roman poets among the Ancients, and in the speculations of Machiavelli and Vico among the Moderns, were capable of encouraging a gloomy cast of mind. Christian eschatology, with its apocalytic vision, has also contributed a sense of despair about the state of the world. In Marxism a similar spirit prevailed which heightened awareness of the wickedness of present social arrangements and pointed to a further deterioration in the moral and physical condition of men before they could attain secular salvation through revolutionary regeneration.

Now it is true that none of these doctrines needs breed any particular emotional response. A cyclical theory of history, like a religious theory of predestination or of the transmigration of souls, is just as compatible with a quiet, even contented acceptance of the unfolding of history or of the Divine Plan, as it is with lamentations or the determination to go down, as down we must, with guns blazing and flags flying. Christians and Marxists have differed, each among themselves, on the vexing question of whether deterioration is a good because good will flow from it, or whether it is an evil which men should struggle as best they can to arrest. A part of the explanation of why this should be so, I suspect, involves nothing more profound than a recognition that the capacity for hope is not spread uniformly throughout mankind.

Since the eighteenth century, concern for the state of western civilization has taken on an increasing urgency in those writers who have attended to it. Burke felt it necessary to shatter the easy optimism of the age of progress and warned that the revolution in France had unleashed forces and given currency to ideas that looked certain to destroy both the Christianity and the classical humanism that were the two pillars of his civilization. Although he was willing to risk kicking against the pricks in hope that the triumph of evil was not providentially ordained, he held grave doubts whether good men would rally to prevent even that part of the evil that was remediable. These doubts were temporarily laid to rest by the success of British and Allied arms against the Napoleonic armies, and the succeeding era of peace and increasing prosperity, though Coleridge, Carlyle and Arnold in England and de Maistre and de Tocqueville in France continued to nag.

Such worries were never completely eradicated. Even so fundamentally an optimistic writer as John Stuart Mill thought it necessary to defend liberty directly by polemic and indirectly by such procedural devices as plural voting to forestall that deterioration in the standards of civilization he thought likely to accompany the rise of an unrestrained democracy. But it was in the German-speaking world of Jacob Burckhardt and Nietzsche that the dread developed with an increased intensity and urgency. In the twentieth century it was again left to the German speaking world, this time in the person of Martin Heidegger to raise the question of the adequacy of the metaphysical presuppositions upon which western civilization was grounded, though his philosophical complexity and obscurity, and his temporary and philosophically problematic association with National Socialism, did much to delay the impact of his arguments in the English-speaking world. These last two thinkers, Nietzsche and Heidegger, have been Grant's acknowledged precursors in the exploration of previously uncharted territories of thought. He has followed their footprints in the snow without approving of what they have found, or of how they intended to exploit their discoveries. He has been like a disgruntled tourist, fascinated by their skill as guides, yet repelled by what they offer on view.

With the twentieth century, the pace of concerned care has quickened. Thus Harold Innis: "The twentieth century has been notable in the concern with studies of civilizations. Spengler, Toynbee, Kroeber, Sorokin, and others have produced works, designed to throw light on the causes of the rise and decline of civilizations, which have reflected an intense interest in the possible future of our own civilization." It would be easy to speculate on the causes of this phenomenon. Two world wars, a great depression, the success of the Bolshevik revolution in Russia, the rise of the European dictators and the widespread appeal of National Socialism and fascism, and later the cold war and the atomic and hydrogen bombs – surely all these, singly or severally would give any reflective man cause for thought and an intimation of impending doom. Yet this answer is far too simple, since for all the prophets of disaster there have been many who have confidently expressed a hope for a happier tomorrow, and many, many, others, intellectuals and ordinary men and women alike, who have seen no cause to allow a public distress to invade their apparent private happinesses.

From its position of marginality, first to the British Empire, and then to the American, Canada has produced a number of eminent thinkers who have avoided the pull of either empire and have exploited Canada's position as a European civilization in North America. I am thinking here of Charles Cochrane, Harold Innis, Northrop Frye, Marshall McLuhan, Brough Macpherson and, of course, George Grant. However diverse their views these thinkers have one thing in common. They have brought to their work a deep and abiding interest in the standards of western civilization and have devoted their intellectual lives to the understanding and the defence of the values they saw embedded therein. It is, to be sure, the thought of George Grant that is the subject of this paper, but it is important to note at the outset that he shares with others of his distinguished fellow countrymen the obvious belief that to be Canadian is not necessarily to be parochial, and that to be Canadian in the highest sense is to be aware of the extent to which Canada is a fragment of a much larger, much older, and much more significant communion.

It is important to put George Grant's writings into this perspective. He shares with the European writers whom I have mentioned a deep dedication to the understanding, preservation and improvement of a cultural tradition of great power and antiquity; and he joins with these other Canadian thinkers in avoiding narrow partiality or concentration on the merely transitory. Yet more than any of these thinkers his work is invoked in topical political controversy. *Lament for a Nation* (1965), Grant's most popular and best-known work, is perhaps most directly responsible for this, but his appearances on television and radio, as well as his contributions to newspapers and magazines, have played a part.

The view that I am at pains to neutralize here is the notion that Grant is in any commonly understood sense a Canadian nationalist, or that his thought about the United States is primarily coloured by emotional dislike. Throughout his work he has developed and reiterated several broad themes of specific interest to Canadians, but of an importance to all who want to enhance the fundamental health of western civilization. To this end I propose to look first at *Lament for a Nation* and argue that this work was an introduction to philosophical speculation addressed to those who were not philosophers, but citizens. I shall then examine Grant's Wood Lectures as a philosophical statement addressed to those whose primary loyalty is not to their state.

Lament for a Nation was a philosophical work enclosed (or even confined) in the form of a topical polemic. The self-conscious casting of his reflections in the poetic form of a lament involved an early awareness of the difficulties of his task of elucidation and of education. As even the superficial reader of Plato's dialogues knows, the beginning and end of a philosophical investigation are not identical, either in details or in the character of the thought. The account of justice that was written down "most carefully and most beautifully in 'the Republic' of Plato"[1] was not a straightforward or didactic account, but rather a bringing to truth by means of dialectic. Plato's account begins with conventions and platitudes (justice is giving each man his due, justice is helping friends and hurting enemies) and then moves on from these partial expressions to give a complex account of the soul's growth to completeness and harmony. It is the character of *Lament for a Nation* to proceed in the same way, beginning with the conventionalities and platitudes of Canadian political and social life, and moving on from there to show the inadequacy and incoherence of common understanding.

The rhetorician, the conjuror with words, has to take his audience as he finds them. Men are most likely to be persuaded or moved to action if a writer or speaker appears to take their beliefs as truths. The philosopher who wants no truck with the ignorant is likely to purchase his purity at the price of obscurity. Grant is well aware of the necessity of appealing at first to sentiment and prejudice, and it is by so doing that he starts his readers on their progress. But it is not to all men that the philosopher can make his appeal; he cannot convince men who refuse to listen. In the present case it is only the man who loves his country and who senses intuitively, as a citizen, that something great and beautiful would be lost in the destruction of his nation, who will be attentive. Such men are at least potentially capable of beginning the ascent toward truth, though it is most likely that many will fall along the way, at best attaining more salutary prejudices.

This attitude to philosophy, as should be obvious, does not stem from egalitarian social or political assumptions. Grant implicitly suggests that those who do not feel the loss of their native land as they would the death of a father or friend are lost to philosophy. And by no means all men, even among those with questing souls, possess the required intellectual capacities or moral character to develop in a philosophic manner. For these a fiction, or noble lie, the kind that poets tell, however badly, is required; for me, the surface teaching of *Lament for a Nation*, is just this kind of gentlemanly myth. It teaches us that in losing our country we will have lost something of real importance, but it does not clarify the nature of the loss, nor does it reveal to us why this loss merits a passionate expression of grief.

Such a reading of Grant's *Lament* presupposes that in the slow unfolding of his argument Grant practices two other classical virtues — irony, the art of indirect speech, and prudence, the art of strategic silence. The very use of these techniques, even without a consideration of the positive message, would suggest that Grant is no democrat. Let me hasten to add that this does not mean he is not a lover of the people. On the contrary, the whole character of his writing indicates decisively that he is guided by a deep affection for the common man, and this sentiment heightens his dislike of the corporate, bureaucratic and political establishments. He once remarked of John Diefenbaker that he had the most marvellous enemies, that all the worst people were against him; and that the finest aspect of Diefenbaker's public career was the great courage he showed in defying them.

The choice of John Diefenbaker as a protagonist in *Lament* is of central importance. At a superficial level, of course, Grant could do no other if he were to talk about Canadian politics in 1965. But, just as obviously, he need not have talked in exactly the way he did. He could have retreated to a discussion of trends and social forces; he could have talked in the language of political science, economics and sociology. A discussion couched in such terms, however, would not have disclosed the most illuminating feature about John Diefenbaker: namely, that he was a great lover of his country, but was a notable failure in protecting the thing that he loved. Passion without philosophy, Grant seems to say, is futile, and may even be dangerous if it provokes powerful enemies into acting more swiftly and more vigorously than they otherwise might have done. If prudence in speech is a virtue for philosophers, prudence in public life is the leading virtue for politicians.

Diefenbaker's failure, as Grant presents it, was in no sense necessary; at least, the failure of the cause for which Diefenbaker stood was not preordained. University students who have read this book and, I presume, others as well, have often misunderstood it as embodying a deterministic prediction about the disappearance of Canada as a sovereign nation-state, with its consequent political and economic absorption into the United States, following ineluctably from the mysterious operation of forces beyond human control called liberalism and technology. No such suggestion could be further from Grant's mind.

Neither technology nor liberalism are things or forces existing independently of the human mind. Although Grant's way of talking about them is to a trifling extent responsible for such confusion, it is clear that he understands by each of these a set of ideas which has eventually taken hold on the western mind and the western imagination over the past three centuries. Both technology and liberalism were the creation of men who persuaded some of their fellows that these new views represented a superior way of regarding nature and the political community. Succeeding centuries of strident and aggressive propaganda on their behalf — as well, it must be conceded, as a remarkable capacity to deliver the goods as promised — turned the defeat of the old values into a rout and almost completely eradicated even the chance of retaining them in the form of thought. These new ways of approaching the world became so firmly entrenched that they became almost the only acceptable mode of talking about important matters. The unfolding of their inner logic led to certain conclusions, while foreclosing the possibility of others. Technology became the defining characteristic and prejudice of the age, and liberalism took on a particular hue by being rubbed so closely against it.

There is a strange myopia which overcomes many men who contemplate the past, which leads them to see it as a fixed tableau which could not have been other than it was. Much thought is given to explaining, not how things came to be as they are, but how it was necessary that things happened as they did. The consciousness of individual men that they are confronted with a range of choices, some involving unanticipatable imagination whose eventual outcome may surprise them as much as others, is lost to those who see history as the dead record of past happenings, rather than a living attempt to reconstruct the thought of the past.

Now it is my contention that Grant does not fall into this trap, although many of his readers do. For Grant the destruction of the economic, political, cultural and military independence of Canada was not inevitable, but was the consequence of many decisions made by many men who thought what they were doing was good, and who were successful (though not unchallenged) in their attempts to persuade their fellow countrymen. Canadians were steadily convinced of the attractiveness of the vision of life which prevailed in the United States, both by the propaganda of that country itself, and by the argument of Canadians who shared that vision and found it in their interests to spread it. The old order crumbled, yielding its place to the new.

Diefenbaker, Grant shows us, had sensed these developments and had sought to arrest them. His keen sense of past achievements allowed him to understand the attempts of the founders of the Canadian nation to construct on the northern half of the continent, in British North America, a state which repudiated many of the central claims of American liberalism, especially the pretension that there was no good other than private good. In claiming to create a state in which the possibility of a public good superior to the satisfaction of private desire was a political fact, the Fathers of Canadian Confederation had attempted to preserve an echo of an older way of thinking on the new continent. It was this possibility that Diefenbaker tried, and failed, to preserve.

His failure came because too many powerful interests were threatened by the attempt to reduce the entanglement. The intimate relations which Canada had with the United States by the time that Diefenbaker came to office were not the result of any sinister conspiracy, and were in many instances the unanticipated outcome of decisions taken for other, often pressing, reasons. Grant urges us to understand that in all this the nature of the United States as an imperialist empire was of key importance. The pressure created by its expansionist urges was a constant factor which Canadians, ignorant or innocent of the character of the American state, were ill-prepared to counteract. And the constant presence of the enemy at the gate meant that the lapses were critical, and cumulatively, fatal. By the time Diefenbaker came to power, businessmen, civil servants, soldiers and the media substantially agreed that this arrangement was a comfortable one, and drew sustenance from their association with a community that incarnated technological modernity at its most dynamic. Let me repeat that to show how something came about is not to show that it must have been so. The question remains: were we sold a bill of goods? Grant thinks we were.

It was an attempt to explain the reasons for this answer that formed the core of Grant's deepest political meditation to date, "English-speaking Justice," first delivered as the Wood Lectures at Mount Allison University in 1974 and recently revised for publication. It is impossible to explore all the themes touched on in these subtle lectures; but it is important to note at the outset that their character is undeniably both political and philosophical. Here he reiterates a theme that has been a central preoccupation in his writings of at least the last decade, namely "the close relation that there has been between the development of technology and political liberalism." But where his prior writings tend to make the point that there was a connection between these two worlds of ideas which had generally been thought of as separate, his concern now is to indicate their distinctiveness, at least seen in the light of their copenetration. As Grant put it, "By thinking about that relation, I hope to throw light on the nature of both our liberalism and technology."

Grant can confuse his readers in his earlier writings by talking about the relationship between liberalism and technology as if the two were different manifestations of the same spirit working in harness to bring about the ultimate realization of the universal and homogenous state. Now he makes it clear that liberalism "in its generic form is surely something that all decent men accept as good — 'conservatives' included. In so far as the word 'liberalism' is used to describe the belief that political liberty is a central human good, it is difficult for me to consider as sane those who would deny that they are liberals." Although he concedes that "progressivism" might be a better characterization of the political doctrine he criticizes, he holds to the use of "liberalism" to highlight two points. "First, the institutions and ideas of the English-speaking world at their best have been much more than a justification of progress in the mastery of human and non-human nature." And, "secondly, the use of the word 'liberalism' rather than 'progressivism' emphasizes the necessary point that our English-speaking variety is not liberalism itself, but a particular species of it."

The apparent naturalness of the alliance between liberalism and technology which was an article of faith to those involved in the assault on Canadian sovereignty and Canadian culture, Grant now calls into question in an explicit way. In *Lament* he had left the conclusion unmoored, arguing poetically and from tradition. Now he addresses the "practical question," namely "whether a society in which technology must be oriented by cybernetics can maintain the institutions of free politics and the protection by law of the rights of the individual."

Put quite simply, technology has eviscerated liberalism. It has called into question both Protestant Christianity and its philosophical analogue, Kantianism; in so doing it has set liberalism adrift from its anchorage, and has made it the captive of "cybernetics — the technology of the helmsman. ... [t]he development of technology is now increasingly directed towards the mastery of human beings." This development, which was impossible so long as liberalism retained a vision of the nature of the human personality and hence of justice as the good a man was fitted for, points toward a political regime that will grow ever more savage and oppressive as its fundamental conceptions become more deeply ingrained. It will, Grant fears, slowly erode, and eventually sweep away, even the last residual institutional embodiments of the older spirit.

To clarify his argument, Grant takes as his protagonist the most comprehensive modern statement of liberalism, that of John Rawls in his *A Theory of Justice*. This analysis, which comprises roughly one third of the lectures, seeks to show that in spite of Rawls' professed Kantian inspiration, his entire edifice collapses because the structure that is grounded on Kant's good will (*ein guter Wille*) cannot sustain weight when Rawls reduces men to rival calculators. In effect, Grant argues, Rawls still depends on the older Kantian conception, whereas the force of the analytical school of which he is a member has been bent on the destruction of such "supra-scientific metaphysical terms." "His writing is typical of much modern liberal thought in that the word 'person' is brought in mysteriously (one might better say sentimentally) to cover up the inability to state clearly what it is about human beings which makes them worthy of high political respect. Where Kant is clear concerning this, Rawls is not." Rawls' whole construction is a house of cards that collapses with the slightest breeze; and it is subject to the entire gale of modern technology!

If modern English-speaking liberalism is so philosophically insubstantial, how did it then come to dominate the political centre of Western civilization? The answer is ironical. It was just that close association between liberalism and technology which now threatens to prove so destructive to liberalism that allowed its earlier success. "The long ascendancy of English-speaking peoples, in the case of England since Waterloo, and the United States since 1914, was achieved under the rule of various species of bourgeois. ... Those shared conceptions of constitutional liberalism seemed to be at one with technological progress, particularly as this progress was being achieved above all by English-speakers. This unity between progress in liberty and in technology, under English-speaking guidance, was often further guaranteed by being enfolded in such doctrines as the ascent of man." In this swelling confidence lay both good and evil. On the one hand the English-speaking world was insulated "from taking seriously the traditions which proceeded either from Rousseau or from Nietzsche. They were for example saved from such a manifestation of those political philosophies as ideology." But on the other hand, as confidence became false confidence, it prevented the reflection that might have been in time to forestall the present crisis. "To rise above the scholars, Churchill's writings may be taken as an example of this confidence in liberalism which did not need to be thought, even at a late date in that British destiny."

The failure of political liberalism to achieve any substantial philosophical support or corrective was not immediately destructive. The strong traditions of Protestant thought, in a sophisticated form in the

United Kingdom, and in a cruder though still powerful form in the United States, provided a substitute. The staying power of this doctrine is only accountable if we "recognise the dependence of secular liberalism for its moral bite upon the strength of Protestantism in English-speaking societies." Even the Kantianism that was adopted in the English-speaking world rested heavily upon this source.

One further step in the argument remains: why treat the situation as one of crisis? Grant thinks that he has seen an indication that the tradition of humane liberalism has given way at its very heart, in the legal institutions which for so long served as its bastion. In his majority decision in Roe v Wade (410 U.S. 113 (1973)) Mr Justice Blackmun "unwittingly looses the terrible question: has the long tradition of liberal right any support in what human beings in fact are? Is this a question that in the modern era can be truthfully answered in the positive? Or does it hand the cup of poison to our liberalism?"[2] By opening a box of such danger he draws attention to the civilisational contradiction which "arose from the attempt of the articulate to hold together what was given them in modern science with a content of justice that had been developed out of an older account of what is." Here, as in *Time as History*, Grant credits Nietzsche with having thought this contradiction through most clearly and most forcefully, and in the course of his arguments, turning all justice into convention. "The English moralists had not discovered that realm of being we moderns call 'history,' and therefore they did not understand the dominance of historicism over all other statements."

Grant puts the consequences of these developments in such stark terms that I must quote them at length:

> Our situation is rather that the assumptions underlying contractual liberalism and underlying technology both come from the same matrix of modern thought, from which can arise no reason why the justice of liberty is due to all human beings, irrespective of convenience. In so far as the contemporary systems of liberal practice hold onto the content of free and equal justice, it is because they still rely on older sources which are more and more made unthinkable in their very realisation of technology. When contractual liberals hold within their thought remnants of secular-ised Christianity or Judaism, these remnants, if made conscious, must be known as unthinkable in terms of what is given in the modern. How, in modern thought can we find positive answers to the questions: (i) what is it about human beings that makes liberty and equality their due? (ii) why is justice what we are fitted for, when it is not convenient? Why is it our good? The

inability of contractual liberals (or indeed Marxists) to answer these questions is the terrifying darkness which has fallen upon modern justice. We have come then to a crisis in modern English-speaking liberalism in which this terrifying darkness threatens to cancel out all the great modern achievements in thought — quantum physics, the biology of evolutionism, and modern logic — and to turn them into stalking monsters, waiting until we have lost the last strength that our institutional preservations of the older tradition of justice retain.

How is it that we in the English-speaking world might be able to lighten this darkness? Grant's answer is ambiguous. "It is folly simply to return to the ancient account of justice as if the discoveries of the modern science of nature had not been made." But just as much, "It is folly to take the ancient account of justice as simply of antiquarian interest, because without any knowledge of justice as what we are fitted for, we will move into the future with a 'justice' which is terrifying in its potentialities for mad inhumanity of action." Grant's formal conclusion is that "It is improbable that the transcendence of justice over technology will be lived among English-speaking people."

The conclusion here speaks in the same mood as *Lament*. Philosophy clarifies the loss to which *Lament* had pointed, but about which it had remained silent. What is ultimately in peril is nothing so little as the loss of Canadian sovereignty, or the economic subordination of Canada to American interests, important though these topics are to Canadians both as citizens and as men. The philosopher can understand where the citizen can only feel; but the loss in either case is the same: the possibility of establishing a just state has been gravely put at risk by men who believe without question that the subjugation and transformation of all nature, both human and non-human, is the only acceptable public programme. This is the will to power with a vengeance!

I have dealt here with *Lament for a Nation* and with "English-speaking justice" because I believe them to be Grant's two greatest contributions to political reflection. But I have also linked them together because I think that the philosophical depth underlying *Lament* has frequently been ignored or underestimated. There is one final question with which we must deal: how seriously are we to take Grant's negative conclusion?

Like the Canadian thinkers I mentioned earlier in this paper, George Grant displays an abiding love for the achievements of his civilization. But, also like them, and like the great European social theorists, he has not inscribed over the gates of his academy, "abandon all hope, ye who enter here." He speaks in his conclusion of an improbability, not an impossibility. Grant's conclusion is enigmatic. I take him to be uttering a prophecy which he hopes is self-defeating. He is, I believe, offering us a challenge to think together the achievements of modern science and of classical philosophy. Only if he can terrify us enough with the prospects of the impending darkness, will we see the need to struggle to remain in the light. By accepting this challenge I think that we bear witness to the desire we share with George Grant not to let pass away through inadvertence the noble achievements in thought of which we are the inheritors, and which, without such a gadfly, we might be beast enough to lose.

The Uses of Philosophy in George Grant
by Laurence Lampert

From the beginning George Grant has been a serious writer, a writer who seeks to make a difference. Although he was for many years a professional philosopher, his work is not a professional exercise and it is philosophy in a sense that would exclude it from most professional philosophy journals. In four slim volumes[1] Grant has offered the Canadian public his reflections on the destiny of modern man. As philosophy these reflections aim not at novelty but at truth and clarity. Hegel has said that philosophy must beware of wishing to be edifying and we can translate this into our own idiom by saying that philosophy must beware of wishing to be relevant. While Grant's work never compromises philosophy by pursuing such a wish, it never fails to be relevant and, who knows, perhaps even edifying. On these matters Grant has learned much from classical Greek philosophers.

For the Greeks, philosophy was a "theoretical" activity, that is to say, it was *theoria* (lit. a looking at), seeing in an intellectual vision, seeing and knowing the way things are through the way they seem to be. It was not "theoretical" in our sense of being opposed to the practical. Rather, as *theoria* philosophy was concerned with the truth of things as revealed and grasped in the array of particulars. Philosophy as *theoria* always had its setting in the city with its conflicting teachings and competing aspirations. Philosophy had a diagnostic purpose in the literal sense of "knowing through," it had a teaching purpose even where the things that needed to be learned could not directly be taught, and it had a healing purpose in holding out the pursuit of wisdom as a search for excellence or virtue.

Philosophy understood in this classical sense remains intact throughout Grant's four books. For Grant, genuine philosophy has always been the pursuit of wisdom and that is necessarily a social activity. It arises in society and serves the purpose of contributing to the well-being of society. It is a peculiar calling reserved for contemplative natures but benefiting the whole in the fruits of reflection. Like the Greek philosophers who knew how cities differed and how their differences affected their inhabitants, Grant has consistently reflected on the particularities of setting; he has tried to understand what it means to be a Canadian in the modern world. This entails knowing something about both Canada and the modern world. His work is addressed directly to Canadians. Again like the Greeks, Grant recognizes that philosophy is not composed of a series of independent fields — metaphysics, ethics, logic, etc. — but rather is a comprehensive rational contemplation of the nature of things with a view to determining the good life for man. As such it is forbidden the luxury of technical specialization. In these ways, as a diagnostic, teaching and healing enterprise, philosophy has been viewed consistently throughout Grant's work.

Still, there have been significant changes in Grant's understanding of the specific uses of philosophy. The most evident changes have concerned what philosophy can do in the world and for it; and, because philosophy is apparently seen to be capable of less and less, these changes have been taken to be a growth in pessimism on Grant's part. The cover blurb on the paperback edition of *Technology and Empire* contains the following phrase: "its pessimism is reasoned and all but complete." Is this an adequate basis for understanding the changes in Grant's view of philosophy? As Grant himself has observed,[2] the word "pessimism," and its contrary, "optimism," entered the language in connection with Leibniz's view of the nature of things. Thus the *Oxford English Dictionary* gives as the first definition of optimism:

> A name given to the doctrine propounded by Leibniz, in his
> *Théodicée* (1710), that the actual world is "the best of all possible
> worlds," being chosen by the Creator out of all the possible worlds
> which were present in his thoughts as that in which the most good
> could be obtained at the cost of the least evil. Also applied [subse-
> quently] to the doctrines of earlier or later thinkers to a like effect.

Optimism in this sense does not refer to a state of mind, but to the state of things, the way things as a whole are; namely, in being at all they are in their optimal condition. Hence pessimism, which came into use as the contrary of optimism, is defined as: "The worst condition or degree possible or conceivable; the state of greatest deterioration" (OED). To hold either of these positions, to be an optimist or a pessimist, is to be committed to a doctrine about the nature of things; it is not to be predisposed to some particular disposition or feeling.

In this original and by now obsolete sense of the term Grant is no pessimist. So far is Grant from a view of cosmic malevolence that he maintains that the totality, or what rules the totality, is not even indifferent. In the obsolete sense, he is something of an optimist; but not one who thinks that things are getting better and better, rather, one who thinks that the nature of things is conducive to human excellence. Grant's changing views of the uses of philosophy do not indicate a growing pessimism but they do indicate Grant's judgment that the course of events in the modern world is increasingly disastrous to mankind in the sense of being increasingly detrimental to human excellence.

The changes in Grant's view of the uses of philosophy have to be understood as other than a growth in pessimism. In this paper I intend to elucidate these changes.

I

On a number of retrospective occasions Grant has retreated from positions that he has come to regard as erroneous. These occasions afford direct access to his changing views on the uses of philosophy. The clearest example of this is the second edition of *Philosophy in the Mass Age* whose new Introduction (1966) retracts and renounces the alleged progressivism of the book with such earnestness that the reader might suppose that he holds in his hand a progressivist tract. While the book is nothing of the sort it does contain expressions of faith in progress. For instance, on page 7 Grant judges that we cannot turn backward to old systems of meaning; such systems cannot be revived by philosophy or by anything else. Philosophy's task is a progressive, even redemptive one. On page 110 Grant envisages a sort of rethink tank in which philosophers join together to consider the destiny of man. As the product of this rethinking Grant anticipates a massive synthesis of the valuable things of ancients and moderns, constructed by comprehensive philosophers and instituted by their teaching. In this vision there is history to be made and thinkers to make it and we will all benefit from this "next stage" of the human spirit.[3]

Certainly in this profound sense the book *is* more of the progressive, and hence the retraction of the Introduction is fitting. Nevertheless, the book is also a thorough indictment of the modern project as characterized by the progressivism of Marxists and Americans. Grant repudiates progress in the ordinary sense[4] and seeks a yet-to-be-formulated answer to this "immensely difficult question":

> The question thoughtful people must ask themselves is whether the progressive spirit is going to hold within itself any conception of spiritual law and freedom; or whether our history-making spirit will degenerate into a rudderless desire for domination on the part of our elites, and aimless pleasure seeking among the masses. Can the achievements of the age of progress be placed at the service of a human freedom which finds itself completed and not denied by a spiritual order?[5]

The book hopes for an affirmative answer and prepares the way for it by clarifying the nature of ancient and modern and seeking the framework for that which it concerns us to know.[6] But in the Introduction Grant judges his hopefulness to have been unwarranted. The unwarranted hope is not that there *exists* that something that it concerns us to know — Grant never repudiates that, not in this book, not elsewhere — rather, the unwarranted hope is that that something lies ahead of us as a future possibility that we may come to know, if not shortly, then eventually.

In *Philosophy* the philosophic task of our time had been to discover and institute the truth that reconciles permanence and time, certainty and change. But this task of philosophical enlightenment and practice is abandoned in the Introduction to the second edition in favour of a much more modest mining of the previously scorned past.[7] Grant mentions specifically Greek philosophy and Plato and Aristotle as worthy of such inquiry[8] and affirms his new conviction that they contain more wisdom than the modern. In the Introduction the role of philosophy is still taken as formative and the task of philosophy is still to understand and teach. It is the content of that which is to be taught that has changed dramatically.

The Introduction simply states these new convictions about the use of philosophy; they are put into practice directly in an essay written in 1964, "Religion and the State." In this essay Grant takes his stand with the classical wisdom and on that ground suggests some practical measures concerning religion in the public schools. The philosopher here sets forth his views explicitly and argues their merits in a public forum *(Queen's Quarterly)*. Grant maintains that it is the philosopher's job "to argue general principles,"[9] to clarify for the public as a whole just what the issues are and how they are to be resolved. The philosopher rises above the impassioned pleading of opposing views in order to permit the light of reason to decide the issue. The result in this case is a masterful essay.

But, in a preface to this essay as reprinted in *Technology and Empire* (1969), Grant retrospectively ridicules his own "virtuous proposals." On this second retrospective occasion, however, Grant does not repudiate the contents of his recommendations, as he had in the Introduction to *Philosophy in the Mass Age*. This time the "folly" lay not in the truths advanced but in the act of advancing them — he had hoped they could have made some difference in policy; he had not yet realized that such classical "conservatism" could have no public appeal.[10] This is not a moral judgement on those who failed to listen; it is a philosopher's judgment on what can be heard. As *proposals* Grant judges his suggestions to have been pointless; there is a distinction that has to be observed between what may be true and what may be told, and with this distinction the philosophical task becomes more complex; or to put it another way, the task becomes Socratic. There are truths to be learned but those truths cannot simply be taught.

The point here turns on a classical or "Platonic" distinction between the public "truths" and the genuine truths that transcend them. The public "truths" are matters of opinion or belief while genuine truth is a matter of knowledge. This distinction is the basis of Plato's distinction between the Sophist as the clever flatterer of the public (or as the flatterer of the spirit of the age to express it in a modern, historical way) and the philosopher as the wise man who seeks the truth in the public setting. Furthermore, as Plato argues in the *Republic*, the public cannot look with favour on philosophy (493e-494a) because philosophy necessarily calls the public "truths" into question and subverts them by holding forth a higher ideal. Hence it appears that philosophers are either useless (to the spirit of the age) or disreputable (having become useful, having become Sophists) (487a-494b). Given this sobering conviction about the setting it occupies, philosophy must always take cognizance of how it is being heard if it is to maintain its frail hope of making some difference.

In Grant's retrospective assessment, "Religion and the State" is flawed because it failed to appreciate this distinction between what is true and what can be heard. Grant's reflection on that failure heralds his new understanding of the philosophical task, namely, the analysis of the public world which we all share and in the midst of which the truth must be grasped if it is to be grasped at all. In Grant's view the public truths of the modern world obscure the truths that transcend it. This, however, is a trait the modern world shares with every public world; more seriously, the truths of *this* public tend to obliterate the very possibility of truths that transcend it. This is something distinctive about the modern world. Hence this public has to be understood because of the danger it represents. What is involved here is not just a shift in strategy on Grant's part; it is not just a determination to say the same things more clearly but in a different way. The question concerns the nature of the modern world as such and how it has framed our ways of thinking and being so as to exclude all other ways of thinking. The task of philosophy then is certainly no longer the making of history with new truths, nor is it the explicit teaching of the ancient truths; it is rather the clarification of the public things, the modern world.

That task of analysis is brilliantly undertaken in Grant's later works and nowhere more energetically than in *Lament for a Nation*. The main argument of that book concerns the *necessity* of Canada's demise as a nation.[11] (Unfortunately that argument is frequently obscured by the force of the polemic, for the polemic pulls in quite a different direction from the main argument; namely, to the affixing of responsibility or blame.) That necessary demise follows from the nature of the modern world, a world committed to an ideology of progressivism, a science of the conquest of nature and a politics of the universal and homogeneous state. So constituted the modern necessarily overthrows or incorporates the national and particular, permitting only that which is consistent with its purpose.

For Grant, philosophy can offer no direct resistance to this public religion; on this he now agrees with Hegel: philosophy comes too late to tell the world what it ought to be. But Grant agrees for a quite unHegelian reason: the world is *not* necessarily what it ought to be. While the necessity of Canada's demise is clear, the goodness of that demise is not; on this Grant opposes Hegel: it is not the philosopher's job to reconcile us to necessity, for historical necessity is not equated to goodness. For Grant, there is no apparent rose in the cross of *this* present. But while philosophy cannot reconcile us to the present it may alienate us from it — that at least is Grant's hope.

Philosophy cannot refute the modern directly and Grant makes no attempt in *Lament* to ground his lament on arguments about the nature of things. Grant bases his lament on tradition, on a sense of "one's own." The matter at issue is clearly what the classical philosophers understood as the most important philosophical issue: the relationship between the public things and truth, between "one's own" and those intrinsically valuable matters that make human excellence possible. It is the modern as such that is increasingly becoming "one's own" in present-day Canada and Grant seeks to clarify the nature of the modern in *Lament* in order to understand just how far it excludes human excellence. In an essay that may be regarded as a sequel to *Lament*, "Canadian Fate and Imperialism," Grant further pursues this central issue — and in doing so considerably clarifies his argument about the necessity of Canada's demise.

> In this era when the homogenising power of technology is almost unlimited, I do regret the disappearance of indigenous traditions, including my own. It is true that no particularism can adequately incarnate the good. But is it not also true that only through some particular roots, however partial, can human beings first grasp what is good and it is the juice of such roots which for most men sustain their partaking in a more universal good?[12]

This admirable statement occurs in the midst of an otherwise murky complaint about critics who explain away Grant's critique of the modern as a function of his personal and psychological preferences.[13] Grant's point against any such explaining away is that while the preferences may be present (and trigger the passion) they are irrelevant to the argument. The argument concerning the relationship between "one's own" and the good itself is not based simply on preferences and cannot be countered on those grounds.

Only through some set of particulars or other can one glimpse or embrace the good.

> In human life there must always be place for love of the good and love of one's own. Love of the good is man's highest end, but it is of the nature of things that we come to know and to love what is good by first meeting it in that which is our own — this particular body, this family, these friends, this woman, this part of the world, this set of traditions, this country, this civilization.[14]

But not all forms of the particular serve equally well as a means for apprehending the good; the particular nature of "one's own" may facilitate excellence or it may inhibit it, or, in the extreme case, it may exclude it. By a benevolent accident of birth Canada is "our own" and Grant attempts to understand just what "one's own" is in this particular case. Grant here enters a most worthwhile debate that began (and continues) among Canadian historians and that has become more widely discussed in recent years.[15] The debate concerns the terms of Canada's rise to nationhood and the forms of imperialism it has had to encounter on the way to achieving or preserving some national identity or particularity. Grant's analysis adds depth and dimension to the historical discussion.

Grant holds that in order to understand Canada's particularity it is necessary to understand Canada's past in relationship to both the United States and Britain. That means appreciating the commitment of Canada's founding statesmen to a form of "public order and common good" that was opposed to American "individualism"; that commitment found its philosophical roots in British conservatism.[16] Grant sees the United States as the embodiment of the modern understanding of man's destiny and it is the encroachment of that *understanding* that has always threatened Canada's existence. Canada was aided in preserving the aims of its founders by the heritage of British conservatism and by the practical relationships with Britain that helped to keep Canada's interests from being wholly identified with American ones. But Britain's abandonment of her conservative heritage and her acceptance of a subsidiary role in the American empire have severed these lines of defence for Canada.[17]

Apart from historical considerations like these Grant has had little to say on "Canadian Identity." It is not difficult to understand why. For any such identity to be significant it must oppose the encroachments of the modern, for the modern is in its essence a demand for homogeneity and universality in essentials. Because Canada cannot succeed in resisting these encroachments, considerations of Canada's identity must take the form of a lament for "the romanticism of the original dream."[18] Grant's lament for Canada is based on the conviction that its particular traditions made excellence possible but that the modern world to which it increasingly succumbs excludes excellence. But laments based on abandoned traditions are not enough and Grant's philosophical efforts quite naturally aim at understanding the modern as such. In the face of the question of our common fate as modern men the question of Canada's particularity becomes secondary, though by no means unimportant.[19] Grant remains concerned with Canada as "one's own" but that very concern requires the investigation of the modern which is increasingly, if not wholly, "one's own" in contemporary Canada. "Canadian Fate and Imperialism" concerns the dilemma one faces when the conviction arises that "one's own" (the modern) is in conflict with the good.[20]

In *Lament for a Nation* and "Canadian Fate and Imperialism" Grant suggests that the universal and homogeneous state of modern Western aspiration is in fact a tyranny. Philosophy as a clarification of the public things is the clarification of a disaster. And philosophy cannot aim to transcend this disaster by making history with new truths, nor can it assuage the disaster by the direct teaching of old truths.

II

In the works considered so far philosophy is used to clarify the public things primarily in terms of political and moral issues. But while political and moral philosophy remain important they are supplanted in later works by a concern with an apparently more extensive and pervasive aspect of modernity. Another passage from "Canadian Fate and Imperialism" indicates this new dimension: "Man cannot help but imitate in action his vision of the nature of things."[21] What is the vision of the nature of things that impels the actions of modern man? The philosopher's task here is to understand in detail just how modern man understands being; it is to inquire into metaphysical matters that Grant "the incipient political philosopher" seemed, in 1964, to hesitate over.[22] Although it is curiously unacknowledged by Grant, his undertaking of this monumental task has been aided greatly by Martin Heidegger.

While there are very few direct references to Heidegger in Grant's work,[23] his influence is apparent in Grant's reflections on language, on thinking, on the nature of technology, on the role of the thinker, and on many other topics. And the influence of Heidegger is clearly evident in the shift in Grant's way of interpreting the modern. No longer is the modern simply a way of thinking about time and nature that differs from the classical. It is that, but more pervasively and overwhelmingly it is a way of being, and consequently a way of taking beings. It is a particular vision of the nature of things, of the being of beings, and as such it is much more than simply a matter of intellectual assent to a new set of propositions about man and world. It is an unquestioned predisposition to a new form of what Heidegger calls the "presencing" of things. Heidegger maintains that the gradual and inexorable development of this new way of thinking and being can be read clearly in our greatest philosophers, Descartes, Kant, Hegel, Nietzsche. And by now the modern has come to seem natural and obvious because it is second nature to us; all our observing confirms it; it is at the deepest level "our own" although it is rarely grasped overtly. Heidegger's exemplary work in clarifying the hidden and historical sense of being presupposed but unthought by contemporary man is effectively utilized by Grant, especially in *Time as History* and in the first and last essays of *Technology and Empire*. Grant has performed the difficult task of fitting Heidegger's thought into our idiom — well, not *exactly* our idiom, for the notions represented are hardly idiomatic and Grant's books still have a strange ring to them. But Grant has avoided the technical jargon of Heidegger's translators and commentators and his utilization of Heidegger's thinking indicates his sensitivity to the English language and what it evokes.[24]

It should be added immediately that for all of this Grant is still no Heideggerian. To mention only the three most important matters: regarding history, Grant is not committed to the historicity of being itself; regarding the philosophical task, he is not committed to awaiting a new beginning in man's way of taking being; regarding the ancients, he is not committed to the view that Plato and Aristotle are the forerunners of our present technological way of taking the being of beings. Nevertheless, from Heidegger Grant has learned a new understanding of the depth of the modern as can be seen in Grant's (Heidegger's) interpretation of Nietzsche as the modern in clearest expression.

> [Nietzsche] lays bare the fate of technical man, not as an object held in front of us, but as that in which our very selves are involved in the proofs of the science which lays it bare. In thinking the modern project, he did not turn away from it. ... In his work, the themes that must be thought in thinking time as history are raised to a beautiful explicitness: the mastery of human and non-human nature in experimental science and technique, the primacy of the will, man as the creator of his own values, the finality of becoming, the assertion that potentiality is higher than actuality, that motion is nobler than rest, that dynamism rather than peace is the height.[25]

In *Time as History* (the title indicates one of the distinctive marks of the modern: time *not* taken as the moving image of eternity) Grant analyzes the public truths of the contemporary world as represented by Nietzsche. The central part of Grant's book is a finely executed account of Nietzsche as the thinker of our time which utilizes to good advantage the insights set forth in elaborate detail in Heidegger's two volume *Nietzsche*. Grant emphasizes two points in particular. First, in an age of apparent relativism, tolerance and pluralism there are in fact dogmas and certainties that we uniformly and automatically assent to by our very way of being. Such absolutes constitute the public religion of our age even though they are infrequently recognized.[26] Second, Grant argues that Nietzsche's central doctrines, such as will to power, nihilism and eternal recurrence, give us insight into these absolutes. Whatever their status as descriptions of man as such, they are not mistaken about *modern* man and his most intimate inclinations. They are descriptions of the way modern man takes himself and his world; Nietzsche's thought is the present metaphysically displayed. "Nietzsche's words raise to an intensely full light of explicitness what it is to live in this era. He articulates what it is to have inherited existence as a present member of western history."[27]

But Grant's book does not end with the exposition of Nietzsche. Appended as a final chapter is a brief refusal. It is not an argument or, *per impossibile*, a refutation; it is quite simply and directly a refusal, a NO to Nietzsche and the modern world he so brilliantly represents. While Grant disagrees profoundly with Nietzsche, he presents no program as an alternative to Nietzsche's position, nor does he elaborate the grounds on which his refusal is based. Presumably the blame for these apparent deficiencies can be laid to the nature of the modern world, to the meanings we are "enfolded in," or "enclosed by." That is, the modern as public ideology is taken by Grant to be a tyranny too thorough to allow a response to be heard, too all-explaining not to explain (away) any objections to its character. Grant is usually careful to give the modern its due even while attempting to say no to it.[28] But he is most sensitive to the power of our public truths to prejudge any propositions contrary to themselves. We all have a natural propensity to embrace the faith of our time and its peculiar formulations of the possibility of human greatness. We are all too educated in its virtues not to have a feel for their rightness.

The nature of language is partly responsible for this state of affairs. Following Heidegger, Grant maintains that language permits the being of beings to disclose itself only in some particular fashion or other.

> It is clear that human beings take much of what they are and what their world is through the way that words bring forth that world and themselves to themselves. ... The very liberation through language takes place by the moulding of particular forms. Like food, language not only makes human existence possible, but can also confine it. It is, therefore, useful to think about those parts of our language which particularly express our civilization, and to judge just how these key words have come to determine our apprehension of what is.[29]

The available language for moderns permits only that disclosure in which being is taken as will. Any understanding of the nature of things which is other than the one that prevails must of necessity sound strange or, even worse, anachronistic. This is the reason for Grant's regular apologies for using such terms as fate,[30] necessity,[31] excellence,[32] in a sense that has become unfamiliar or archaic.

In such a setting a refusal must be carefully presented. The gist of Grant's refusal of the modern is this: we are not fit for it. The truth of the modern world is untrue to man; that is to say, unnatural to human nature, for man *has* a timeless nature. This is not demonstrated; presumably no demonstration is possible. But Grant tries to make clear the strategy of refusal: he is not "inoculating" against the modern project nor is he refuting it. His point is this: the thinness and deficiency of the modern must become apparent from within, and this is so even in its noblest form, in Nietzsche. Then, out of dismay at the inadequacy of "one's own," the rights of the tradition to a hearing may be recognized. Grant's confidence is in the modern world's capacity to dissatisfy, to be at bottom unacceptable. That is the extent of the philosophical hope as expressed here; namely that the poverty of the opinions of the public world will become apparent. The philosopher's single task is to facilitate this disillusionment with the public truths in order that the search for a timeless wisdom will be initiated.

Grant's hopes are given a somewhat firmer expression in the last essay of *Technology and Empire*, "A Platitude" — the title indicates how fragile and clichéd Grant recognizes his proposals to be; we have heard them all before and they are boring. Once again, Grant's hopes are expressed following a statement of the limitation of the available language. And yet, in the face of the almost insurmountable difficulty of what language permits, the hope is expressed that along with what the modern world reveals about man and beings it will elicit "intimations of deprival." Grant maintains that the precise content of what we are deprived of is "unthinkable in the public terms"; hence he has no hope that the public world is going to change through any urging on his part — or on the part of any other philosopher. The modern world is inexorable in its movement towards an all-encompassing technical mastery. The hope so hesitantly expressed seems to be (to continue the contrast with Nietzsche) that Nietzsche is wrong to maintain that man is the as yet undetermined animal. For Grant there is that which belongs to man as man; man has an essential nature, a trans-historic nature, a nature that resists infinite manipulation by technique, a nature that will revolt against being taken as infinitely malleable and infinitely free. Furthermore, the hope is expressed that this revolt will consist of a recalling or remembrance of the permanently valuable things resident in the tradition that the modern must despise, or, worse, celebrate as primitive curiosities, as so many stages on the way to the very best, that is to say, ourselves.

It is clear that from his very few remarks on remembering[33] that Grant's remembering is *essentially* different from Nietzsche's praise of remembrance, his espousal of the "antiquarian" as one of the possible uses of history (in *The Use and Abuse of History*). The contrast is instructive. In Nietzsche's account – a beautiful and evocative account – such a use of history places it purely and simply at the disposal of man in the present. The aim is not to preserve the valuable things; the aim is, by the activity of preserving, to nurture something noble in mankind in the present. What is preserved and how it is preserved are irrelevant; only the creative act of ennobling is important. Furthermore, there is nothing essential about preserving as such; for human dispositions other than the "antiquarian," for men with an other than "conservative and reverent nature," the past can just as well be put to use by being criticized and condemned or by being culled for useful models of action. Only certain kinds of men find it valuable to revere the past and Nietzsche condescendingly finds such revering appropriate to "the less gifted races."[34]

Grant apparently maintains that the past contains a particular set of valuable things and that it is human to preserve them. Preserving is not an optional mode that may or may not contribute to man in the present; nor are the things preserved arbitrary. Grant's hope is that the intimations of deprival arising from the nature of the modern world will engender the quite unmodern task of reverent remembering of the valuable things. That is the platitude.

III

In the face of Grant's analysis and hopes one cannot escape a sense of dissatisfaction. It is a dissatisfaction familiar to the readers of Plato's Socratic dialogues. Socrates can make his contemporaries look foolish in their commitments but what does *he* stand for? What is *his* program? If piety is none of the things Euthyphro says it is then what is it? Socrates' silence seems to indict him. Grant has undertaken the immensely difficult task of thinking through *his* contemporaries' commitments. There are two matters (at least) concerning which one feels an initial dissatisfaction. The first is the matter of the verification of the analysis of the modern age. With Socrates, of course, we have a series of arguments whose validity and force can be judged directly. With Grant however we have a description of a state of affairs, not simply a series of arguments subject to the rules of logic. Grant does not presume to be able to prove his description in any narrow sense of proof, and indeed it does not admit of proof. The description of a state of affairs has to carry its own verification; that it *is* a description (that it truly describes) cannot be proven (or disproven[35]) by anything but more description. Beyond indicating the nature of the problem involved here I can of course make no attempt to settle the matter in this paper. This issue is the heart of Grant's philosophical enterprise and it amounts to an invitation to think through the claims set forth.

It is the second matter of dissatisfaction that I will consider, namely, what are the grounds of Grant's platitudinous hopes? Or to put it another way: Why *isn't* Grant a pessimist? Grant regularly disclaims any authority to present the grounds of his hopes adequately.[36] While some grounds of certainty must be present for such hopes to be held, Grant vouchsafes none of them. This reticence must be strategic; like Socrates he "knows nothing" for a purpose.

This matter of strategic reticence (which I will be concerned with for the rest of this paper) is raised by Grant himself in "Tyranny and Wisdom," an essay included in *Technology and Empire*. The essay discusses the book *On Tyranny*,[37] an altogether remarkable encounter between Leo Strauss and Alexandre Kojève on the ancient and the modern. Grant sides with Strauss and the ancients in the debate but his essay contains a plea for Strauss to declare himself more directly on a number of central points. (The author of *Persecution and the Art of Writing*, Leo Strauss well knows the eloquence of strategic reticence. His explications of the dialogues of Plato and Xenophon are astounding in their sensitivity to the strategic reticence of the philosopher or, more specifically, to the studied indirection of the wise man who seeks to teach.) Grant requests of Strauss more information on many points: the alleged rejection by the classics of a science which aims at a conquest of nature; the character of the virtue and piety that were normative in the classics; how one can hail the classics and still recognize the achievements of the modern; the relation of modern philosophy to Biblical religion; Strauss' own stand towards Biblical religion.[38] In the main these requests aim at a single issue: can the ancient ways be shown to be viable? This would include stating directly just what Greek wisdom is, but on Strauss' understanding of the necessary indirection of the wise man no such direct statement is possible. This difficulty (or evasion or obscurantism) about the classical wisdom has led frequently to the conclusion argued in detail by Hans Kelsen in an essay on the Greek view of justice, namely, that Plato's assurance about justice in the *Republic* and the *Laws* amounts to an unsupported and unsupportable assertion that the Sophists are wrong.[39] That is, regarding any alleged classical wisdom, the problem is not that the King has no clothes, it is that the regal clothes have no King. Grant's series of requests directed at Strauss amounts to a plea to a leading defender of the classical wisdom to say it isn't so, and to say why.

These are legitimate requests made of Plato's defenders and Grant's essay puts the issue clearly. But the same kind of requests can be made of Grant, for his own writings lack a direct statement of those positive teachings which he occasionally alludes to as his own means of survival,[40] and which may seem to be presupposed as the ground of his critique of the modern. Grant gives only the most fragmentary intimations of their content. While the philosophical model for this sort of indirection is of course Socrates, another figure that casts light on this aspect of Grant's understanding of the use of philosophy is Søren Kierkegaard. Kierkegaard reflected deeply on the strategic irony of Socrates' teaching and he devised for himself fantastic schemes of oblique indirection to get a hearing from a jaded and self-assured public. These strategic machinations can be instructive as a model that elucidates Grant's philosophical purpose. For Grant, to clarify the modern means exhibiting it as deprival, revealing it even in its rewards as "unnatural" for human beings, the hope being that the recognition that "one's own" is inimical to the good faciliates a search for the good in our tradition. Kierkegaard's pseudonym John the Climber puts it this way in the *Concluding Unscientific Postscript*: the task is to make things hard, as hard as possible, but not any harder than they are.[41] That is (for both Grant and John the Climber), the things that technological mastery makes easier are only accidental matters, however impressive they might be; the essential thing, being a human being, is as problematic and fearful as always.

John the Climber explains his sense of mission clearly; it came to him after he had witnessed a scene of great sadness – an old man, a Christian, buried his son who had died outside the faith, carried away as he was by the modern, by modern philosophy in fact.[42] John determines "to discover where the misunderstanding lies between speculative philosophy and Christianity."[43] It was "a very complicated criminal case" that needed to be unravelled. Here, and through all the stratagems of the pseudonyms and their indirect communciation, Kierkegaard aims ultimately to reintroduce Christianity into Christendom. Grant's case would seem to be similar: how is the modern world and its technological promise of a Kingdom of God among us, if not within us, related to the wisdom of the Greeks and to Christianity? And the direct task is similar: to clarify what the modern world is in relation to the human as such, namely, *not* a new and higher stage of the human spirit, but a specific and limiting modification of the human as such.

But the example of Kierkegaard breaks down because Kierkegaard's intentions are clear; when the left hand offered the pseudonymous works the right hand offered the *Edifying Discourses*, and when Kierkegaard ruefully observed that the world took only with its right hand what he offered in his left he explained the whole strategy in *The Point of View of my Work as an Author.* But no *Edifying Discourses* accompany Grant's laments and critiques, although Grant has from the beginning been a religious author.[44] Furthermore, in Kierkegaard there is a willful holding back of what could, but for the strategic aims, just as easily have been said. When the strategy of "wounding from behind" had clearly failed, Kierkegaard redirected his attack away from the overly subtle use of pseudonyms to the hammer blows of bitter denunciation in the *Fatherland* and the *Instant*; through it all the truth to be conveyed was never in doubt. No such steadfast assurance can be located with certainty in Grant's elusive hints of a better way, and it is pointless to try to read into Grant's hints just what it is that he really believes about the real nature of things.

But it is pointless, too, to demand of Grant an outline of what he takes the ultimately true things to be. As far as strategy is concerned, he must already have judged that such a declaration would serve no useful purpose – from his works so far one can judge that he sees it as no part of philosophy's task to engage in such unSocratic didacticism. Rather than an expounding of doctrines, philosophy as a clarification of the public things is initially an invitation to despair –just as Kierkegaard's Judge William, the ethical man, invites A, the aesthetic pursuer of the interesting, to despair at the hopelessness and inhumanity of his aspirations. Grant's reputation for "pessimism" rests on this: there is no hope in the aspirations of the public world, and that public world shows no likelihood of changing. Grant's books are calls to disillusionment with what has become "our own."

But beyond the strategic purpose Grant's reticence arouses dissatisfaction because of the supposition that the real grounds of his critique are to be found in what remains undisclosed. Is this supposition legitimate? As a critic of the modern age Grant clearly appeals to other outsiders, outsiders who are as far as possible from Grant's own intimated assurances. That is, the criticism is communicable directly because the modern is inadequate and can be known to be so on its own grounds. It is misleading to call Grant's work on the modern "criticism" for, as Grant sees it, when the modern is clarified in its fundamental nature its deficiency is simply apparent, it convicts itself; it need not be "criticized," only understood. This is a cardinal point. Grant's analysis of the modern is not conditional on the truth of some particular historical conception of man's nature. The fact that Grant apparently holds one of these historic conceptions to be true does not imply that his account of the modern is valid only if that conception *is* true. In fact, Grant maintains that it is the evident inadequacy of the modern that confirms the truth of the historic conception and not *vice versa*. Whatever the strategic interests, the analysis stands or falls on its own account.

And it is this that we are slow to realize, predisposed as we are to search out that telling psychological or sociological fact that explains everything – that explains why anyone would hold these odd views, why anyone, that is, would *like* them better than the prevailing ones. We want motives where only reasons are fitting. But the logic of the attack is not based on some secret bias or even on some veiled conviction. Just as his being the grandson of the author of *Ocean to Ocean* is not the reason Grant laments the defeat of Canadian nationalism, so it is that holding some version of the ancient wisdom to be true is not the reason he analyzes the modern world as he does. It is fruitless to suppose that there are any biographical or personal facts worth knowing if we are inquiring into the legitimacy of Grant's attacks and laments. Can the independence of the accounts from psychological and sociological bias be demonstrated? Not apart from the attacks and laments themselves. The question is not whether Grant is free of bias; of course he is not. The question is whether his account of the modern world is free of bias, that is, whether the account is true of the modern world. Once again, the adequacy of the descriptions depends solely on the descriptions and the described.

We come back in the end to Socrates. The changes in Grant's view of the uses of philosophy signify an increasing appreciation of the Socratic notion that the wisdom that needs to be learned cannot be taught directly. With Socrates, Grant holds that the task of the philosopher is not to list the good things and encourage pursuit of them; such naivete defeats the aim of discovering wisdom at the beginning. In addition, any inferences that might be made from the nature of the modern to the nature of the true and valuable things are passed over in silence by Grant. Perhaps the only task for the philosopher as teacher is to undo the assurances that move us to pursue the less than highest ends, to clarify, that is, the nature of the public truths we find ourselves committed to so readily and so unthinkingly. Philosophy in this sense is surely subversive if it is not ineffectual. It must subvert for it treats of a public world that can be understood but not reformed by philosophy.

PART V. A GRANT BIBLIOGRAPHY

George Parkin Grant: a Bibliographical Introduction
by Frank K. Flinn

In this brief introduction to the writings of George Parkin Grant I cannot hope to give an exhaustive account of the many directions which his thinking has taken. What I can do is to indicate what I believe to be Grant's key writings and how these reflect the dominant concerns and important shifts in his thinking.

As for the published evidence, I think we can discern three major phases in Grant's thinking. The first phase I call "The Time of Chastened Hope" — a title which I derive from Grant's second published writing *The Empire: Yes or No* (1945a). The second I name "An Era of Retractions: *la memoria di quel bene.*" This title stems from Grant's self-avowed changes of mind, particularly in the new preface to the second edition of *Philosophy in the Mass Age* (1966a: ii-ix) and in the new introductory note to "Religion and the State" (1963a), reprinted in *Technology and Empire* (1969a: 43-45). The third phase I designate "The Face of Moloch: Intimations of Deprival." This title is the most dubious of the three in my own mind. The phrases, of course, are taken from Grant (1970a: x; 1969a: i43), but the theo-political metaphor of Moloch evokes echoes of a deep-felt concern which transcends all the phases of Grant's thinking.[1]

1. *The Time of Chastened Hope.* This period of Grant's thinking roughly embraces the writings from *Canada: an Introduction to a Nation* (1943) to "Religion and the State" (1963a). The word "hope" is included because during this time Grant was still thralled by the North American Liberal Dream and the philosophical vision of Hegel. "Chastened," because the events of WW II seriously challenged the Liberal Dream of perfectionism (1945a: 9). The culminating work from this period was *Philosophy in the Mass Age* (1959a; reprinted, 1966a).

The elements of liberal hope, in Grant's mind, were grounded on the equation of human freedom with history (rather than, e.g., with harmony with nature) and the concurrent equation of history with the idea of progress. Still Grant clung to the hope that the ancient conception of time as "the moving image of an unmoving eternity" (see Plato, *Timaeus* 37d) and as the arena of God's providential action could be reconciled with the conception of time as history made by man (1966a: 20, 77). *Philosophy in the Mass Age* not only unfolds the dialectic between the ancient and the modern, but also uncovers the nerve ends of the two forms of liberalism in modernity: Marxism and pragmatism.

The chastening of Grant's hope in part resulted from the uncovering of the alternatives in the modern world. First, Canada, with its unbroken links to the European traditions of French logic and form and English compromise and sagacity, faced the danger of being enfolded in the continental isolationism either of the Soviet Union or of the United States after Yalta and Teheran. Grant's earliest hope was rooted in Canada's triadic relation to both Europe and North America as opposed to the exclusive collectivism of the USSR or the exclusive individualism of the USA (1945a: 31; 1945b: 163). Secondly, Grant had noted the tendency of North American liberalism to drift into a shallow positivism (1952; 1954a; 1956), just as Western theology was wandering in the direction of Barth's radical revelationism and naive biblicism (1953b: 3; 1954a: 191).

Besides uncovering the dialectic between antiquity and modernity, as well as the dialectic between communism and pragmatism, *Philosophy in the Mass Age* also opened the question about nature. To what extent is nature to be contemplated as the limit of a Creator God? To what extent is nature to be conquered by humans who believe in a God of Redemption? The first question, first posed by the ancients, calls for awe and reverence. The second, first posed by the moderns, calls for action and mastery. Grant saw that the problem for North Americans would be how to hold the two questions together. "What doctrine of nature," asked Grant, "will be adequate to express that nature is a sphere for our timeless enjoyment and yet is also a sphere which we must organize, that it has meaning apart from our ends and yet is also a part of redemptive history?" (1966a: 110-111). From a theological perspective, Grant wondered how North Americans could retain even a tenuous awareness of the doctrines of the Fall and of Providence, the two doctrines which mediate the ideas of creation and nature, on the one hand, and freedom and history, on the other. The idea of progress tends to obliterate both and, as Grant noted with undue calm, "North America is the only society that has no history of its own before the age of progress ..." (1966a: 2).

In the first phase of his thinking Grant called for a new kind of transcendence which could encompass a vision of nature which is to be contemplated and a vision of nature which is to be dominated. At this time Grant was only dimly aware that he had posed a contradiction which did not lend itself to a mediation in the Hegelian mold.

2. *An Era of Retractions: la memoria di quel bene.* The era of retractions is first made explicit in the new introduction to the second edition of *Philosophy in the Mass Age.* The word "retractions" is to be taken in the sense of Augustine's *Retractiones,* luxuries of thought which one cannot allow oneself in an era of urgency. In the new introduction Grant announced that he once considered Hegel the greatest of all philosophers because that German Olympian had been able to synthesize Greek philosophy, Christianity and the Enlightenment. Grant, however, began to have doubts about the idea of progress, which presented itself as an inevitability, and about the idea of technological mastery, which was presented by modern thinkers as a neutral means to a justified end. To Grant the relentless quest for technological mastery came to mean the closing of access to human excellence and what Plato and Augustine had called the Good. He finally asserts without equivocation: "I have come to the conclusion that Plato's account of what constitutes human excellence and the possibility of its realization in the world is more valid than that of Hegel" (1966a: viii).

Grant's disavowal of a trust in modernity is anticipated in two essays: "Tyranny and Wisdom — the Controversy between L. Strauss and A. Kojève" (1963b; reprinted with a prefatory introduction in 1969a: 81-109) and "Value and Technology" (1964a). In the former Grant came to a new recognition: Hegel's universal and homogenous state not only crowns the advent of technical reason but also programs the demise of philosophy.[2] Kojève, according to Grant, sees Hegel's state as a fusion of Greekness with secularized Christianity (1969a: 104). Strauss, in turn, argues on Platonic terms: Hegel's state is based on the modern emancipation of the passions which recognizes no sacred restraints. This philosophy of the state, Strauss stresses, is neither classical nor biblical, but Hobbesian. Grant faults Strauss for not giving the biblical side of the argument, but Strauss lets him see for the first time that Hegel possibly represented the subversion of the ancient way (what Strauss called 'the oblivion of eternity') and the end of philosophy itself.

In "Values and Technology" Grant homes in his new insights on North American continentalism. North Americans, in Grant's view, are not merely the subjects of technology; they are its masters. Canada, which once held a tenuous link to the ancients by not joining "the Republic" to the South (1945b), was now caught in the very web of Empire itself. (For Grant, Canada's future was never about empire *per se* but about *which* empire.) As Grant saw it, North America was now the example *par excellence* of the universal and homogenous state, animated by a desire for technological mastery which "... makes problematic the very idea of value itself" (1964a: 22).

The era of retractions comes to a peak with the publication of *Lament for a Nation* (1965; reprinted, 1970a). It is a lament in the double sense that, while celebrating the passing of something good (Canadian nationalism), *Lament for a Nation* is also a clarion call against a fate not chosen. On the surface the book was an attempt to explicate the reasons for the defeat of John Diefenbaker as Prime Minister of Canada in 1963 at the hands of the liberal establishment, north and south of the 49th parallel. On the deep level, the book was about the demise of the possibility of what might be called "social conservatism" (1970a: 66). Grant faced Canada's "fate" head on: Canada had become a "branch-plant" society. Earlier, Grant had seen the danger of the Behemoth to the south as an external threat (1945b). In *Lament for a Nation* he asserts that the Leviathan is now within in the guise of the Canadian liberal establishment, which capitulated to the American Empire. In particular, Grant mentions the political and social policies of MacKenzie King, C.D. Howe and the economic individualism of the entrepreneur E.P. Taylor.

The public reaction to *Lament for a Nation* ranged from accusations of nostalgia for the *ancien régime* to charges of unremitting pessimism. Grant's dour assessment of Canada's outlook in "A Critique of the New Left" (1966c) and "Canadian Fate and Imperialism" (1967a) seems to confirm the charge of pessimism. Yet Grant was to point out that the distinction between optimism (Leibniz) and pessimism (Voltaire) is itself a product of modernity (1970a: xii).

In his second phase Grant came face to face with the hidden implications of the modern project. As he had taken Hegel as his guide during his first phase, so now he found in Jacques Ellul and Leo Strauss intimations of the darkness that comes with the copenetration of North American continentalism and technological mastery (1966a: ix).

3. *The Face of Moloch: Intimations of Deprival.* Throughout the first two phases of his thinking Grant was guided by the Augustinian hermeneutic in which human existence was a steady, if uneven, process from images and shadows into the light — *ex umbris et imaginibus in veritatem* (1954b: 10). In his new introduction to "Religion and the State" he recognized something he could not face before: "I could not face the fact that we were living at the end of *western* Christianity. I could not believe that the only interpretation of Christianity that technological liberalism would allow to survive publically would be that part of it (e.g. the thought of Teilhard) which played the role of flatterer to modernity" (1969a: 44). Modernity, as Grant now understood it, was not motion

leading to rest but action as a preamble to further action. Modern motion is grounded on human will-to-power and the finality of becoming, in Nietzsche's sense. In this third phase, Grant radically alters, if he does not reverse, his earlier hermeneutic. No longer does he pretend to be a "spectator of time and eternity" (1964a: 21). In the end Grant hopes simply and starkly only "... to bring the darkness into light as darkness" (1976a: 131).[3]

The writings which most clearly indicate Grant's third phase are "The University Curriculum" (1969a: 133-133), "A Platitude" (1969a: 137-143), *Time as History* (1969g) and " 'The computer does not impose on us the ways it should be used' " (1976a). In these writings Grant takes for his guides into the darkness both Nietzsche and Heidegger, two thinkers who have thought the darkness of modernity to its depths.

It is interesting that *Time as History* did not receive the public recognition given to *Philosophy in the Mass Age* and *Lament for a Nation*. This, in part, is due to the emergence of a new terminology in Grant's thinking. Words like "enucleate," "enfold," "diremption," and "recognition" preempt easy analysis. What Grant learns from Nietzsche in his very rejection on him is the confluence of the will-to-power with the mastery of not only nature but humanity itself. Grant notes that Nietzsche's *amor fati* is not passive but "... a call to dynamic political doing" (1969g: 46). From Heidegger Grant learns that technology is the "ontology of the age" (1976a: 128).

In his third phase Grant comes to the recognition that the essence of modernity is a co-penetration of knowing and making (1974) such that contemplation, reverence and awe are ruled out in the modern world. In sum, for Grant both Plato's 'wonder' and Simone Weil's 'ultimate attention' (1954a: 10) are relics from a past which can only be remembered and recollected in an age of dynamic willing (1969g: 50-51).[4]

Grant has often described his own life in terms of Plato's cave (see 1969a: 36-37). The cave from which he felt himself dragged is the cave of modernity. Philosophically, modernity is a belief in progress. Theologically, it is a naive trust in radical revelation which can consort easily with a scientific positivism that separates "facts" from "values." Politically, it is the dream of liberalism and its scientific mistress — "neutral" technology. In his emergence from the cave of forgetfulness, Grant has had many guides — Hegel, the existentialists, Ellul, Strauss, Nietzsche, Heidegger — but only two thinkers have proven to be the true compasses to the lodestar of his thinking: Plato and Weil, the modern Diotima.

The question remains: what is the lodestar? An answer attempted: the beauty of the Gospel.

Bibliography of George Parkin Grant (1918-   )

1943.   *Canada: An Introduction to a Nation.* Toronto: Canadian Institute of International Affairs (Special Series). Five subsequent editions (1943-46).

1945a.   *The Empire: Yes or No?.* Toronto: Ryerson Press.

1945b.   "Have we a Canadian nation?" *Public Affairs* (Institute of Public Affairs. Dalhousie University) 873: 161-165.

1951.   "Philosophy," *Royal Commission Studies* (The Massey Report), 119-135. Ottawa: Edmond Cloutier, Printer to the King.

1952.   "The Pursuit of an Illusion: a Commentary on Bertrand Russell," *Dalhousie Review* 32: 97-109. (Summer).

1953a.   "Philosophy and Adult Education," *Food for Thought* (Toronto) 14: 3-8 (September-October).

1953b.   "Two Languages in the Ethical Tradition – Hebrew and Greek." An address delivered to the Maritime Philosophical Association. Mimeograph, 5 pp.

1954a.   "Plato and Popper," *Canadian Journal of Economic and Political Science* 20: 184-195 (September-October).

1954b.   "Adult Education in an Expanding Economy," *Food for Thought* (Toronto) 15: 4-10 (September-October).

1955a.   "The Minds of Men in the Atomic Age," *Texts and Addresses Delivered at the Twenty-Fourth Annual Couchiching Conference* (Toronto: Canadian Institute on Public Affairs), 39-45.

1955b.   "Jean Paul Sartre," in *Architects of Modern Thought* (1st & 2nd Series), ed. by John A. Irving (Toronto: Canadian Broadcasting Corporation Publications), 39-45.

1955c.   Reprint of 1954b in *The Anglican Outlook* (Montreal) 10/7: 8-10 (May).

1956.   "The Uses of Freedom – a word in our world," *Queen's Quarterly* 65: 515-527 (Winter).

1958.   "Philosophy," *Encyclopedia Canadiana* (The Grolier Society of Canada) 8: 184-189.

1959a.   *Philosophy in the Mass Age.* Toronto: The Copp Clark Publishing Company: New York: Hill and Wang. Reprinted with a new introduction in 1966a.

1959b.   "Fyodor Dostoevsky," in *Architects of Modern Thought* (3rd & 4th Series), ed. by John A. Irving (Toronto: Canadian Broadcasting Corporation Publications), 71-83.

1961a.   "Philosophy and Religion," in *The Great Ideas Today,* ed. by Robert M. Hutchins and Mortimer J. Adler (Chicago: Encyclopedia Brittanica, Inc.), 337-376.

1961b. "An Ethic of Community," in *Social Purpose for Canada*, ed. by Michael Oliver (Toronto: The University of Toronto Press), 3-36.

1962a. "Conceptions of Health," in *Psychiatry and Responsibility*, ed. by Helmut Schoeck and James W. Wiggins (Princeton: The Van Nostrand Co., Inc.), 117-134.

1962b. "Carl Gustav Jung," in *Architects of Modern Thought* (5th & 6th Series), ed. by John A. Irving (Toronto: Canadian Broadcasting Corporation Publications), 63-74.

1963a. "Religion and the State," *Queen's Quarterly* 70: 183-197 (Summer). Reprinted with a new introduction in 1969a: 43-60.

1963b. "Tyranny and Wisdom — the controversy between L. Strauss and A. Kojève," *Social Research* 31: 45-72. Reprinted with a new introduction in 1969a: 81-109.

1964a. "Value and Technology," *Canadian Conference on Social Welfare: Proceedings* (Ottawa, Printer to the Queen), 21-29 (August). See 1964b.

1964b. "Progres technique et valeurs humaines," *Canadian Conference on Social Welfare: Proceedings* (Ottawa: Printer to the Queen), 30-39 (August). French translation of 1964a.

1965.   *Lament for a Nation: the Defeat of Canadian Nationalism.* Toronto: McClelland and Stewart, Ltd. Reprinted with a new introduction in 1970a.

1966a. *Philosophy in the Mass Age.* Toronto: The Copp Clark Publishing Co. Second edition, with a new introduction, of 1959a.

1966b. "Protest and Technology," in *Revolution and Response*, ed. by Charles Hanly (Toronto: McClelland and Stewart, Ltd.), 122-128.

1966c. "A Critique of the New Left," in *Canada and Radical Social Change*, ed. by D.I. Roussopoulos (Toronto: McClelland and Stewart, Ltd.), 55-61.

1967a. "Canadian Fate and Imperialism," *Canadian Dimension* 4: 21-25. Reprinted in 1969a: 63-78 and 1973c: 100-109.

1967b. "Wisdom in the Universities: Part One," *This Magazine is About Schools* 1/4: 70-85. See 1968b.

1967c. Comments on the Great Society in *Great Societies and Quiet Revolutions* (The Thirty-Fifth Annual Couchiching Conference), ed. by John Irwin (Toronto: The Canadian Institute on Public Affairs and the Canadian Broadcasting Corporation), 71-76.

1968a. "The University Curriculum," *This Magazine is About Schools* 2/5: 52-57 (Winter). The continuation of 1967b; revised and reprinted in 1968b and 1969a: 113-133.

1968b. "The University Curriculum," in *The University Game*, ed. by Howard Adelman and Dennis Lee (Toronto: House of Anansi Press), 47-68. See 1967b, 1968a & b, 1969a: 113-133.

1969a. *Technology and Empire: Perspectives on North America.* Toronto: House of Anansi Press. Contains 1963a & b (with new introductions) and 1968b (with alterations).

1969b. "A Conversation on Technology," *Journal of Canadian Studies* 4/3: 3-6 (August). With Gad Horowitz.

1969c. "Is Freedom Man's Only Meaning?," *Saturday Night* (Toronto) 84: 31-33 (March). Excerpts from 1969a.

1969d. "Horowitz and Grant Talk," *Canadian Dimension* 6:18-20, (Dec.-Jan., 1969-70).

1969f. "Thoughts about Politics and the Practice of Politics." The George Nowlan Lectures, delivered at Acadia University.

1969g. *Time as History.* The Massey Lectures, 9th Series. Toronto: Canadian Broadcasting Corporation. Printed by The Hunter Rose Company, Toronto.

1970a. *Lament for a Nation: the Defeat of Canadian Nationalism.* Toronto: McClelland and Stewart, Ltd.). Second edition, with a new introduction, of 1965.

1970b. "Revolution and Tradition," *Canadian Forum* 50: 88-93 (April-May). Reprinted with alterations in 1971b.

1971a. "Nationalism and Rationality," *Canadian Forum* 50: 336-337 (January). Translated into French for *Le Devoir* (Montreal).

1971b. "Revolution and Tradition," in *Tradition and Revolution*, ed. by Lionel Rubinoff (Toronto: MacMillan of Canada, Ltd.), 81-95. Reprint, with alterations, of 1970b.

1973a. "Ideology in Modern Empires," in *Perspectives of Empire* (Essays Presented to Gerald S. Graham), ed. by J.E. Flint and G. Williams (London: Longman's Group, Ltd.), 189-197.

1973b. "Canadian Fate and Imperialism," in *The Evolution of Canadian Literature in English 1945-1970,* ed. by Mary Jane Edwards, George Parker and Patrick Denham (Toronto: Holt, Rinehart & Winston), 100-109.

1974. "Knowing and Making," *Transactions of the Royal Society of Canada* (4th Series, Number 12), 59-67.

1975a. "The University Curriculum and the Technological Threat," in *The Sciences and the Humanities and the Technological Threat*, ed. by William Roy Niblett (London: The University of London Press, Ltd.), 21-35.

1975b. Book Review: *The Collected Papers of Walter Bagehot*, Volumes V-VIII – The Political Writings, ed. by Norman St. John Stevas (London: The Economist, 1974), in *The Globe and Mail* (Toronto, March 1).

1975c. Book review: *The Gladstone Diaries*, Volume II (1840-47) and IV (1848-54), ed. by M.R.D. Foot and H.C.G. Matthew (Oxford: The Oxford University Press, 1975), in *The Globe and Mail* (Toronto, September 20), 30.

1976a. " 'The computer does not impose on us the ways it should be used,' " in *Beyond Industrial Growth*, ed. by Abraham Rotstein (Toronto: The University of Toronto Press), 117-131.

1976b. "Abortion and Rights," in *The Right to Birth: Some Christian Views on Abortion*, ed. by Eugene Fairweather and Ian Gentiles (Toronto: The Anglican Book Centre), 1-12. Written with Sheila Grant.

1976d. "Role Conflict in the Humanities." Unpublished paper presented to the Symposium on the Future of the University, General Session on Role Conflicts (Royal Society of Canada and the Association of Universities and Colleges of Canada, Ottawa, May 4-7).

1977a. Book review: *Simone Weil* by Simone Petremont, tr. by Raymond Rosenthal (New York: Random House, 1977), in *The Globe and Mail* (Toronto: February 12), 43.

1977b. Book review: *Nietzsche's View of Socrates* by Werner J. Dannhauser (Ithaca: *Cornell University Press*, 1974). In *The American Political Science Review*, vol. LXXI, Sept. 1977 #3, p. 1127.

1977c. Book Review: *John Stuart Mill: The Collected Works*, Volumes XVIII & XIX, ed. by J.M. Robson (Toronto: The University of Toronto Press, 1977), in *The Globe and Mail* (Toronto, August 6), 31.

1977d. "Faith and the Multiversity," in *Proceedings: The Sixth International Conference on the Unity of the Sciences* (San Francisco, November 25-27), 18pp. To be published.

1977g. *Grant and Lamontagne on National Unity*. (Toronto: Cermasco Management, Ltd.), 4-9.

1978a. *English-speaking Justice*. (Sackville, New Brunswick: Mount Allison University). These are The Wood Lectures, delivered at Mount Allison University in 1974.

Footnotes

References to Grant's work are given the following abbreviations: *PMA, Philosophy in the Mass Age*, 2nd edition, (Vancouver, 1966); *LN, Lament for a Nation: The Defeat of Canadian Nationalism*, (Toronto, 1970); *TE, Technology & Empire: Perspectives on North America*, (Toronto, 1969); *TH, Time as History*, (Toronto, 1971).

A Imperio Usque Ad Imperium

1 Abraham Rotstein, *The Precarious Homestead: Essays on Economics, Technology and Nationalism* (Toronto, 1973), p. 242.
2 Lawrence Lampert, "The Uses of Philosophy in George Grant," *Queen's Quarterly*, 81 (1974), p. 495.
3 Eric Voegelin, *Anamnesis: Zur Theorie der Geschichte und Politik* (Munich, 1966), p. 352.
4 Bernard J.F. Lonergan, S.J., *Insight: A Study of Human Understanding* (New York, 1957), pp. 176-177.
5 Donald Creighton, "The Decline and Fall of the Empire of the St. Lawrence" in *Towards the Discovery of Canada* (Toronto, 1972), p. 167.
6 *Public Affairs*, 8 (1945), pp. 161-166.
7 Toronto, 1945. A pamphlet published by Ryerson Press.
8 Frank Underhill's running commentary on Mackenzie King, conveniently collected in *In Search of Canadian Liberalism* (Toronto, 1960), pp. 114-140, provides a clear documentation of Grant's point.
9 "Philosophy," in Canada, Royal Commission on National Development in the Arts, Letters and Sciences, *Royal Commission Studies* (Ottawa, 1951), p. 120. This Royal Commission is generally known as the Massey Commission.
10 It was not until the second edition of *PMA* (pp. vii-ix) in 1966 that Grant reflected upon the impact of Hegel's thought on his own.
11 "Philosophy and Adult Education," *Food for Thought*, 14: 1 (1953), p. 4.
12 *Ibid.*, p. 8
13 "Adult Education in the Expanding Economy," *Food for Thought*, 15: 1 (1954), p. 4.
14 *Ibid.*, p. 8
15 *Ibid.*, p. 10
16 Grant first touched upon this theme in "The Uses of Freedom," *Queen's Quarterly*, 62 (1956), pp. 515-527, and has repeated it or alluded to it in nearly all his subsequent writings.
17 The term was borrowed from Jacques Ellul's book, *La Technique, ou l'enjeu du siècle* (Paris, 1954), translated as *The Technological Society*. Recently Grant has made clear the distinction between technique, a "particular means of making" and technology, "studies from which

they [i.e., techniques] came." "Knowing and Making," *Proceedings and Transactions of the Royal Society of Canada*, 4th Series, vol. 12 (1974), p. 63.

18 "Macdonald and Canadian Historians" in *Towards the Discovery of Canada*, p. 204.

19 A good biography of O.D. Skelton, the biographer of Laurier, who removed to Ottawa to serve King as Undersecretary for External Affairs, might be of assistance here.

20 R.B. Bennett's attempt during the 1930s to regulate the economy was eventually declared *ultra vires* the Dominion government by the JCPC. Left intact, presumably it could have performed some of the tasks Grant had in mind. In any event, the major crown corporations, both federal and provincial, have all been established by Conservative governments. Consider, in this connection the thesis of Herschel Hardin on "The Canadian Economic Culture," *A Nation Unaware* (Vancouver, 1974).

21 See Grant's later remarks comparing our last three Prime Ministers, "Nationalism and Rationality" in A. Rotstein, ed., *Power Corrupted: The October Crisis and the Repression of Quebec* (Toronto, 1971), p. 51.

22 Recently there has been advocated the curious opinion that the national purpose is to be found in preserving a multitude of "ethnic and cultural values." Whatever the difference, if there is one, between the Canadian "mosaic" and the American "melting pot," it is certain that no *political* principle is involved.

23 The behaviour of Trudeau, a convert to the liberal faith who has decisively rejected his own tradition, when the "cultural diversity" of Quebec grew serious is instructive. For an analysis see my "Rhetoric and Violence: Some Considerations of the events of October, 1970" in David Shugarman, ed., *Thinking about Change* (Toronto, 1974), pp. 71-87.

24 What Grant is alluding to here in his criticism of Ellul's condescending opinion of North American production can be seen at the other end of the cycle as well: whereas until very recently North Americans consumed their LTDs and Black Label with gusto, Europeans were essentially bored by their BMWs and Pernod. "North American Society was till recently both more innocent and more barren than Europe" (*TE*, p. 122), and so avoided both thought and nihilism.

25 Grant's account in "Tyranny and Wisdom," *TE*, pp. 79-109, is generally reliable. He accepts, however, Strauss's interpretation of Kojève's argument, "that the universal and homogeneous state is the best social order and that mankind advances to the establishment of such an order" (*TE*, p. 86). According to Kojève, the universal and homogeneous state is not "best," it is necessary; or better, it simply is, which is to say that mankind *has advanced* to it.

26 In Grant's discussion of the controversy between Kojève and Strauss, he seemed to have forgotten this existential aspect of philosophy and tacitly accepted the understanding shared by the antagonists, namely that philosophy is first of all a consistent and coherent account of things (*TE*, p. 92).

27 By articulating it so thoroughly it is arguable that he added to the crisis since he enabled more poeple to understand their fate. A similar criticism, which Grant admitted was serious, had been made of *Lament for a Nation*. By speaking of Canada's fate, it was said, Grant invited the fulfillment of what was in truth a prognostication. He answered that it was perhaps better to ridicule ignoble delusions than prop up noble ones. See *LN*, Carleton Library edition, p. xi and compare with *TH* pp. 24-25.

28 Grant's use of the distinction between optimism and pessimism is close to the original eighteenth-century meaning, which implied not one's state of mind but rather the state of the whole. An optimist, therefore, was one who, as the Jesuits who first applied the term to Leibniz remarked, thought this the best world possible. A pessimist held the contradictory opinion.

29 *LN*, p. xii.

George Grant's Anguished Conservatism

1 Letter dated March 26, 1926 from Frank H. Underhill to J.W. Lothian, Underhill Papers National Library, Ottawa. Elsewhere in this letter he says: "I have been reading a good deal of Bertrand Russell too".

2 *PMA*, pp. 48-49.

3 *Ibid.*, p. 49.

4 *Ibid.*, p. 15.

5 *LN*, p. 94.

6 *TE*, p. 44.

7 *Ibid.*, pp. 27-30.

8 *Ibid.*, p. 28.

9 Sheila and George Grant, "Abortion and Rights: the Value of Political Freedom" in Eugene Fairweather and Ian Gentles (ids.) *The Right to Birth: Some Christian Views on Abortion*, (The Anglican Book Centre: Toronto, 1976) p. 2.

10 *Ibid.*, p. 3.

11 *PMA*, p. 35. Here Grant uses the growing acceptability of abortion to indicate departure from belief in the Natural Law.

12 Grant and Friedenberg cassette recording of CBC programme, *Ideas*.

13 *LN*, p. 4.

14 See in particular Ramsay Cook, *The Maple Leaf Forever: Essays on Nationalism and Politics in Canada* (Toronto, 1971), p. 64.

15 *LN*, p. 96.

16 *PMA*, p. 113.

17 *TE*, pp. 75-76.
18 *Ibid.*, p. 44.
19 *Ibid.*, p. 143.

George Grant: Liberal, Socialist Or Conservative?

1 Gad Horowitz, "Conservatism, Liberalism, and Socialism: An Interpretation," *The Canadian Journal of Economic and Political Science*, XXXII, no. 2 (Toronto: University of Toronto Press, May, 1966), p. 159.
2 *Ibid.*, pp. 143, 158, 169. Horowitz's main point is that the Canadian political tradition is unique in North America, primarily because of the presence of toryism, which has influenced both the strength of socialism and the distinctiveness of Canadian liberalism.
3 *PMA*, pp. 108-109.
4 *TE*, p. 11.
5 *LN*, p. 40.
6 Informal autobiographical reflections by Grant at a colloquium at Erindale College, Mississauga, October 15, 1977.
7 Grant's 1969 "Introduction" to "Religion and the State," *TE*, p. 43.
8 Grant, *The Empire: Yes or No?* (Toronto: The Ryerson Press, 1945), p. 11.
9 Laurence Lampert, "The Uses of Philosophy in George Grant," *Queen's Quarterly* 81 (1974), p. 497.
10 *PMA*, p. 108, 181.
11 Sheila and George Grant, "Abortion and Rights: The Value of Political Freedom," *The Right to Birth* ed. by Eugene Fairweather and Ian Gentles (Toronto: The Anglican Book Centre, 1976), p. 11.
12 *Ibid.*, p. 80.
13 *PMA*, p. 65. This is not to say that Grant agrees with Marx's view of science, although, as we see, Grant does at this time have a more positive view of science than he does later.
14 *LN*, p. 59.
15 Grant, " 'The computer does not impose on us the ways it should be used'," *Beyond Industrial Growth*, ed. by Abraham Rotstein (Toronto: University of Toronto Press, 1976), p. 123.
16 "Horowitz and Grant *Talk*," *Canadian Dimension*, VI, 6 (1969-70), *passim*.
17 *Ibid.*, p. 19.
18 *LN*, p. 73.
19 Robert Lindsay Schuettinger, *The Conservative Tradition in European Thought* (New York, 1970), pp. 12-17.
20 *TE*, p. 73.
21 *LN*, p. 66.
22 *Ibid.*, p. 74.
23 *TE*, p. 43.

24 *Ibid.*, p. 44.
25 Abraham Rotstein, *The Precarious Homestead* (Toronto: New Press, 1973), p. 242.
26 See Darrol Bryant's "The Barren Twilight" in this volume.
27 *LN*, p. xi.
28 *TE*, pp. 139, ff.
29 *LN*, p. xii.

Some Influences Of Simone Weil On George Grant's Silence

1 An example is Laurence Lampert, "The Uses of Philosophy in George Grant", *Queen's Quarterly*, 81 (1974), pp. 495-511.
2 George Grant, *English-speaking Justice* (Sackville, New Brunswick: Mount Allison University, 1978), p. 95.
3 *TE*, p. 137.
4 *English-speaking Justice*, p. 93.
5 *TE*, p. 133.
6 *English-speaking Justice*, p. 93.
7 George Grant, "The computer does not impose on us the ways it should be used," *Beyond Industrial Growth*, ed. Abraham Rotstein (Toronto: University of Toronto Press, 1976), p. 128. (Hereinafter referred to as The Computer).
8 *Technology*, p. 142.
9 *TH*, p. 48.
10 Simone Weil, *On Science, Necessity and the Love of God*, (London: Oxford University Press, 1968), p. 21. (Hereafter referred to as *On Science*).
11 *Ibid.*, p. 24
12 Untitled unpublished paper, 1973, p. 26.
13 *English-speaking Justice*, pp. 93f.
14 Simone Weil, *Gateway to God*, (Glasgow: William Collins Sons and Co., 1974), p. 52, (Hereafter referred to as *Gateway*).
15 Simone Weil, *Intimations of Christianity among the Ancient Greeks*, (London: Routledge and Kegan Paul), 1957, pp. 186-187. A similar statement is found in *On Science*, p. 186.
16 *On Science*, p. 195.
17 *Ibid.*, p. 70.
18 *Ibid.*, p. vii.
19 George Grant, "Role conflict in the 'humanities'," (unpublished paper prepared for the Symposium on the Future of the University, General Session on Role Conflicts, sponsored jointly by the Royal Society of Canada and the Association of Universities and Colleges of Canada, held in Ottawa May 4-7, 1976), p. 6.
20 The Computer, p. 131.
21 *Gateway*, p. 55.
22 *LN*, p. 89.

23 Simone Weil, *The Need for Roots*, (Boston: Beacon Press, 1955), p. 282. (Hereafter referred to as *Roots*).

24 *Ibid.*, p. 271.

25 *Ibid.*, p. 270.

26 *TE*, p. 63.

27 *Ibid.*, p. 36.

28 *Ibid.*, pp. 131-32.

29 *English-speaking Justice*, p. 94f.

30 *Ibid.*, p. 86.

31 *On Science*, p. 148.

32 *Roots*, p. 263.

33 *Gateway*, p. 46.

34 Classroom comment, October, 1975.

35 *PMA*, p ix.

36 *Gateway*, p. 72.

37 *On Science*, p. 104.

38 *PMA*, pp. 99-100.

39 *LN*, p. 3.

40 *Roots*, p. 234

41 *Ibid.*, p. 235.

42 *On Science*, p. 197.

43 *Roots*, p. 244.

44 Simone Weil, *Waiting on God*, (London: Routledge and Kegan Paul, 1951), p. 114.

45 *On Science*, p. 187.

46 *Gateway*, p. 54.

47 *Ibid.*, p. 65.

George P. Grant and Jacques Ellul

1 Page numbers for Grant's works in the text refer to editions mentioned at the beginning of these notes and in Frank Flinn's bibliography. Works by Jacques Ellul consulted for this essay are as follows, arranged chronologically:

1960 *The Theological Foundation of Law*. Translated by Marguerite Wieser. London: SCM Press. Published originally as *Le Fondement Théologique Du Droit* by Editions Delachaux and Niestle S.A., 1946.

1964 *The Technological Society*. Translated by John Wilkinson. Introduction by Robert K. Merton. New York: Vintage Books. Published originally as *La Technique ou l'enjeu du siècle* by Librairie Armand Colin, 1954.

1967 *The Political Illusion*. Translated by Konrad Kellen. New York: Alfred A. Knopf, Inc. Published originally as *L'illusion politique* by Robert Laffont, 1965.

1972   *False Presence of the Kingdom.* Translated by C. Edward Hopkin. New York: Seabury Press. Published originally as *Fausse Présence au monde moderne* as part of the series "Les Bergers et les Mages," 1963.

1975   *The New Demons.* Translated by C. Edward Hopkin. New York: Seabury Press. Published originally as *Les nouveaux possédés* by Librairie Artheme Fayard, 1973.

1976   *The Ethics of Freedom.* Translated and edited by Geoffrey W. Bromiley, Grand Rapids: Wm. B. Eerdmans Publishing Co. Published originally as a part of *Ethique de la Liberté* by Labor et Fides, n.d.

Grant's Critique of Values Language

1 *TH*, p. 44.
2 *Ibid.*, p. 45.
3 *TE*, pp. 38-39.
4 *Ibid.*, p. 39.
5 *Ibid.*, p. 128.
6 *PMA*, p. 40.
7 *Ibid.*, p. 90. In creating one's values one is at the same time creating one's *self*. Cf. "Value and Technology" in Canadian Conference on Social Welfare, *Conference Proceedings: Welfare Services in a Changing Technology*, 1964, p. 24.
8 "Value and Technology," p. 25.
9 *TE*, p. 118.
10 *Ibid.*, pp. 119-120.
11 Cf. *Ibid.*, p. 123: "The fact-value distinction led generally to the conclusion that there was no rational way of knowing that one way of life was nobler than another." For a similar criticism see Leo Strauss, *Natural Right and History* (Chicago: University of Chicago Press, 1953), pp. 42-50.
12 *Ibid.*, p. 119.
13 *Ibid.* For the same point attributed to a Marxist critique see Grant's essay " 'The computer does not impose on us the ways it should be used' " in Abraham Rotstein ed. *Beyond Industrial Growth* (Toronto: University of Toronto Press, 1976), p. 123.
14 *TH*, p. 1.
15 "Value and Technology," p. 22.
16 *TE*, p. 120.
17 Cf. *Ibid.*, pp. 25-32.
18 *TE*, p. 32.
19 *Ibid.*, p. 34. Cf. also "The University Curriculum," *Ibid.*, p. 131.
20 Cf. *TH*: p. 47. "All of us are increasingly enclosed by the modern account."

21 *PMA*, p. 107.
22 *TH*, p. 44f.
23 *TE*, p. 141.
24 " 'The computer ...'," p. 127. In a different context Grant explains
    why the scientific mode of knowing is unable to grasp the notion of
    "goodness". See "Knowing and Making," *Transactions of the Royal
    Society of Canada*, ser. 4, xii (1974), 65.
25 "Values-clarification exercises differ from most other work-book
    assignments in one way: Any and all answers are considered 'right' as
    long as one can give a reason for them. Asked whether a youngster
    might not, therefore, end up reaffirming 'wrong' values, such as in-
    tolerance or thievery, the designers of the approach reply: 'Our
    position is that we respect his right to decide upon that value'." Amitai
    Etzioni, "Do as I say, not as I do", *New York Times Magazine* (Sept.
    26, 1976), p. 45.
26 *TE*, p. 126.
27 Cf. *PMA*, p. 81.
28 *TH*, p. 45.
29 "How can we think 'morality' as a desiring attention to perfection,
    when for the last centuries the greatest moral philosophers have writ-
    ten of it as self-legislation, the willing of our own values?" *Ibid.*, p. 48.
30 *Ibid.*, p. 47.
31 *Ibid.*, pp. 51-52.
32 Cf. *Ibid.*, and *TE*, pp. 140-143.
33 *TH*, p. 52.
34 *TE*, p. 40.
35 " 'The computer ...' ", p. 130. Grant's 1976 Wood Lectures also
    conclude with an extended delineation of the present darkness.
36 *TH*, p. 52.

The Barren Twilight:
History and Faith in Grant's Lament

 1 *LN*, p. 4.
 2 *TE*, p. 78.
 3 Harvey Cox, *The Secular City* (New York, 1965), p. 1.
 4 *TE*, p. 44.
 5 A. Brady, *University of Toronto Quarterly*, 35 (1966), p. 459.
 6 K. McNaught, *Canadian Forum*, 80 (Aug. 1965), p. 8.
 7 *The Canadian Banker*, 73 (Sum 1966), p. 124.
 8 R. K. Crook, *Queen's Quarterly*, 81 (1974), 495-511.
 9 *LN*, p. 2.
10 *Oxford Dictionary of the Christian Church*, (London, 1958), p. 882.
11 *Ibid.*
12 Here prophecy is meant in its oldest Greek sense: *prophetes* as "say-
    ing," "speaking," "public proclamation." See A. Siirala, *The Voice of
    Illness*, (Philadelphia, 1964), p. 42 ff.

13 Lamentations 1:7a.
14 *LN*, p. 3.
15 *LN*, p. 6.
16 *LN*, p. 94.
17 *LN*, p. 5.
18 Genesis 24:29-34.
19 George Grant, "Tradition and Revolution," *Canadian Forum*, 50 (Ap.-My. 1970), p. 91.
20 A. Brady, *op. cit.*
21 *TE*, p. 44.
22 The idea of multiple citizenship in relation to the life of a people is developed in Eugen Rosenstock-Huessy, *Out of Revolution: Autobiography of Western Man*, (Norwich, Vt., 1969), especially p. 468 ff.
23 *LN*, p. 89.
24 *LN*, p. 6. I am thinking especially of the poetry of Dennis Lee, *Civil Elegies.*
25 *LN*, p. 97.
26 Lamentations 5:19-21.
27 Cf. E. Rosenstock-Huessy, *The Christian Future: Or the Modern Mind Outrun*, (New York, 1966), pp. 61-134.
28 *Ibid.*, p. 83.
29 *LN*, p. 87.

The Significance Of Grant's Cultural Analysis

1 *PMA*, p. 7.
2 *TE*, p. 7.
3 *Ibid.*, p. 16.
4 Vol. XXX, No. 18 (Nov. 2-16, 1970), p. 226.
5 "To this day our shallow intellectual streams are kept flowing by their rain." *TE*, p. 16.
6 *PMA*, p. 3.
7 *PMA*, p. 5.
8 See the essay by Professor Wm. Christian.
9 *PMA*, p. 7.
10 *TE*, p. 137.
11 *PMA*, p. viii.
12 *LN*, p. 43.
13 *TE*, p. 141.
14 *TE*, p. 40.
15 *TE*, p. 19.
16 I have developed this thesis at length in my book, *Lighten Our Darkness: Towards an Indigenous Theology of the Cross* (Philadelphia, The Westminster Press, 1976).

George Grant And The Problem Of History

1 *TH*
2 *Ibid.*, p. 7.
3 *Ibid.*, p. 10.
4 *Ibid.*, p. 49.
5 *PMA*, p. v.
6 *TH*, p. 50.
7 *Ibid.*, p. 4.
8 *PMA*, p. v.
9 *Ibid.* p. ix.
10 E.F. Miller, "Leo Strauss: The Recovery of Political Philosophy" in E. de Crespigny and K. Minogue, *Contemporary Political Philosophers* (London: Methuen & Co.: 1976), p. 68.
11 *Ibid.*
12 *TE*, p. 81.
13 *TH*, p. 52.
14 *Ibid.*, p. 48.
15 *Ibid.*, p. 6.
16 *Ibid.*, p. 7.
17 *TE*, p. 44.
18 *Ibid.*, p. 72.
19 Cf. *Ibid.*, pp. 30-40.
20 Cf. M. Heidegger, *Being and Time* (London: SCM Press, 1962).
21 Cf. R. Bultmann, *Jesus Christ and Mythology* (New York: Charles Scribner's Sons, 1958).
22 Cf. E. Voegelin *Order and History, Volume One: Israel and Revelation* (Baton Rouge: Louisana State University Press, 1956).
23 Cf. O. Barfield, *Saving the Appearances* (New York: Harcourt Brace and World, 1965).
24 J. Lukacs, *Historical Consciousness* (New York: Harper & Row, 1968), p. 235.
25 G. Grant, "Role Conflict in the Humanities," p. 3.
26 *TH*, p. 4.
27 *Ibid.*
28 E. Voegelin, *Order and History, Volume Four: The Ecumenic Age* (Baton Rouge Louisana State University Press, 1974), p. 2.
29 *Ibid.*, p. 2-10.
30 *Ibid.*, p. 6.
31 Cf. conversations in this volume.
32 E. Voegelin, *The Ecumenic Age*, p. 9.
33 *PMA*, p. 40.
34 Cf. E. Voegelin, *The Ecumenic Age*, pp. 2-10.
35 *Ibid.*, p. 6.
36 L. Strauss, *What is Political Philosophy* (Glencoe, Illinois: The Free Press, 1959), pp. 39-40.

Philosophy, Revelation And Modernity

1 *TH*, p. 44.
2 George Grant, "Revolution and Tradition," in Lionel Rubinoff, ed., *Tradition and Revolution* (Toronto: MacMillan, 1971), p. 86.
3 Leo Strauss, *What is Political Philosophy?* (New York: The Free Press, 1959), p. 10.
4 Eric Voegelin, *The Ecumenic Age* (Baton Rouge: Louisiana State University Press, 1974), p. 242.
5 *TH*, p. 47.
6 George Grant, "Ideology in Modern Empires," in J.E. Flint and G. Williams, eds., *Perspectives of Empire: Essays Presented to Gerald S. Graham* (London: Longmans, 1973), p. 195.
7 *TE*, p. 106.
8 *TE*, p. 94.
9 Nicholas Lobkowicz, *Theory and Practice: History of a Concept from Aristotle to Marx* (Notre Dame: University of Notre Dame Press, 1967), p. 7. See also Hannah Arendt, *The Human Condition* (Chicago: University of Chicago Press, 1958).
10 *TE*, p. 106f.
11 *TE*, p. 53f.
12 *TE*, p. 35; cf. p. 18.
13 *TE*, p. 59.
14 *TE*, p. 50f.
15 *TE*, p. 35.
16 *TE*, p. 108.
17 Cf. *TE*, p. 35.
18 *TE*, p. 35.
19 *TH*, p. 21.
20 "Revolution and Tradition," p. 88.
21 *TE*, p. 18.
22 *PMA*, p. 48.
23 *PMA*, p. 43f.
24 *PMA*, p. vii.
25 *TE*, p. 106.
26 *TE*, p. 138; cf. 129n.
27 *TE*, p. 103.
28 *TH*, p. 22.
29 *TE*, p. 19.
30 *TE*, p. 18.
31 *TH*, p. 34n.
32 *TH*, p. 17.
33 *TH*, p. 15.
34 *TE*, p. 105.
35 *TH*, p. 21f.

The Technological Regime

1 *TE*, p. 32.

2 *English-Speaking Justice* (Sackville, New Brunswick: Mount Allison University, 1978), p. 88.

3 It would be misleading to speak here of "technical competence" inasmuch as the competence most highly regarded is something broader than this term suggests. What is involved at the highest level perhaps must include some measure of technical competence but as well a blending of self-discipline and freedom from all that might impede the will to mastery. For an account of these requisites see C.I. Barnard, *The Functions of the Executive* (Cambridge: Harvard University Press, 1968), pp. 258-284.

4 *TE*, p. 131.

5 *Ibid.*, p. 39.

6 *LN*, p. 68.

7 *TE*, pp. 30-31.

8 Simone Weil, *Oppression and Liberty* (London: Routledge and Kegan Paul, 1958), pp. 39-56.

9 *LN*, p. 56.

10 *Ibid.*, p. 57.

11 Socialist thought has assumed that the desires of men will not conflict with each other or with a "happy social order" once scarcity is removed. See, eg., C.B. Macpherson, *Democratic Theory* (Oxford: Clarendon, 1973), p. 74.

12 *TE*, p. 101 (my underlining).

13 See, e.g., Hobbes, Leviathan 1.11 (near the beginning) and consider Montesquieu's remark preceding his praise of the English regime understood as the expression of Locke's principles that the English regime alone has political liberty as the direct end of its constitution. *De L'Esprit des Lois* 11.5.

14 James Madison, *Federalist Papers* No. 10.

15 Consider Montesquieu's conjecture that there may be no instances where free labour might not take the place of slavery "par la commodite des machines." *Op. cit.*, 15.8. Kojeve writes: "Dans le Monde naturel, donne, brut, l'Esclave est esclave du Maitre. Dans le monde technique, transforme par son travail, il regne — ou, du moins, regnera un jour — en Maitre absolu." *Introduction a la Lecture de Hegel* (Paris: Gallimard, 1947), p. 28.

16 Both the lack of liberty outside the centre of the liberal empire and the directing of technology towards cybernetics and other modes of control over human beings at the very centre of liberalism must cause us to question this identity. "English-speaking justice," p. 5. Citations of this work in the balance will normally be given in parenthesis in the text.

17 *Roe v. Wade*, U.S. Law Week 4214-1-23-73.

18 *English-Speaking Justice*, p. 76.

19 Similarly in John Rawls, *A Theory of Justice* (Cambridge: Harvard U. Press, 1971), which Grant also examines in these lectures, we see a decisive reliance upon the concept of persons with little support for the connecting of that concept to the possession of a right to justice, as well as the priority of right to good, and an assumed moral pluralism or agnosticism.

20 *Utilitarianism* (Indianapolis: Bobbs-Merrill, 1957), p. 66.

21 *English-Speaking Justice*, p. 49.

22 *Ibid.*, p. 74.

23 Speech at Springfield, Illinois, June 26, 1857 in R. Basler, ed., *Collected Works* (New Brunswick, New Jersey: Rutgers, 1953) II, p. 406.

24 The inequality of negro slaves in status, natural assets, or even acknowledged legal rights did not remove the negro slave from the intention of the Declaration expressed in the statement that all were equal "in certain inalienable rights, among which are life, liberty, and the pursuit of happiness" for its authors "did not mean to assert the obvious untruth, that all were then actually enjoying that equality, nor yet, that they were about to confer it immediately upon them. ... They meant simply to declare the right, so that the enforcement of it might follow as fast as circumstances should permit ... to set up a standard maxim for free society which might be a last obstacle to those who might seek to establish tyranny." *Ibid.* If ratification of the constitution required a compromise with the evil of slavery yet the Declaration forced those like Taney, who sought to demand more for that institution, to sophistic evasions of its language, to enter into the same ontological issue as does Blackmun. Indeed Lincoln understands the consequences of opening that issue almost exactly as does Grant. *Ibid.*, p. 407. Lincoln's foe Douglas who claims the constitution requires an attitude of moral indifference towards slavery is again forced to interpret the words of the Declaration so as to reduce their "moral bite."

25 Compare 546D and 549B with 551C-552B. See also Aristotle, *Politics* 1309b18-35.

26 *English-Speaking Justice*, p. 66.

27 I assume with Grant in what follows that what distinguishes Locke from Hobbes is Locke's "marvellous caution and indirectness of rhetoric and ... some changes of emphasis at the political level." *Technology and Empire*, p. 22, I shall confine myself to Hobbes's account, therefore, assuming it to be essentially the same and in many respects clearer.

28 *TE*, p. 22. See, also, *English-Speaking Justice*, p. 80.

29 *English-Speaking Justice*, p. 92.

30 Consider, e.g., Aristotle *Politics* 1267a10-14 and the "education" of Glaucon in Plato's *Republic*; see, especially, 519D, 521A-B, 592A-B.

George Grant And The Terrifying Darkness

1 George Grant, *English-speaking Justice* (Sackville, New Brunswick: Mount Allison University) 1978. All subsequent direct quotations are from these lectures (The Wood Lectures).

2 For Grant, when Mr Justice Blackmun raises the question whether a foetus is a person, he is making an ontological statement, and not a scientific one. "But once ontological affirmation is made the basis for denying the most elementary right of traditional justice to members of our species, ontological questioning cannot be silenced at this point." Blackmun's opinion, however, in my reading, raises nothing so profound. There, as I understand the argument, the question of "person" is raised in a legal, not a philosophical context; namely, whether the word "person" as used in the American constitution can be extended to cover foetuses. Blackmun concludes that it cannot, and this, I think, corresponds to the use of "person" in normal English speech. In this way, he avoids the potential conflict, while leaving open the question of whether abortion is a moral wrong which the legislatures are nonetheless constitutionally debarred from legislating against.

The Uses Of Philosophy In George Grant

1 *LN*, p. xii; *TE*, p. 63.

2 A similar perspective more detailed in its analysis of present conditions in Canada and more direct in arguing its conclusions is presented in George Grant, "An Ethic of Community," in *Social Purpose for Canada*, ed. Michael Oliver (Toronto: University of Toronto Press, 1961), pp. 3-26.

3 *PMA*, pp. 68-81.

4 *PMA*, p. 76.

5 *PMA*, p. 96.

6 *PMA*, p. v.

7 *PMA*, p. viii.

8 *TE*, p. 46.

9 See *LN*, pp. 66 f.

10 *LN*, pp. 45-87, 5, 14, 37.

11 *TE*, pp. 68-69.

12 See also *TE*, p. 140.

13 *TE*, p. 73.

14 The issues are conveniently set forth in Carl Berger, ed., *Approaches to Canadian History* (Toronto: University of Toronto Press, 1967). See also D.L. Creighton, *Towards the Discovery of Canada* (Toronto: Macmillan, 1972); Ramsay Cook, "La Survivance English-Canadian Style," in Ramsay Cook, *The Maple Leaf Forever: Essays on Nationalism and Politics in Canada* (Toronto: Macmillan, 1971), pp. 141-165.

15 *LN*, pp. x, 3, 4, 68.
16 *LN*, pp. x, 68-74; *TE*, pp. 70-71.
17 *LN*, p. xi.
18 *LN*, pp. xi-xii; *TE*, p. 78.
19 Cf. Leo Strauss, *What is Political Philosophy? and Other Studies* (Glencoe, Illinois: Free Press, 1958), p. 35: "All human love is subject to the law that it be both love of one's own and love of the good, and there is necessarily a tension between one's own and the good, a tension which may well lead to a break, be it only the breaking of a heart."
20 *TE*, p. 72.
21 *TE*, p. 77.
22 There are no explicit discussions of Heidegger. He is mentioned in *PMA*, p. viii; *LN*, p. ix; *TE*, p. 192n; *TH*, p. 18n.
23 See all of *TH*, especially chapters 1 and 2.
24 *TH*, p. 44.
25 See also *TE*, 26-30.
26 *TH*, p. 24.
27 See *PMA*, pp. 11, 26, 78, 108 where the praise of the modern is much less ambiguous than later: *LN*, p. 94; *TE*, "In Defence of North America," pp. 15-40, 103.
28 *TH*, pp. 1, 2.
29 *TE*, p. 63.
30 *LN*, pp. 88 f.
31 *TE*, pp. 140 f.
32 *TH*, pp. 50-52; pp. 141 f.
33 Friedrich Nietzsche, *The Use and Abuse of History*, trans., Adrian Collins (Indianapolis: Bobbs-Merrill, 1947).
34 That Grant's account is difficult to disprove is a conclusion one inescapably draws from all the attempts to disprove it. See for instance, R.K. Crook, "Modernization and Nostalgia: A Note on the Sociology of Pessimism," *Queen's Quarterly*, 63, 2 (Summer 1966), 269-284; Robert Blumstock, "Anglo-Saxon Lament," *Canadian Review of Sociology and Anthropology*, 3, 2 (May 1966), 98-105; Ramsay Cook, "Loyalism, Technology and Canada's Fate," in Ramsay Cook, *The Maple Leaf Forever*, pp. 46-67. These essays assure us that Grant is mistaken but in doing so they simply invoke the very criteria that Grant's work attempts to question.
35 See for instance *PMA*, pp. 100 f.; *LN*, p. 98; *TE*, pp. 76 f. Grant frequently seems to give away too much, as for instance on page 18 of *TH* where he confesses that he is incapable of the very analyses necessary to substantiate his claims.
36 Leo Strauss, *On Tyranny*, revised and enlarged edition (Ithaca: Cornell University Press, 1963).
37 *TE*, pp. 100-109. See, now, Leo Strauss, "Preface to Spinoza's Critique of Religion," in Leo Strauss, *Liberalism: Ancient and Modern* (New York: Basic Books, 1968), pp. 224-259.

38 Hans Kelsen, "The Metamorphoses of the Idea of Justice," in Paul
   Sayre, ed., *Interpretations of Modern Legal Philosophies: Essays in
   Honor of Roscoe Pound* (New York: Oxford University Press, 1947),
   pp. 390-418.
39 See for instance *TE*, p. 36; *TH*, p. 47.
40 Søren Kierkegaard, *Concluding Unscientific Postscript*, trans. David F.
   Swenson and Walter Lowrie (Princeton: Princeton University Press,
   1941), pp. 166, 340.
41 *Ibid.*, pp. 213 ff.
42 *Ibid.*, p. 216.
43 See for example George P. Grant, "Philosophy," *Royal Commission
   Studies: a selection of essays prepared for the Royal Commission on
   National Development in the Arts, Letters and Sciences* (Ottawa: E.
   Cloutier, King's Printer, 1951), pp. 119-133.

George Parkin Grant: A Bibliographical Introduction

1 The biblical metaphors of Moloch, the Behemoth and Leviathan have
   not only theological ramifications but also evoke Plato's reflections on
   the Great Beast as refracted in the thinking of Simone Weil. See Weil,
   The Simone Weil Reader, ed. by George A. Panichas (New York: David
   McKay Co., 1977), 391-396.
2 The exchange between Strauss and Kojève is contained in Leo Strauss
   On Tyranny, revised and enlarged (Ithaca: Cornell University Press,
   1968).
3 The theologian Douglas Hall has argued persuasively that Grant's
   hermeneutic of darkness proffers to North Americans the first
   occasion for appropriating the theology of the Cross. See Hall, *Lighten
   Our Darkness: Toward and Indigenous Theology of the Cross*
   (Philadelphia: The Westminster Press, 1976), pp. 203-225.
4 The influence of Weil on Grant's thinking has been constant, if not
   always noted (see, e.g., 1954b: 10; 1955a: 45; 1966a: 99). It is only in
   his third phase that Grant has come to speak openly about his relation
   to Weil (1977a & d). This openness may mark a new phase in Grant's
   thinking.

Notes On The Contributors

John Badertscher received his Ph.D. from the University of Chicago and has been a member of the Department of Religious Studies, University of Winnipeg, since 1971.

Darrol Bryant attended the Harvard Divinity School (S.T.B.) and the Institute of Christian Thought, St. Michael's (M.A., Ph.D.). He has taught at Wilfrid Laurier, University of Windsor, and is presently an Assistant Professor of Religion and Culture at Renison College, University of Waterloo.

William Christian was educated at the University of Toronto and the London School of Economics. He is currently Associate Professor of Political Science at Mount Allison University. He is co-author of *Political Parties and Ideologies in Canada*, and has recently published articles on Harold Innis in the *Canadian Journal of Political Science, Journal of Canadian Studies*, and the *Queen's Quarterly*. He is currently editing Innis's *Idea File* for publication.

Barry Cooper was born in Vancouver, educated at UBC and Duke University, and presently teaches Political Science at York University.

Frank K. Flinn did his undergraduate work at Harvard and his graduate studies at St. Michael's College, University of Toronto. He is presently Director, Graduate Program in Religion and Education, in the Department of Theological Studies at St. Louis University.

Douglas John Hall, born in Ingersoll, Ontario, studied at the University of Western Ontario and Union Theological Seminary. He has served as Principal of St. Paul's United College, University of Waterloo, and McDougald Professor of Systematic Theology, St. Andrew's College, Saskatoon. He is currently Associate Professor of Christian Theology at McGill University's Faculty of Religious Studies. He has written three books, *Hope Against Hope, Lighten Our Darkness*, and *The Reality Of The Gospel And The Unreality Of The Churches*, as well as numerous articles and reviews.

The brothers **Edwin** and **David Heaven**, are native Hamiltonians, having studied at McMaster University. Edwin Heaven is presently Provost and Vice-Chancellor of Thorneloe University in Sudbury, Ontario, and David Heaven is in business for himself in Hamilton.

Laurence Lampert was born and raised in Winnipeg. He is currently Associate Professor of Philosophy at Indiana University — Purdue University at Indianapolis. His published work includes essays on Nietzsche, Heidegger and Leo Strauss.

William Mathie (B.A., McMaster; A.M. Ph.D., University of Chicago) teaches political philosophy in the Department of Politics at Brock University. He has written several articles on the concept of political community in ancient and modern philosophy.

John Muggeridge received his B.A. in Modern History from Jesus College, Cambridge, and his M.A. in Canadian History from the University of Toronto. Since 1957 he has taught English, History and French at various Canadian schools and has worked as a free-lance journalist. He is now the Canadian Studies' specialist at Niagara College of Applied Arts and Technology, Welland, Ontario.

Father Joseph F. Power, an Oblate of St. Francis de Sales, is completing doctoral studies in the Institute of Christian Thought, St. Michael's College, Toronto. He holds a licentiate in theology from the University of Fribourg, Switzerland and a Th.M. from St. Michael's, and has taught theology in Maryland and New York.

A. James Reimer graduated from the University of Toronto in 1974 with a Master's degree in European intellectual history and is now a Ph.D. candidate in Theology at the Institute of Christian Thought, St. Michael's College, Toronto. He holds his B.A. from the University of Manitoba and has studied at Union Theological Seminary, New York, under a Rockefeller Theological Fellowship.

Larry Schmidt was educated at St. Michael's College where he received his Ph.D. in 1975. Currently, he is assistant professor of Religious Studies at Erindale College, University of Toronto.

Since 1968 **Bernard Zylstra** has been senior member in political theory at the Institute for Christian Studies, Toronto. He studied at Calvin Theological Seminary, the University of Michigan Law School, and the Free University of Amsterdam, and is the author of *From Individualism to Collectivism: The Development of Harold Laski's Political Thought*, as well as several articles on politics and theology.

Index